APPLIED PSYCHOLOGY IN LAW ENFORCEMENT AND CORRECTIONS

Publication Number 905
AMERICAN LECTURE SERIES®

A Publication in
The BANNERSTONE DIVISION *of*
AMERICAN LECTURES IN SOCIAL AND REHABILITATION PSYCHOLOGY

Consulting Editors
JOHN G. CULL, Ph.D.
Director, Regional Counselor Training Program
Department of Rehabilitation Counseling
Virginia Commonwealth University
Fishersville, Virginia

and

RICHARD E. HARDY, Ed.D.
Chairman, Department of Rehabilitation Counseling
Virginia Commonwealth University
Richmond, Virginia

The American Lecture Series in Social and Rehabilitation Psychology offers books which are concerned with man's role in his milieu. Emphasis is placed on how this role can be made more effective in a time of social conflict and a deteriorating physical environment. The books are oriented toward descriptions of what future roles should be and are not concerned exclusively with the delineation and definition of contemporary behavior. Contributors are concerned to a considerable extent with prediction through the use of a functional view of man as opposed to a descriptive, anatomical point of view.

Books in this series are written mainly for the professional practitioner; however, academicians will find them of considerable value in both undergraduate and graduate courses in the helping services.

APPLIED PSYCHOLOGY

IN LAW ENFORCEMENT

AND CORRECTIONS

RICHARD E. HARDY

JOHN G. CULL

CHARLES C THOMAS • PUBLISHER

Springfield • Illinois • U.S.A.

Published and Distributed Throughout the World by
CHARLES C THOMAS · PUBLISHER
Bannerstone House
301–327 East Lawrence Avenue, Springfield, Illinois, U.S.A.

© 1973, by CHARLES C THOMAS · PUBLISHER
ISBN 0–398–02862–1
Library of Congress Catalog Card Number: 73–4695

*With THOMAS BOOKS careful attention is given to all details of
manufacturing and design. It is the Publisher's desire to present books
that are satisfactory as to their physical qualities and artistic possibilities
and appropriate for their particular use. THOMAS BOOKS will be true
to those laws of quality that assure a good name and good will.*

Library of Congress Cataloging in Publication Data

Hardy, Richard E.
    Applied psychology in law enforcement and corrections.

    (American lecture series, publication no. 905. A
publication in the Bannerstone Division of American
lectures in social rehabilitation psychology)
    1. Criminal psychology.   2. Law enforcement.
3. Corrections.   I. Cull, John G., joint author.
II. Title.
[DNLM: 1. Crime—U.S.   2. Criminal psychology.
3. Psychology, Applied.   4. Rehabilitation.   HV 6080
A652   1973]
HV6080.H35   364.3   73–4695
ISBN 0–398–02862–1

Printed in the United States of America
K–8

CONTRIBUTORS

DAVID B. COFFLER: B. A. in Psychology, California State University, Northridge; Master's Degree in Counseling, California State University, Los Angeles. Chief of Rehabilitation Services, Acton Rehabilitation Center and Los Angeles County Health Services.

WILLIAM A. CRUNK, JR.: B. A., Mansfield State College. Master's Degree in Rehabilitation Counseling, Virginia Commonwealth University. Currently Evaluator and Coordinator, Chesterfield School Unit, Virginia Department of Vocational Rehabilitation.

JOHN G. CULL: Ph.D. Director, Regional Counselor Training Program and Professor, Department of Rehabilitation, School of Community Services, Virginia Commonwealth University, Fishersville, Virginia; Adjunct Professor in Psychology and Education, School of General Studies, University of Virginia; Technical Consultant, Rehabilitation Services Administration, U.S. Department of Health, Education and Welfare; Lecturer, Medical Department Affiliate Program, Woodrow Wilson Rehabilitation Center; Consulting Editor, *American Lecture Series in Social and Rehabilitation Psychology,* Charles C Thomas, Publisher. Formerly Rehabilitation Counselor, Texas Commission For The Blind and Texas Rehabilitation Commission; Director, Division of Research and Program Development, Virginia Department of Vocational Rehabilitation. Dr. Cull has contributed more than fifty publications to the professional literature in psychology and rehabilitation.

CHARLES W. DEAN: Ph.D. Superintendent, Connecticut School for Boys, Meriden, Connecticut. Lecturer, Department of Psychology, Yale University. Formerly, Chief of Program Planning, Connecticut Department of Correction; Director of Research, Kentucky Department of Correction; Consultant, South Carolina Department of Correction; Assistant Professor of Sociology, University of Kentucky; Assistant Professor of Sociology, University of South Carolina. Dr. Dean has contributed numerous articles to the professional literature in Sociology and Corrections.

WAYNE S. GILL: Ph.D. Rehabilitation Psychologist in independent practice, San Antonio, Texas; Member, Texas State Board of Examiners of Psychologists; Consultant, Texas Rehabilitation Commission, State Commission for the Blind, Goodwill Industries and various school districts; Lecturer,

Graduate Program in Rehabilitation, Our Lady of the Lake College. Dr. Gill is the author of more than twenty articles in various psychology and rehabilitation journals.

RICHARD E. HARDY: Ed.D. Chairman, Department of Rehabilitation, School of Community Services, Virginia Commonwealth University, Richmond, Virginia; Technical Consultant, Rehabilitation Services Administration, U.S. Department of Health, Education and Welfare; Consulting Editor, *American Lecture Series in Social and Rehabilitation Psychology*, Charles C Thomas, Publisher; and Associate Editor, *Journal of Voluntary Action Research*. Formerly Rehabilitation Counselor in Virginia; Chief, Psychologist and Supervisor of Training, South Carolina Department of Vocational Rehabilitation and member South Carolina State Board of Examiners in Psychology; Rehabilitation Advisor, Rehabilitation Services Administration, U.S. Department of Health, Education and Welfare. Dr. Hardy has contributed more than fifty publications to the professional literature in psychology and rehabilitation.

STEPHEN A. LEVINE, M.D.: Staff psychiatrist, N.I.M.H. Clinical Research Center, Lexington, Kentucky. Dr. Levine received his M.D. degree in 1966 from the University of California at San Francisco. He completed his psychiatric training at the Langley Porter Neuropsychiatric Institute, San Francisco, in June, 1970. He is now fulfilling a two-year selective service obligation as a commissioned officer with the U.S. Public Health Service. In addition to the present chapter Dr. Levine has collaborated in a number of professional articles and is engaged in the research of street addict values.

JOHN M. MACDONALD: M.D. Associate Professor of Psychiatry of University of Colorado School of Medicine and Director of Forensic Psychiatry at the University of Colorado Medical Center. Also Dr. Macdonald is active as Consulting Psychiatrist to the District Courts of Colorado. He has published widely; his books include *Rape: Offenders and Their Victims, The Murderer and His Victim, Homicidal Threats,* and *Psychiatry and The Criminal.*

J. GARY MAY: M.D. Child Psychiatrist, Associate Professor of Psychiatry, Associate in Pediatrics, University of Louisville Medical Center, Louisville, Kentucky; Chairman, State Mental Health Representative for Children and Youth; Former Deputy Commissioner for Child Psychiatry, Kentucky Department of Mental Health, Frankfort, Kentucky; Member, Steering Committee for National Consortium on Mental Health Services for Children. Dr. May has written for professional literature regarding group processes, group therapy, and mental health consultation, in addition to contributions in the child psychiatry literature. He has served in various capacities as consultant in welfare agencies, law enforcement agencies and other community groups.

WILLIAM A. REICHART: B.A. Political Science, Perdue University, M.A. Political Science University of Kentucky. Associate Director of the Experimental Police District. Formerly, Assistant Professor of Political Science, Bellarmine College. Taught in ghetto schools in Chicago area. Participated in police training, police selection and community relations.

EDWARD S. ROSENBLUH: Ph.D. Research Professor of Psychology. Director, Law Enforcement Education and Research Programs, Bellarmine College, Louisville, Kentucky. Formerly, Dr. Rosenbluh was a Teaching and Research Assistant at the University of Oklahoma, Norman, Oklahoma. He has published widely in the area of psychology and corrections. Director of federal projects in Police community relations, police selection and police psychology.

RICHARD C. STEPHENS: Ph.D. Research Sociologist, N.I.M.H. Clinical Research Center, Lexington, Kentucky. Dr. Stephens received his B.A. in Sociology from Louisiana State University in New Orleans (1964), and his M.A. (1966) and Ph.D. (1971) in Sociology from the University of Wisconsin, Madison, Wisconsin. Among his contributions to the professional literature are a follow—up study of narcotic addicts, an analysis of the reliability of addicts as respondents in research projects, a description of demographic and sociological characteristics of addicts, and papers on evaluation of drug treatment programs. One of his principal ongoing research interests is the "street addict" about whom he has already published some work.

MINTAUTS MICKEY VITOLS: M.D., F.A.P.A. Psychiatry Associate at the Westbrook Psychiatric Hospital in Richmond, Virginia and is Director of the Henrico Mental Hygiene Clinic. Dr. Vitols is a Consultant to the Virginia Institute of Pastoral Care, Inc., and is a Clinical Assistant Professor in Psychiatry, Virginia Commonwealth University, Health Sciences Center, Medical College of Virginia. He is a Diplomat in Psychiatry.

This book is dedicated to

Sheriff Emmerson C. Hardy and his wife Kathleen of Lunenburg County, Virginia.

Sheriff Hardy has been in office since being elected in 1955.

PREFACE

CRIME AND ITS CONTROL have become major political, moral and public concerns in the United States. Massive efforts are being made to control crime and retard its development. Although a great deal of research has been done and some improvements have been made, many persons do not venture from their homes at night for fear of being molested. In short, crime control and prevention have met with major obstacles.

The contributors of this book have been concerned with these and related problems throughout their professional lives. All of them have been outstanding practitioners in one role or another in the area of law enforcement or corrections. Without their help and cooperation the development of this book would have been impossible. We owe a real debt of gratitude to them for tolerating our constant calls, letters, negative and positive criticisms.

This book represents diligent efforts to demonstrate the use of principles from the general body of knowledge of psychology in order that techniques can be developed and applied toward the effective control of problems associated with and related to crime.

Richard E. Hardy
John G. Cull

Richmond, Virginia
1973

CONTENTS

APPLIED PSYCHOLOGY IN
LAW ENFORCEMENT
AND CORRECTIONS

HUMAN NATURE AND CRIMINAL BEHAVIOR

PART I

- CAUSES OF CRIME
- CRIME, CORRECTIONS AND TRENDS
- SOME ASPECTS OF CRIME AND DELINQUENCY
- HUMAN PERSONALITY AND ITS ADAPTIVE AND DEFENSIVE DEVICES

Chapter 1

CAUSES OF CRIME

RICHARD E. HARDY AND JOHN G. CULL

- RAPID SOCIAL CHANGE
- IMPORTANCE OF PEER GROUPS AND ROLE MODELS
- WHERE CRIME OCCURS
- REFERENCES

THIS IS SURELY A TIME in American history when the concern of most people has reached an all time high over crime, violence, and law and order concepts. Over five million crimes were reported to the police in 1971. This number represented an increase of 11 percent over 1970. Persons in many areas, both rural and urban, are fearful of leaving their homes at night because of violence. It has been estimated that more than 31 billion dollars is the annual economic cost of crime.

Theoreticians and researchers have varied in their explanations of what causes crime. Some have discussed problems within the society and its constantly changing nature and increasing complexity. Others have written concerning chromosomes and genealogy as factors related to crime.

The bias of this chapter will be seen quickly. In the minds of the authors there seems to be a definite relationship between poverty and crime (especially those aspects concerning housing, educational opportunity, and mental or physical health) and rapid social change and crime. It is not the purpose of this chapter to review and report on the various research projects concern-

5

ing the causes of crime. The authors simply wish to present some of their opinions to the reader for the reader's evaluation. This chapter is concerned mainly with the psychosocial aspects of the "normal" offender, and not with abnormality.

RAPID SOCIAL CHANGE

Institutions such as the church, the family, governmental structures of service, the university, and other educational systems are changing so rapidly that many persons are losing their anchor points for emotional stability. People look around them and find little or no certainty in their jobs, in their family life, or in traditional and religious beliefs formerly held sacrosanct. All of us are deeply influenced by the effects of the mass media such as television. These media to us depict what the outside world seems to have. The outside world seems to have so much more than so many think they have.

Diminishing Value of Work

In the early days of the development of this country, the Protestant Ethic played a most important part in bringing about advancements in agriculture, technology, and the social services. The amount of hard work which an individual did was a direct indication in many cases of his status in the community. Work for work's sake was highly respected. The Protestant ethic is now much less an influencing factor on attitudes of persons toward work than it once was. In fact, by the year 2000 it may well be that family attitudes in teaching children such characteristics as dependability and diligence related to work may be drastically modified. Society is moving toward a much greater leisure time involvement. At the present time the effects of this accelerating movement away from the Protestant ethic are being felt. This means that convincing persons that the way to success is through hard work of an honest nature is becoming even more difficult. Even vocational specialists such as vocational rehabilitation counselors in state and federal agencies are now talking about deemphasizing vocational aspect of rehabilitation services which in itself indicates some drastic changes in the philosophy of many persons in the social service area on vocations and work.

With an increased amount of leisure time and a deemphasis on full work days or full work weeks, there is more time for all types of activities, including unlawful activities. There seems to be a definite emphasis toward getting what we want the easy way. This emphasis is perpetuated and reinforced by many white collar workers who are able to "get around the law" by various methods. An example is the landlord who puts enough pressure on tenants to receive monthly payments for rent but does not maintain his buildings according to city ordinances. Persons often see different applications of the law applied according to socioeconomic status of the individual accused. Sentences can vary enormously according to whether an individual brings an attorney with him to court, whether the offense is a traffic violation or a more serious one.

Some Characteristics of the Society Which Lead to Crime

We live in a violent society. One which idolizes prize fighters and war heroes. One in which the western robber of the movies is idolized until he is caught—a world in which heroes such as Ian Fleming's James Bond who is "licensed to kill" is respected because he is more violent and gruesome in his treatment of criminals than they are of him and their other victims. Our young military men are taught to kill. The emphasis on violence does not always end with the discretionary thought of the one who is taught to be violent and this fact has been indicated also in the battles of Vietnam when innocent villagers have been killed as well as those who were obviously the enemy.

Americans have necessarily had a somewhat violent and, in addition, fighting spirit. This characteristic has been most important in conquering the wilderness of the West and forging a new nation. Our highly competitive physical effort is constantly depicted in television programs of the wild west. Even the bad man often does not seem so bad when he robs or takes what he needs. The so-called bad guy is even respected as long as he is getting away with his activities. The most thrilling scene of a technicolor western movie is often at the beginning of the movie when the train is robbed and the bandits are able to elude the sheriff and his posse.

Our city areas are particularly vulnerable to violence. A factor which always causes increased social interaction of all types, and crime in particular, is overcrowding. When persons are heavily concentrated in our cities in areas of ugliness, which include poor housing and general discomfort, violent and criminal behavior will occur. When people are concentrated in small areas there are more persons of every type. There are more mentally ill persons including psychotics. There are more physically unhealthy persons, including individuals who are uncomfortable due to injuries which have been ill attended or not attended. Many persons are taking drugs which compound already existing problems and create new ones. Stability is not enhanced by overcrowding. We can expect only a higher incidence of various types of behavior including criminal behavior in that overcrowding in the cities is worsening as our population becomes more urban.

IMPORTANCE OF PEER GROUPS AND ROLE MODELS

Pressures for conformity come from all sides. Persons in the ghetto feel pressure to conform to the ways of behaving of persons of the ghetto. These behavior pressures are particularly strong among the adolescent groups and especially influential among adolescent boys. The emphasis seems to be on beating the "system" somehow, and this attitude should not be considered an unhealthy emphasis. It represents the wish of most Americans—to somehow get established and find happiness within a social system which is now in constant turmoil and within a society which is in many ways unhealthy.

In order for the person from the ghetto to beat the system, he must either "fake out" some bureaucratic program such as the Department of Public Welfare and get on the public dole, or behave as two different persons. He must demonstrate one type of behavior which will secure his position within his own peer group and demonstrate another type of behavior which will allow him to secure employment in the outside world. His only other alternative is to leave his peer group and those things which he has felt important in order to enter another man's world. It is much easier for all of us to remain in a world which we have known and adjusted to than it is to modify behavior in order to become members of a different society. Think how difficult it would be for most of us to move into a culture different and distinct from our own. The same types of problems and equal in complexity exist for persons who are from impoverished areas, either rural or urban, when they face finding employment and security in the world of work.

Another problem which often leads to crime is that of the lack of sufficient role models for individuals to follow. One of the earliest influences on all persons is that of the parents and much of the early child's play involvement is concerned with the work behavior of adults. When adults within the family are not able to work, children simulate the behavior which they exhibit and this behavior is often characterized by frustration and idleness.

Many individuals who find themselves in trouble need to understand their own motivations—reasons for behavior. The most prevalent reason, for instance, for dismissal from employment is that of inability to get along with fellow workers. Certainly a real cause of crime is inability to get along with persons within the family on the street, and within the community. This is often due to personal immaturity. When there is a basic lack of understanding of human nature, the weaknesses and strengths of all of us, there can be a real tendency to misunderstand the intentions of our neighbors. "Rap sessions" held in various community centers may be of substantial value to young persons and older ones too, who wish to come into a group situation in order to discuss problems which they may be having. In addition, they will find support and interest in them as individuals which they may have never found before. Many persons in crime are involved in order to gain attention or recognition after having failed in other areas of life in the highly competitive society of today.

Idleness and hopelessness can be the handmaidens of crime. When persons attempt time and again to find acceptance within their families, but can find no work and no acceptance and must remain idle, crime often results. The hopelessness of many persons is profound, especially in ghetto areas where they must sit on porches or in apartments with inadequate facilities and are unable to join in meaningful activity. Many middle-class white collar workers have experienced what might be called "Sunday neuroticism," those hours on weekends when they can find little that they may want to do. Many persons are unable to find meaningful activities for themselves outside of their employment. Many are just plainly bored. When employment opportunities are lacking, chances for crime or delinquent behavior are compounded. When employment is found, and is of a menial and meaningless nature to the individual in terms of what he is able to gain from it intellectually, emotionally, or materially, an inadequate adjustment pattern can be established. When the individual has a job which is not commensurate with his capabilities and interests, and the job does not provide what the person needs in terms of materialistic possessions, then the possibilities for crime are again increased. When skills are limited and the work hard and the obvious fact is that most other people have more in terms of material possessions, the thoughts of delinquent behavior again arise.

All of us are susceptible to our own innate aggression. Some of us are able to control it better than others through sublimation. A highly "developed" man is able to live and let live without unduly imposing his will or his hurt upon others. Many have not mastered this.

Many people will say that they are not interested in violence and this innate aggression and tendency toward violence does not apply to them. Certainly it applies to all of us in various ways. Many like prize fighting, some enjoy bull fighting, many are able to vicariously satisfy their violent cravings through hard work, professionalism, or risky activities in sports, etc. Through the ego (will power) we can suppress and, in general, control or handle our tendency toward violence, especially if we understand our own nature—tendencies to behave in various ways.

WHERE CRIME OCCURS

When we look at the areas of the cities in which crime is most prevalent, we find in those areas dilapidated and run-down housing facilities, poor plumbing, unsatisfactory health conditions, both mental and physical, a real lack of the aesthetic aspects of life, poor streets, poor garbage collection, poor transportation in and out of the area, few offices of governmental state or Federal service agencies, few pharmacies or drug stores, poor schools with some of the most ill prepared teachers. All these factors and others lead to poor attitudes, poor adjustments, poor mental and physical health, and a feeling of inability to escape.

Questions are often raised in rehabilitation service groups concerning how we motivate people. We do not motivate them in our plush offices through counseling and esoteric information when they have to return to poverty or ghetto areas to live. In fact, they feel in an unreal world when they are in the office of the counselor and it is difficult for them to respect his judgment when they feel he is not fully aware of their world.

It should be remembered that crime is more prevalent in the areas just described, but also exists in all segments of the society and in all geographic areas. The auto mechanic who may steal parts for his automobile from his employer, the highly educated white collar worker who fraudulently files his income tax reports, the businessman who cheats on his expense accounts—all commit crime—and of course, we know that persons in every strata are involved in drug dependency and abuse. It is important for us to be certain not to brand all persons who live in the ghetto as criminals or prospective criminals. Most people who live in poverty never commit a serious crime.

Prisons and Their Contribution to Crime

The purpose of this chapter is not to outline methods of rehabilitation, but to indicate certain causes of crime. We cannot doubt the prison is a training ground in crime. The prison system must be vastly revamped into a rehabilitative and vocationally oriented training program if we are to cut back the high recidivism rate that exists and the high continued crime rate which is prevalent among those who have "attended" prisons.

Karl Menninger has written a book entitled *The Crime of Punishment.*[2] One of the crimes of punishment is certainly the training which individuals get while in prison—training in being more effective criminals. Imagine yourself a young man who has stolen an automobile and who is imprisoned for several years as a result of maybe a second offense. Your initiation to prison life during your first night consists of your being forced into homosexual behavior by the stronger inmates. This continues far beyond an initiation period and may happen every night when the lights go off in the prison cells. You talk with persons who are third and fourth "timers" who can teach you a great deal about how to be more successful in stealing automobiles and other more expensive items. You get ideas beyond your dreams concerning the possibilities in crime. There you may meet the leaders in the criminal underworld who will locate jobs for you in crime once you have completed prison training. Violence becomes a way of life. The taking from the weak by the strong is accepted. Those who can defraud others and get away with it are the most highly respected members of this community. The person who can "con" the psychologist or the counselor or the other inmates is also highly respected.

Ramsey Clark in his book *Crime in America* [1] has called prisons "factories of crime," and certainly this is an apt description of what takes place within the prison system which is manned in some cases by prison guards with less training and education than the inmates. As long as poorly paid and poorly trained guards and other personnel work in these institutions, we cannot expect for prisons to be less than training programs in crime. As long as there are large dormitory rooms where many live within prisons where guards do not remain at night there will continue to be mass violence. What has been indicated about prisons also can be said about local jails. Much must be done to improve situations in both.

Karl Menninger has indicated that the use of prisons in punishment only causes more crime. Punishment has actually increased the amount of criminal behavior which the public must bear. There must be massive rehabilitation programs to eliminate these conditions within prisons which are so segregated from the normal community in terms of the basic necessities of life. A very high percentage, approximately 70 percent of those persons who are in the Federal prison system, never have a visitor while in prison.

It should be noted that a high percentage, approximately 25 percent of the prisoners in some state penitentiary systems are mentally retarded. Certainly rehabilitation services, in particular vocational rehabilitation, to those who are physically and mentally impaired can be most helpful.

REFERENCES

1. Clark, Ramsey: *Crime In America*. New York, Simon and Schuster, 1970.
2. Menninger, Karl: *The Crime of Punishment*. New York, Viking Press, 1968.

Chapter 2

CRIME, CORRECTIONS, AND TRENDS

Charles W. Dean

- ■ Historical Background
- ■ Who Goes to Prison?
- ■ What Are Inmates Like?
- ■ Changes in Corrections
- ■ Rehabilitation as a Basic Right
- ■ References

THE PRESENT state of correctional rehabilitative programs is characterized by a mixture of progressive and outmoded practices which vary from state to state, sometimes within the same state, and not infrequently within the same institution. Thus any attempt to describe current trends will be fraught with exceptions. This resembles census data which indicate that, over the last two decades, population migration has been to the west, to urban areas, and from inner city areas to the suburbs. While no one questions this, everyone knows a lot of people who have moved eastward, to rural areas and from suburbs to the inner city. Any attempt to summarize contemporary trends in correctional rehabilitation will have to be equally as general and based on far less data, since there are numerous and notorious exceptions to the progressive trends that have characterized correctional rehabilitative efforts over the last half century.

14

The following chapters discuss in detail program areas presently emphasized in the correctional field. The purpose of this chapter is to point out the underlying patterns, the conditions which have determined these and problems that must be met. Awareness of these conditions and problems is requisite to understanding the pace at which change can be introduced, the success of such programs and the support, both in terms of financial resources and public acceptance, that correctional rehabilitation receives at the present time.

HISTORICAL BACKGROUND

The development of those program areas that are likely to be found in a typical correctional agency at present evolved over the last two centuries. Some understanding of their historical origins is essential to explaining their present form. The first prisons were the functional equivalent of the death penalty which they replaced, since they completely and often permanently removed the offender from the community. Early penology was simple. A punitive ideology dominated the system and there was little concern for inmate welfare. Prisoners were seen as comprising a homogeneous category of people whose past behavior had been so reprehensible that individual differences were insignificant. The law of the time was far behind the ancient code that specified an eye for an eye since the seriousness of the crime was not considered. During this period, the offender, by his act of offending, was considered to have forfeited his membership in the community and his claim to any social concern. During this period, confinement was the sole purpose of prisons. Adequate security was provided by thick stone cells and high stone walls patrolled by armed guards. Inmates often wore leg irons or were chained to walls. Such facilities were constructed to house criminals who were perceived as dangerous animals requiring strong cages. This philosophy is evident in the architecture of many ancient prisons currently in operation.

It is generally agreed that the eighteenth century was remarkable for its emphasis on the concepts of the rights of men. Becarria, Voltaire, and later Bentham and Romilly all contributed to extensive practical reforms of criminal jurisprudence. The English criminal code was completely transformed between 1820 and 1861. In 1822 the death penalty was removed from some one-hundred petty offenses. During this period incarcerated males were segregated from females, the old from the young, and the more hardened offenders from the inexperienced. Some crimes were considered to be more serious than others and the recognition of this necessitated differential treatment of offenders. Although this was severely limited in the prisons of that day, some were allowed to leave their cells to participate in work activities and attend religious services. Later, it was recognized that housing all inmates under maximum security conditions was unnecessary and extremely expensive. Other institutions were constructed for inmates not considered to be serious escape risks and dangerous to society. This ranking of prisoners according to risk of escape and dangerousness was the first step toward the recognition of individual differences in corrections.

With the recognition that all offenders should not be treated identically and that expensive and harsh maximum security penal institutions were not necessary for all inmates, the seeds were sown for the recognition of individual differences among criminals convicted of the same offense. Also during this period, there was initial awareness that offenders would eventually be released to the community and thus, in order to protect society adequately, it was necessary to alter their behavior and attitudes during incarceration. Early efforts to implement this rather simple philosophy were quite crude but there was considerable optimism. The opening of the Elmira, New York, Reformatory for Men in 1870 appeared to mark the beginning of a golden age in the correctional movement although the optimism was short-lived. This reformatory, as well as others patterned after it, failed to realize the high hopes of the founders. This was due largely to an unrealistic faith in the effectiveness of unselective education for all and other mass treatment programs. By 1910 it was generally admitted that the adult reformatory idea as put into practice was almost a complete failure.

In the period just before World War I, attacks on prison conditions which had been made intermittently since the early 1800's was given impetus by the reports of state commissions set up by

New York and New Jersey to investigate their prison systems. Generally it was agreed that corrective efforts up to that time had been dismal failures, as rehabilitative devices, punishment, religious services, industrial activity, and mass education had been weighed in the balance and found wanting.

By the end of a century that had been a virtually worldwide abolition of slavery, the only two classes of people completely under the domination of the state were the hospitalized insane and the incarcerated criminal. The attitudes toward the mentally ill shifted from perceiving the mental patient as evil or as possessed of a devil to defining the person as ill. There was increased professionalization of treatment and liberalization of laws in this respect. Still, the criminal was viewed as a person who, of his volition, chose to commit an act which was contrary to the law. In an intellectual atmosphere which was increasingly skeptical of all simple philosophies and ethics, the doctrine of moral culpability began to weaken. Denied this prop, what George Bernard Shaw called "the ruthlessness of the pure heart" began to appear even more ruthless. At this point the issue was complicated by the new doctrine of psychiatry which suggested that criminality could result from disease as well as immorality.

Once the traditional doctrine of moral responsibility was undermined, the possibility arose that those who inflicted pain rather than those who endured it were morally culpable. This led to a change in the law called the Durham Act. This ruling exempted from criminal liability not only those who did not know that they were doing wrong but those who knew but could not keep from doing what they knew to be wrong. Thus the social-psychiatric form of justice which had been developing since the M'Naghten rule was accepted by the court. In effect, society became to some extent a codefendant of the accused. Moral indignation against the offender as an enemy of society was ameliorated. The prisoner became the victim of a questionable ideology and those who punished him at least shared in his guilt. In a book written by a prisoner in 1914, the manifesto of the new convict reads:

> My business in this book was to show that penal imprisonment is an evil and its perpetuation a crime . . . and to show that it does not protect the community but exposes it to incalcuable and calcuable

perils. Men enfeebled by crime are not cured by punishment or by homilies and precepts but by taking off our coats and showing them personally how honest and useful things are done. And let every lapse and failure on their part to follow the example be not counted against them but against ourselves who fail to convince them of the truth and hold them up to the doing of good.[1]

From this time on, penology was no longer single-minded. Psychiatry and related disciplines were considered to be a necessary part of any prison program. It was fairly well agreed that incarceration alone constituted adequate punishment. This resulted in steadily increased emphasis on treatment. This solved the moral dilemma facing the public. There was no longer any need for them to feel uncomfortable about sentencing convicted criminals since prisons were places where treatment was provided. An ambivalent and capricious public assumed punishment and treatment, all hidden in the confines of the correctional institution.

The double purpose of the prison was reflected in a staff dichotomy. The new staff introduced to provide rehabilitative services was labeled "treatment" and the old staff "custody." Members of the treatment staff, generally referred to as "professionals," were better educated and better paid. While outnumbered in over-all prison personnel, the treatment staff usually outnumbered the custody staff on classification committees and other decision-making bodies. Yet, the custody members' votes usually carried the weight of a veto since they were responsible for security, the primary goal of the institution. There was little communication between the two groups. Each represented different social classes both inside and outside the institution, with the higher class being the newcomer and contributing less to organizational maintenance. Basically the prison had not changed but a few new staff members had been placed in the institution. These usually were regarded as appendages having little to do with the real business of the institution. The treatment staff was expected to perform their rituals without interfering with the custody function.

Professionals throughout the field recognized the difficulties of the schism between treatment and custody and considerable efforts were made to minimize the consequences of this split and to bring the two together. At various times and at various places, major improvements were made in particular systems between the turn of the century and 1950. During the 1950's, a wave of riots and other mass disorders swept over prisons in every section of the country. The American Prison Association's committee on riots stated that "the immediate causes given out for prison riots are only symptoms of more basic causes." The committee listed the basic causes as inadequate financial support, public indifference, substandard personnel, enforced idleness, lack of professional leadership, excessive size, overcrowded institutions, political domination and motivation of management, unwise sentencing, and unfair parole practices. These riots precipitated a new wave of correctional reform which has continued to the present. During the last decade, new innovations by the social and behavioral sciences have been incorporated into rehabilitative programs. Also, the Federal Government has started to make substantial investments in state correctional agencies.

Programs now provided by correctional agencies more nearly reflect traditional views of the offender and the correctional agencies' task than awareness of the needs of inmates and the society to which they will return. The first prisons were characterized by work, religious and educational services. Eventually, psychological and social services were added. Presently, correctional agencies appear to be a collage which was constructed by adding one new piece of material per decade over the last century. New programs have been superimposed on old structures or new structures over old programs. Programs seem more nearly geared to the needs of the institution than of the population it serves. A paucity of funds prevents development of program areas that require intensive individual care. The unique qualities of the population served by the correctional agency and the impact of the correctional setting on programs has not been adequately accounted for. Consider the characteristics of the population.

WHO GOES TO PRISON?

The criminal is defined as a person who commits an act which violates a criminal law. It is generally assumed that criminals usually go to prison. A closer examination indicates that while all prison inmates have been legally declared to be criminals, not all criminals are necessarily inmates. In fact it seems that the prison population contains a small and unrepresentative fraction of the total criminal population since there is only a slight possibility that a person who violates a criminal law will be confined in a penal institution. An examination of the differences between criminals and prisoners will provide considerable insight into the task of a correctional institution and of the highly selective process by which a person gets there.

There are several categories of criminals seldom observed in a correctional setting. First, many criminals do not go to prison because the laws they violate are not enforced by the police. There are many laws in criminal codes that are not enforced because they were designed to regulate conditions which no longer exist. Other laws are not enforced even though they regulate conditions that do exist in the modern community but are not considered morally repugnant. Examples of these are laws prohibiting gambling, prostitution, the sale of marijuana, and in some localities the sale of alcoholic beverages. In many states it is not unusual to find nightclubs and gambling casinos operating in full view of everyone although operating such establishments is contrary to law. Generally speaking, laws will not be enforced if they prohibit behavior which is socially acceptable.

Those who commit crimes where there are no victims is the second category of criminals seldom appearing in correctional institutions. Examples of this type of crime are abortion, gambling, homosexuality and the sale of narcotics. These criminals are seldom apprehended because those who are their "victims" go to them voluntarily and by their voluntary participation are somewhat guilty themselves.

A third type of criminal seldom appearing in a prison population is the white collar or occupational criminal. This type of criminal is defined as the person of high socioeconomic status who violates the laws designed to regulate his occupational activities. Financial losses due to this type of crime are many times greater than the financial cost of all acts customarily included in the so-called "crime problem." Financial loss to the community through white collar crime would be many times the amount of money stolen through burglary or robbery-type crimes by all inmates of all correctional institutions. These crimes include embezzlement, violation of anti-trust laws, advertising fraud, income tax evasion, and other illegal business practices.

Those participating in organized crime constitute a fourth type of criminal that seldom appears in correctional institutions. This type of crime provides services prohibited by law, such as alcoholic beverages, narcotics, gambling, and prostitution. At present, organized crime has grown to the point where it is no longer a special field of activity but rather a technique of violence, intimidation and corruption which, in default of effective law enforcement, can be applied to any business or industry which produces large profits. The underlying motive is always to secure and hold a monopoly on some activity which will produce large profits. Generally speaking, those involved in organized crime are well accepted by the larger population. This type of criminal is becoming an increasingly significant part of American society as politicians feel they are forced to accept contributions from organized crime in order to wage the increasingly expensive campaigns which are necessary to gain and hold office.

A fifth category of criminal is seldom incarcerated in spite of the fact that their behavior is in violation of laws which are supported by community mores and that there are victims in their crimes. Certain general categories of people seem to be exempt from imprisonment if not from arrest. Various self-reporting studies show that middle class people frequently commit crimes which are detected but which are not dealt with in such a way as to result in the offenders being considered criminal. One study reported that a random sample of high school boys admitted to committing two-thirds as many delinquent acts as the inmates of a reform school. Another study reported that of 1,020 men and 678 women who were asked whether they had ever committed any of 49 offenses, 99 percent had committed one or more. The average number of offenses committed in adult life was 18 for all men, with a range of 8.2 for ministers and 20.2 for laborers, and 11 for all women. Of the 49 offenses listed, 14 were felonies. Sixty-four percent of the men and 29 percent of the women admitted having committed a felony-type offense.[2] From the above studies it appears that many respectable citizens have at one time or another been involved in behavior which is criminal in nature. This behavior has failed to bring these individuals to the attention of the law because their respectable social class positions in the community have afforded them insulation against the legal process as it exists today.

A sixth category of criminal seldom appearing in correctional institutions results from the tremendous discretion police officers have in arresting people. If the individual is polite and contrite or of a respectable social class position in the community, or if the behavior that brought him to the attention of the police is unlikely to arouse widespread community indignation, there is a strong possibility that he will be released by the policeman. This decision places the policeman in an extremely powerful position with the responsibility of psychiatrist, diagnostician, and judge in each situation. Policemen are usually untrained in the law and the dynamics of human behavior and must make their decisions according to some criteria. Their interpretation of the immediate behavior of the person they are dealing with, the reaction of the community, and the wishes of their superiors seem to be the most important criteria in their decision. There are no adequate data but it is estimated that well over half of those apprehended by the police are released without court referral.

From the above, it appears that the inmates of correctional institutions are not average criminals but are selected from the lower economic segments of our society and are convicted of committing particular kinds of crimes. A glance at the type of crimes for which inmates are sentenced indicates that theft-type crimes are by far the most common. These, along with crimes against persons, such as murder, assault, and sex offenses, comprise the bulk of most prison populations. These are the same types of crimes which are reported in FBI statistics. Such crimes account for over 95 percent of all reported crimes and an equally large proportion of inmates in correctional institutions. Even so, those who commit crimes in these categories comprise a small proportion of those offenders who are sentenced. The 1970 FBI statistics report that burglary and larceny account for over two-thirds of all crimes reported. If auto thefts are added, this type of crime totals over 85 percent of all crimes reported. FBI statistics indicate that less than 25 percent of these crimes are cleared by arrest. This means that 75 percent of those committing such offenses get away with their crime. This does not apply to those who commit crimes against persons, since murder is cleared by arrest in 92 percent of the cases, manslaughter in 83 percent, and assault in 75 percent. An additional large number of offenses are not reported to the police for a variety of reasons.

Once a person has been arrested there is some chance that he will not be found guilty. Assaultive type offenders are found innocent in approximately 40 percent of the cases. Those arrested for larceny, auto theft, burglary, etc., are found innocent in about three-fourths of the cases. Thus of one hundred burglaries and larcenies, there usually are only twenty-five arrests. Of the twenty-five who appear in court for such offenses, only 70 percent or seventeen are likely to be found guilty. Of the seventeen convicted, many are sentenced to short-term jail sentences, to probation, or are released with a warning. Thus it is very unlikely that a person who commits a crime will be sent to prison even if he is of the social class from which prison inmates are drawn and if he commits the type of crime for which one is likely to be sent to prison. It appears that a prison population is drawn from a highly selected proportion of a particular kind of criminal and represents but a small fraction of the total *criminal* population. This leads one to conclude that prisoners are an atypical and relatively homogeneous population.

WHAT ARE INMATES LIKE?

The initial impression laymen get when walking through a prison is that inmates seem to be different from the people they see on the streets of a city. Such observations led early criminologists to conclude that criminals were physiologically unique, with different skull measurements, body characteristics, and were less sensitive to pain, since so many had tattoos. One of the basic weaknesses of this research was considering prison inmates and criminals to be one and the same. Later research, which accounted for this factor, corrected these notions and gradually it was recognized that there was no such thing as a special inmate type. To treat all prisoners alike would be like treating all sick people alike, for there seem to be as many types of prisoners as there are types of people and illnesses. However, we do use types. The law classifies all criminals into types and treats robbers, murderers, burglars, and rapists all differently. Besides the type of behavior for which the person is sentenced, prisons classify offenders according to age and length of criminal record. The youthful offender and the first offender are often separated from the older offender and the hardened criminal. However, there are no data which support the conclusion that the prison inmate is a special type of person. Rather, inmates seem to represent a cross-section of the lower socioeconomic segments of our society. Nevertheless, many people are convinced that inmates are very much like each other and very much unlike the people on the outside. How can the initial impression that inmates are different be accounted for? If there are differences, what are they? To answer these questions, it will be helpful to compare inmates with non-inmates. First, consider inmates' educational and occupational characteristics.

Education and Occupation

Over *30 percent* of the general population above age twenty-five have twelve or more years of education, while only *10 percent* of the inmates have this much. Thus, a much smaller proportion of the inmates are high school graduates. Occupationally, *15 percent* of the male work force are professionals, businessmen, managers, or officials while only *one-fourth of one percent* of inmates are in this group. On the other hand, half of the inmates are unskilled laborers; whereas only 20 percent of the labor force is engaged in unskilled labor. Also, only 4 percent of the inmates are sales or clerical workers; whereas of the general population, 11 percent are in this category. From these data, it appears that inmates are drawn from the lower educational and economic levels of our society. To compare people selected from any subsegment of a group with the total group is inappropriate. Thus, inmates cannot be compared with the general population.

Intelligence Levels

It has often been maintained that inmates have inferior intelligence. This idea is an old one and not too many years ago it was accepted as fact. In 1914 a team of researchers who studied 200 penal institutions reported that at least half of the inmates were mentally retarded. In 1928 another larger study concluded that only twenty per cent were retarded. This difference was not the result of inmates becoming smarter over a period of time but of improved testing and scoring techniques. Although even today it is generally agreed that inmate IQ scores are slightly lower than those of the general population, two factors account for most of this difference. First, inmates are from homes of the lower educational and economic levels; and people from such homes, whether in prison or not, usually do not perform well on intelligence tests. It is generally agreed that such tests are biased in favor of the middle classes and that they measure exposure rather than native intelligence. All IQ tests are subject to this criticism. If a group of inmates is compared with a group of their educational and economic equals, these differences will be greatly reduced if they do not disappear completely. Second, duller individuals are more likely to get caught at crimes since they are less likely to be clever at concealing their criminal acts. This latter factor would seem to account for a large portion of whatever differences that do exist after educational and economic levels are accounted for.

It seems safe to conclude that the distribution of inmates' intelligence is near normal for people of their socioeconomic level. While there are some differences, these are slight. The success of prison education and vocational training programs and the complex and responsible jobs performed by many inmates further supports the argument that prisoners are much like the general population relative to intelligence levels.

Mental Illness

Another commonly held misconception about inmates is that they are mentally deranged. This distorted conception of the criminal is often based on the belief that a person has to be mentally diseased to commit crimes. Those who hold this position usually use extreme cases to support their argument and fail to consider the large number of their neighbors who regularly commit crimes. While some criminals are mentally ill, most are not. As in the case of mental retardation, the proportion of inmates who actually evidence serious personality disorders is usually exaggerated. Most prisons have facilities for psychotic prisoners, but the proportion of inmates who are in these is quite small. For example, of the 2,300 inmates under the care of the South Carolina Department of Corrections, only around thirty reside in these special quarters at any given time. There are others who receive out-patient care just as is the case in the free community. Of those thirty, often there is no evidence as to whether their problems existed prior to incarceration. In many cases, there is a strong possibility that the seriousness of the problem has been increased greatly by the adjudication process and by imprisonment.

Such concepts as the "criminally insane," "psychopath," and "sociopath" are frightening words and are often believed to characterize most prison inmates. However, such labels are not applicable to most prisoners. The highest guesses of the proportion of sociopaths, whatever this means, in a prison population is 20 percent. Most people believe that this is far too high a figure. While there is little agreement among experts as to what a sociopath is, it is generally agreed that most sociopaths are not in prison and most prisoners are not sociopathic.

There are no data to compare outside rates with the frequency, the type, and the seriousness of personality problems which appear in prisons. Also, there is no information which enables us to identify the source of these problems. Without doubt, some psychological problems were expressed in the criminal behavior which caused many inmates to be sent to prison. However, other disorders may be caused by the arrest-trial-conviction process or by the pains of incarceration. Everyone values privacy, visits with families and contacts with members of the opposite sex. All of these suddenly become unavailable to the inmate and this in itself may be a serious adjustment problem. While the rate of mental illness may be slightly higher among inmates than among people on the outside, and while the typical inmate may show evidence of a more serious adjustment problem than the average person on the outside, the differences are slight and probably result from the abnormality of the prison setting more than from any unusual characteristics of inmates.

From the above, it appears that prison inmates represent a small proportion of the total criminal population and that they generally are a cross-section of the lower social and economic segments of our society. Whatever differences that exist between these people and those in the segment of society from which they are selected do not seem to be significant. In spite of this, many people are convinced that inmates of correctional institutions are not ordinary people. This is to be expected since the average person has even less chance for direct contact or for gaining accurate information about inmates than about criminals in general. Even well-informed citizens are often surprised when they have their first contacts with inmates. To understand the correctional institution it is necessary to understand that prisoners are people, but a highly selected group of people.

CHANGES IN CORRECTIONS

The above description of prisoners and prisons clearly suggests that traditional rehabilitative techniques are unlikely to be effective unless drastically altered to meet the needs of a very special kind of client in a very special kind of situation. Prisons have been referred to as black boxes. We know what goes in and we know what comes out, but we do not know much about what happens in-between. While there is a paucity of research to guide the direction of rehabilitative efforts, the studies that are available have altered the emphases considerably. Daniel Glaser[3] conducted a five-year study on the effectiveness of the federal prison and parole system. There were numerous conclusions reached in the study but two of these have had direct implications on programming in the Federal Bureau of Prisons.

The first of these resulted in a redefinition and elevation of the role of the correctional officer. The Glaser research clearly indicated that the correctional officer was the most significant rehabilitative agent in the institution. The dichotomy between the treatment and custody staff produce organizational chaos and splintering of efforts that the treatment staff efforts are largely negated. The results of this study were available about the same time other studies reported that rehabilitative relationships were not necessarily dependent upon the formal training of the person attempting to produce behavior change. Such studies led on one hand to the increased professionalization of correctional officers and to a subsequent reduction of the split between professional and custody staff. On the other hand, there is general agreement that a psychiatric or psychological evaluation is a necessary tool to the custodial person. Thus, in some instances the effects of the treatment-custody dichotomy has been reduced considerably. Prisons are still characterized by a quasi-military form of organization which complicates rehabilitative efforts by restricting communication between levels. This communication is essential to the rehabilitative task. A parallel might be the defining of commissioned officers in military service as counselors of enlisted men.

The elevation of the correctional officer's role has clearly pointed to the ineffectiveness of traditional rehabilitative techniques and methods in the correctional setting. While the bottom has been raised, the top has also been lowered so that the level of effectiveness of correctional programs may not have increased greatly although the negative effects of the treatment-custody dichotomy has been reduced, thereby reducing one of the major organizational barriers to development of effective programs.

A second research finding of the Glaser study pointed out that a sizeable portion of parole violations occur within the first ninety days after release from a correctional institution. Another study on the post-release employability of prisoners suggested that the vocational training within correctional institutions is far less closely related to post-release employment circumstances than is desirable and necessary. As a result of these two studies, increased emphasis has been placed on parole supervision during the first ninety days after release.

Still another study [4] which had its roots in the Glaser study, but which was conducted on releasees from the state institution, divided the variables associated with post-release success or failure into three theoretically relevant classes. These were as follows: (a) the situation, i.e. the external, social, and economic world in which the individual was located; (b) identifications, or the groups whose norms and values the individual accepts as his own; and (c) value orientations which the individual has internalized. This study utilized an interactional statistical model which made it possible to combine the effects of two classes of variables at a time. While the economic situation, Identification with criminal values, and the degree of criminality in the individual's value orientation were each significantly related to parole outcome, when any two variables were considered together, the strength of the relationship increased markedly. This research suggests that any effective rehabilitation program will have to deal effectively with the releasees' legitimate economic opportunities, the group affiliations which support criminal and noncriminal values, and the preference for criminal means of goal attainment which relates to the amount of criminality in the value orientations. Each of these variables suggests a program area that must be included in a successful rehabilitative program. Unfortunately, programs are selected on other criteria than research findings.

The custodial function is such a primary part of the prison's responsibility that those rehabilitative programs which contribute to custody goals tend to survive while those which do not, even though they may be in the best interest of the inmates, tend not to survive. For example, education occupies inmates for a period of time during the day and breaks up the monotony thereby reducing tensions. Recreation is considered a necessary part of any correctional agency because it provides necessary tension release as well as occupying idle time. Prison work programs minimizing the cost of operating the institution also occupy the time of the inmates. While there is strong feeling that traditional psychotherapy is not effective in a correctional setting, the effectiveness of this discipline has never really been tried since such services which must be provided on a one-to-one basis are extremely expensive.

While there are numerous instances of programs which challenge the above generalizations, it seems safe to conclude that the composition of most correctional rehabilitative programs has not been based on therapeutic needs but upon custody needs, the availability of funds, and tradition. Even the emphasis on community corrections has been born of necessity since this is the one means of preventing correctional institutions from becoming over-crowded and explosive. At this point in time, there is a serious need to rationally review the conditions under which the correctional rehabilitative agent must work, the characteristics of his client and the nature of the setting both in the institution and after release. Development of new programs must be based on whatever knowledge is available.

There is no question that many inmates will need academic and vocational training before they will be able to compete in the economic world they will face after release. Neither is there question that social relationships the releasee finds available in the community will, to a significant extent, determine whether he will become a recidivist in crime. Awareness of this is evident in parole regulations which forbid socializing with other parolees or persons with criminal records, but too little is done to provide the releasee with a new set of social relationships to replace those available to him prior to his incarceration.

The fact that a person committed a crime as a means of solving a situation he was encountering is explicit evidence that his values need to be redirected so that he is likely to select noncriminal methods of problem solving. No matter how great his economic opportunities may be and how legitimate his friends, unless the releasee prefers noncriminal problem solving techniques, he will become a recidivist in crime. To place a thief in an institution with a thousand other thieves to cure him of thievery is, to say the least, a questionable process. The question of value modification has received relatively little attention and usually it is assumed that if a person has a good job and does not have to steal, then he will not. All the data suggest that this is a false assumption. Altering criminal values in a society of criminals is indeed a difficult task. Nevertheless, until some method is devised for meeting this need, efforts will continue to be unsuccessful.

This brings corrections to the issue of its relationship to the larger community. Such value changes are likely to be induced only in a situation where the offender receives less gratification from noncriminal than from criminal responses. This requires shaping an environment in the community after release which would encourage such value modification. While preliminary efforts may be made in a correctional setting through use of a therapeutic milieu, behavior modification, psychotherapy, etc., little change is likely to be observed after release unless the program continues for a period of time after the offender is released to the community.

Corrections is now in the midst of conditions which may for the first time produce basic changes. For the last two decades there has been strong support and greatly improved public relations although, in spite of this, prisons are considered even a greater social problem than they were at the start. Also with the commitment of people for narcotics offenses, conscientious objectors and Black militants, prison inmates have leadership that has never existed before. Finally, and related to the above conditions, the courts of the land have shown an increasing willingness to intervene in the operation of correctional institutions.

Correctional authorities have only themselves to blame for the intrusion, if this is what it is, by the courts into what was once the exclusive domain of the executive branch of government. Just as gross action on the part of police officers has brought about vast changes in law enforcement, so has gross action on the part of prison officials brought about vast changes in corrections. Historically, correctional agencies have ignored or looked the other way when a guard was brutalizing or harassing an inmate. When the inmate expressed dislike for the treatment, he was written up by the guard in a report which ultimately resulted in the loss of institution privileges. This is not to say that every time a prisoner found himself in segregation that it was the result of unfair treatment. This is not a blanket indictment but rather is intended to point out that all of the fault does not lie with inmates. For this and other reasons, correction officials now find themselves living in a glass house with their every move relative to treatment of prisoners subject to scrutiny.

The evolutionary process which has characterized correctional change has gone from a period of time when prisoners had no rights and could be killed, mutilated, etc., to a period typified by the classical Virginia ruling that inmates were slaves to the state. Now inmates can be deprived only of those rights specified by law and requisite to operating the institution. In one case, a court ruled that undifferentiated fear or apprehension of disturbance is not enough to overcome the right to freedom of expression. Any departure from absolute regimentation may cause trouble. Where there is no finding that engaging in the forbidden conduct would materially and substantially interfere with the requirements of appropriate discipline, the prohibition cannot be sustained. Such rulings make it clear that the burden of proof has shifted from the inmate to the correctional agency in withholding privileges or assigning punishment. Furthermore, budgetary considerations and preservation of the treasury are not valid concerns of state officials charged with the care and welfare of inmates who have been given constitutional rights.

REHABILITATION AS A BASIC RIGHT

Rights are what inmates are entitled to upon their entry into an institution and administrators are held responsible if these are not fulfilled. These include such things as safe and healthful living conditions, the right to wear clothing, a balanced diet, medical care, and fair treatment. Privileges can be withheld upon unsatisfactory performance or when granting them interferes with order and discipline within the institution. Mail, packages, and reading materials are examples of items generally considered to be privileges.

Rehabilitative services generally are considered to be privileges. Thus correctional authorities can exclude the violent and the more difficult. However, over time, privileges have a way of being escalated to the level of rights. Even though rehabilitation did not originate from a constitutional or statutory foundation, it has captured the attention of legislators and courts. Some states have passed laws which require treatment. For example the South Carolina legislature, in 1968, passed a Youthful Offender Act geared to provide "corrective and preventive guidance and training designed to protect the public by correcting the antisocial tendencies of youthful offenders." The same year the Arkansas legislature recognized the important place of training and rehabilitation in the Arkansas penal code and directed the Department of Corrections to initiate and conduct such a program. When there are statutory requirements for rehabilitative programs, offenders can initiate cases against authorities when they are deprived of the opportunity to participate. In several states, administrators have had to justify their decisions to exclude certain individuals. It appears that the view that rehabilitation is a privilege may gradually lose ground. Increasingly the courts are challenging correctional autonomy and requiring services. Presently while the inmate does not have the absolute right to rehabilitation, the courts have shown a willingness to intervene in correctional procedures when an inmate is not given fair and equal treatment and when such services do not interfere with the proper functioning of the correctional system. In the future, there is likely to be growing concern for inmates' rights and more court intervention relative to rehabilitative services. Such actions will tend to upgrade the standards of corrections by requiring reform in less progressive areas.

It has been suggested by one of no less stature than the former Attorney General of the United States, Ramsey Clark,[5] that prisoners need a bill of rights. In this statement he says the following:

> Why then do we fail to try to rehabilitate? Because we deny a common humanity. We fear persons convicted of crimes. We want to punish, failing to see that punishment is itself a crime, soon visited upon the public which causes or condones its usage . . . If prisons are to rehabilitate, the government must have a duty to provide certain essential services to prisoners. The prisoners must have a right to obtain those services. Foremost among them, insofar as the condition of the individual prisoner is concerned will be the rights to health, to education and vocational training, and to employment . . . Prisoners should have rights to an education and to be immediately placed in an appropriate academic program and, where needed, to all remedial help that can be reasonably given. For those who have exhausted their academic potential, there should be vocational training with special programs for the handicapped.

The field of mental health was drastically changed by a rule that stated that if a person was committed to an institution under statute which provided for treatment, and the committed person did not receive that treatment, his constitutional rights were violated and he must either be treated or released. Rehabilitation of prisoners was originally conceived in corrections as a response to contemporary psychological and social theories. The concept was introduced and has been cultivated by the initiative and devotion of correctional authorities. However, it has been a philosophical and theoretical development which has been voluntary. Thus administrators are endowed with discretion in rehabilitative decisions such as what programs and services to provide and who is eligible. There has been meager financial support of rehabilitative programs so these services both in terms of quantity and quality have been far from adequate. With the interest of courts in the provision of services and with the strong possibility that such services will be considered a constitutional right, correctional agencies and those disciplines related to them are likely to be called upon in the relatively near future to demonstrate their wares. It seems obvious that procuring funds to do more of the same things or to do them better will result in certain failure. Corrections is on a frontier. There must be new directions, new methods, new forms of organization, new attitudes and a great deal more effort.

REFERENCES

1. Hawthorne, J.: The subterranean brotherhood XVII–XVIII, 1914, quoting from R. Korn, and L. McKorkle: *Criminology and Penology.* 1965, pp. 410–411.
2. Wallerstein, James S., and Wyle, Clement J.: Our law-abiding law breakers. *Probation,* April, 1967, pp. 107–112.
3. Glaser, Daniel: *The Effectiveness of a Prison and Parole System.* Indianapolis, Bobbs Merrill, 1964.
4. Dean, C. W., and Duggan, T. J.: Interaction and parole prediction. *Br J Criminol,* October, 1969, p. 345 ff.
5. Clark, Ramsey: Needed: a bill of rights for prisoners. *Hartford Courant,* Nov. 7, 1971, p. 1A.

Chapter 3

SOME ASPECTS OF CRIME AND DELINQUENCY

Edward S. Rosenbluh

Delinquency has been "defined by two essential elements: it is the behavior that violates basic norms of the society, and when officially known, evokes a judgment by agents of criminal justice that such norms have been violated" (Cloward and Ohlin, 1960). As noted by Sherif and Sherif (1956), deviation from one norm may be conformity to another. Sykes and Matza (1962, p. 253) note that ". . . deviation from certain norms may occur not because the norms are rejected, but because other norms held to be more pressing or involving a higher loyalty, are accorded precedence." For many years slum societies had been considered disorganized, but Whyte found that the

35

Street Corner Society (1943) was in fact highly organized, with its own norms and values, although from the outside world, that is the "conforming world," this small Italian community seemed highly disorganized.

One need but read the daily newspaper to see that every women's league, church group, and civil betterment organization has come up with the final answer to the "cause" of delinquency. We all know that comic books are at the bottom; we also know that television is the basic offender; and again we know that the movies have caused the greatest deviation from societal standards. Several theoretical approaches have been advanced as the complete explanation of the delinquency problem, however, none of them, according to Cloward and Ohlin (1960), actually provides the answer to the broad cross section of delinquent behavior. Talcott Parsons, for example, feels that the American kinship system prevents the young male from properly identifying, at an early age, with the adult male, and, therefore, a certain disorganization results when the youthful male attempts to define his status in the adult world. However, such an outlook does not take into account the need for "collective behavior" which leads to the delinquent norms created by groups of these youngsters interacting to control their worlds. Bloch and Niederhoffer have theorized that conflict in the transition to adulthood is the major source of delinquent subcultures. However, this fails to determine the basis for equality between "adolescent gangs" and the "delinquent gangs." Not all adolescent groups have been shown to be delinquent. "The 'adolescent protest,' like the 'masculine protest' may lead to delinquent acts—assaults, vandalism, and the like—in many adolescent groups, but these acts may or may not be supported by specifically delinquent norms" (Cloward and Ohlin, 1960, p. 60). In somewhat the same light, Miller theorized that conformity with lower-class values, is enough to automatically cause violations of the law. However, he neglects to note that many delinquent acts performed by the delinquent subculture violate lower-class norms also. At the same time, Miller neglects to mention how these differing norms originated, with the possible exception that they may have been derived from the European cultures which were the bases of many of our subcultures. This, though, does not take into account the flaws in our own society which have tended to bring about many of the deviant responses to be found among the delinquent subcultures. Another theory of interest is *Techniques of Neutralization* by Sykes and Matza (1962, p. 251). It is their contention "that much delinquency is based on what is essentially an unrecognized extension of defenses to crimes, in the form of justifications for deviance that are seen as valid by the delinquent but not by the legal system or society at large." That this thesis leaves something to be desired will be demonstrated below.

For one to grasp the societal foundations of delinquency, it is first necessary that one explore the continuous interaction between the individual and his society. In the great "group mind" debate of the early Twentieth Century, William McDougall felt that groups, institutions, and culture have reality apart from the particular individuals to be found in them. On the other hand, Floyd Allport stated that only individuals are real, and that groups or institutions are phenomena to be found only in the individual mind (Cartwright and Zander, 1960). Freud (1922), in a somewhat different light, felt that the individual was basically a storehouse of evil, and needed society in order to learn how to control the desired transgressions of the Id. Theories such as these have provided a beginning in the study of man in his environmental relationship with society, but they, as the theories mentioned above, do not answer the extremely important question of, "Why does the delinquent subculture evolve?"

REFERENCE GROUPS

Max Wertheimer, the founder of Gestalt psychology (Allport, 1955), demonstrated the importance of points of reference. He showed that the individual, in all of his perceptual relationships, always attempts to judge that which he is perceiving against a firm anchorage which will maintain his equilibrium. This apparent need in the human for a point of reference, or anchorage, seems also to carry over to the daily socialization process of the individual (Sherif and Sherif, 1956). The young child, for example, takes his cues from the immediate family. He learns to react to various stimuli as he observes those close to him reacting. As the child matures and begins to associate with peer groups outside the family, he seems to acquire the responses of those with whom he aspires to associate. For the child of school age, the teacher often becomes the anchor point. In the working world, those who have succeeded in his particular area of endeavor take on a certain positive allure which newly conditions his reactions. Newcomb (1943) found that new students at Bennington College tended to become more liberal in their outlooks, as they advanced toward senior standing, if they demonstrated a desire to be a part of the college community, while those whose reference groups remained outside the campus tended to retain their more conservative views. Piaget (1932) stated that the child only begins to acquire an autonomous moral sense when he begins to play in a reciprocal give-and-take relationship with other children. Without a cooperative participation, the individual considers the norms to be imposed by sheer authority, and, therefore, as nuisances to be avoided. Throughout one's life are to be found many instances where the individual desires to enter a group other than that to which he belongs. The new affiliation may be religious, educational, military, or fraternal, but if its norms are somewhat different than those of the group to which he belongs, he will find it necessary to discard those of his former anchorage and he will tend to conform to those of his new reference group.

It often occurs that in the process of acquiring a new role, such as that of foreman in a factory, the individual finds it extremely difficult to adjust to the conflicting norms. Such a marginal man still retains ties with the workers to whose ranks he recently belonged, but is no longer accepted by them, while at the same time, he is not fully accepted by management, whose norms he, too, does not fully espouse (Sherif and Sherif, 1956). While delinquency of some sort seems to pervade all strata of society, there seems to be a much greater concentration of organized deviation in the lower or working-class. Here one finds a tendency toward marginality. The individual is a member of a group which in-and-of itself does not possess all the material comfort and privilege that its members can often observe in those classes somewhat higher on the scale. When such occurs,

these marginal people may exhibit conflict feelings of belongingness and not belonging in their society. Such occurrences may
be likened to Karl Marx's (1964) theory of Alienation.

ALIENATION

Alienation, as described by Seeman (1964, p. 527–536), may
be characterized by the "expectancy or probability held by the
individual when his own behavior cannot determine the occurrence of the outcomes, or reinforcements he seeks. Also meant
is "the individual is unclear as to what he ought to believe when
the individual's minimal standards for clarity and decision making are not met." That is to say, "the individual cannot choose
appropriately among alternative interpretations (cannot 'act
intelligently' or 'with insight') because the increase in functional
rationality, with his emphasis on specialization and production,
makes such choice impossible." Again, "it is characterized by a
lower expectancy that satisfactory predictions about behavior can
be made." Those who are alienated from society tend to be somewhat isolated from that society, that is, they "assign low reward
value to goals or beliefs that are typically highly valued in the
given society." The individual has little feeling for that which he
does and looks only upon it for its reinforcing qualities. That is,
the individual seeks rewards that lie outside the activity itself.
This "self estrangement refers essentially to the ability of the
individual to find self rewarding activities that engage him."
Quoting Glazer, Seemen summarizes alienation as "our modern
'. . . sense of the splitting assunder what was once together, the
breaking of the seamless mold in which values, behavior, and
expectations were once cast into interlocking forms.'" As a part
of alienation, Seeman also delves into Durkheim's "Anomie,"
". . . a situation in which the norms regulating individual conduct have broken down or are no longer effective as rules of
behavior."

ANOMIE

Man, according to Durkheim (1951), learns to maintain an
equilibrium through the forces of society, whereby he does not

discharge his passions freely. Society alone, felt Durkheim, could play the moderating role through its authority to stipulate laws and to set the point beyond which man's desires may not go. So long as this societal structure is maintained, each person remains in harmony with his situation. However, ". . . it is not enough for the average level of needs for each social condition to be regulated by public opinion, but another, more precise rule, must fix the way in which these conditions are open to individuals" (Durkheim, 1951, p. 249). When the individual is not satisfied with his place, as with Marx's Alienation, his societal rules will tend to lose their value for him. "In normal conditions the collective order is regarded as just by the great majority of persons" (Durkheim, 1951, p. 250). However, ". . . when society is disturbed by some painful crisis or by beneficent but abrupt transitions, it is momentarily incapable of exercising this influence; then . . ." comes Anomie (Durkheim, 1951, p. 251). "The state of deregulation or *anomie* is . . . further heightened by passions being less disciplined, precisely when they need more disciplining" (Durkheim, 1951, p. 252). ". . . the less one has the less he is tempted to extend the range of his need indefinitely. Lack of power, compelling moderation, accustoms men to it, while nothing excites envy if no one has superfluity" (Durkheim, 1951, p. 252). Merton (1949) took the concept of Anomie and used it to define those pressures which cause particular groups to demonstrate high rates of deviant behavior. His aim was to ". . . discover how some social structures exert a definite pressure upon certain persons in the society to engage in noncomformist rather than conformist conduct" (Merton, 1949, p. 125). His central hypothesis was that ". . . aberrant behavior may be regarded sociologically as a symptom of dissociation between culturally-prescribed aspirations and socially-structured avenues of realizing these aspirations" (Merton, 1949, p. 128). Man, he feels, seeks the most efficient means of attaining that which is culturally approved and valuable. However, this does not say that the most efficient means are also legitimate. When this attenuation continues, we have what Durkheim called "Anomie." At this point, only achieving the goal is important: the means of achievement are of little consequence. Such a situation may well lead to the conclusion that "luck" or "pull" is what is needed to get ahead. This last sentiment was evidenced by Shaw in *The Jack Roller* (1930), where Stanley is convinced that fate has determined his lowly standing in the socio-economic hierarchy and that to get along in the world requires the deviant behavior which has continued to keep him in a state of Anomie. Merton feels that deviant behavior will ensue on a large scale when the cultural values make certain success goals for the society extremely important while the social structure restricts the approved methods of goal achievement to only a certain part of the general population. For the excluded members, deviation may be the only avenue of achievement. As Cohen (1955, p. 95) points out: "Both in preachment and in practice the working-class boy is liable to find the middle-class ethic much attenuated in the lives of his parents and the parents of his neighborhood peers. Their aspirations with respect to jobs and income are likely to be well below what a middle-class person would consider necessary for respectability. If they are 'ambitious,' they are likely to be ambitious for a working-class job recognized by their mates as better than the average job available or better than that from which they started. They do not typically aspire to middle-class jobs." Rather, their tendency is to seek middle-class goals through working-class means. This occurs, to a great extent, because the overall societal goals are in fact determined by middle-class representatives. "One of the situations in which children of all social levels come together and compete for status in terms of the same set of middle-class criteria and in which working-class children are most likely to be found wanting is in the school" (Cohen, 1955, p. 112). "Despite reservations such as 'with due regard to individual differences,' this conception of 'democratic' education implies that a major function of the schools is to 'promote,' 'encourage,' 'motivate,' 'stimulate,' in brief, *reward* middle-class ambition and conformity to middle-class expectations" (Cohen, 1955, p. 113). Such is also to be found in the entertainment and news media: television, magazines, newspapers. However, in slum areas, where organized delinquency seems to predominate, one finds a lack of opportunity to achieve these middle-class standards due to the segregation of those ethnic groups deemed least desirable (often the most recent newcomers to the country) by the *better* classes of people.

Bell (Cloward and Ohlin, 1960, p. 196) noted that "the coalition of crime and politics has been a crucial factor in the assimilation of many immigrant groups during the past century. Blocked from legitimate access to wealth, the immigrant feels mounting pressures for the use of illegal alternatives. This has resulted in the progressive encroachment by the descendants of each new immigrant group upon the rackets structures established by preceding ethnic or nationality groups." In the early 1930's, Italians were excluded from the better jobs both in and out of government. At that time, Italians tended to dominate youthful delinquency roles, and now they predominate in gambling and "mob" positions. ". . . twenty years ago children of Eastern European Jews were the most prominent figures in organized crime, and before that individuals of Irish descent were similarly prominent." As children born for the most part in the U.S.A., the offspring of immigrants seek the goals they have learned to expect, but in their transitionary stage: with parents who retain 'old country' values—they find they do not fit in and are often rebuffed as undesirables. Shaw states in *The Jack-Roller* (1930, p. 35), "The original settlers, who moved in the area to work in the Chicago stock yards, were predominantly Irish, German, and Scandinavian; while the present population is largely Polish, Russian, and Lithuanian." He adds: "Such marked changes in the cultural composition of the neighborhood has undoubtedly entailed considerable disorganization and confusion of moral standards." And he concludes: ". . . there is a definite break between the foreign-born parents and their native-born children. In many of the families the relation between the child and parent assumes the character of an emotional conflict, which definitely complicates the problem of parental control and greatly interferes with the incorporation of the child into the social milieu of his parents." The fact that middle-class goals are shut off from the working-class child does not, however, make the goals undesirable, but achievable only through other than normal channels. Thrasher (1927, p. 22) adds, "The gang is almost invariably characteristic of regions that are interstitial . . . 'the poverty belt'—a region characterized by deteriorating neighborhoods, shifting populations, and . . . mobility. . . .''

DELINQUENCY

When a cluster of people finds itself in a position whereby certain desires of its members are thwarted by some outside pressure, the individuals tend to come together with the express purpose of finding a solution to their dilemma (Sherif and Sherif, 1956). Since they have a common goal—to get ahead—they soon acquire an informal and spontaneous kind of organization. Some members become leaders: they tend to take more responsibility and tend to develop more and better plans toward solution. Various duties are divided up among the members of this newly forming group, and unwritten norms of behavior and a certain *espirit de corps* begin to develop. Eventually a single leader with his lieutenants emerges. After a while, a complete hierarchy evolves, with some members being at the bottom of the heap while others assume positions between the top and the bottom. As long as this group can continue to provide solutions to the problem of goal achievement, it will remain intact, with little change in its purpose or structure, with the possible exception of continual changes in membership. This group now takes on the stature of reference group for new or growing members of the community. The group or gang thereby perpetuates itself with a continual infusion of aspiring members. The gang has now become the primary anchor for achievement for the youth of the area. Cohen (1955) states that the delinquent subculture offers the status which could not be achieved by normal means. Cloward and Ohlin (1960, p. 197) add:

> During this stage the integrated slum organization comes into being. Alliances develop between racketeers and police, politicians, and other legitimate elements of the community. The power of the politician grows, partly financed by the newly won and enlarging wealth of the racketeer. Increased political power makes it possible for the racketeer not only to gain entry to 'respectable' ruling groups within the larger urban structure but also to open channels of legiti-

mate ascent for others. Thus illegal activity contributes to social mobility by legitimate as well as illegitimate channels.

In *The Professional Thief,* Sutherland (1937, pp. 211–213) offers an insight into the means of entry into organized delinquency by his theory of Differential Association: "Professional theft is a group way of life. One can get into the group and remain in it only by the consent of those previously in the group." "A professional thief is a person who has the status of a professional thief in the differential association of professional thieves." The mere desire to become a professional is not enough, however. "Selection and tutelage are the two necessary elements in the process. . . ." "A person cannot acquire recognition as a professional thief until he has had tutelage in professional theft, and tutelage is given only to a few persons selected from the total population." Those who eventually enter the professional ranks do so ". . . as a result of contact with professional thieves, reciprocal confidence and appreciation, a crisis situation, and tutelage." The type of crisis which ellicits the entry into apprenticeship may be the loss of a job, getting "caught in amateur stealing," or the need for money. During his apprenticeship, the ". . . neophyte is assimilating the general standards of morality, propriety, etiquette, and rights which characterize the profession, and he is acquiring 'larceny sense.' " In *Principles of Criminology* (1955, pp. 77–79), Sutherland and Cressey list the nine precepts of the Genetic Theory (Differential Association) of criminal behavior as:

1. Criminal behavior is learned.
2. Criminal behavior is learned in interaction with other persons in a process of communication.
3. The principal part of the learning of criminal behavior occurs within intimate personal groups.
4. When criminal behavior is learned, the learning includes (a) techniques of committing the crime, which are sometimes very complicated and sometimes very simple; (b) the specific direction of motives, drives, rationalizations, and attitudes.
5. The specific direction of motives and drives is learned from definitions of the legal codes as favorable or unfavorable.
6. A person becomes delinquent because of an excess of definitions favorable to violation of law over definitions unfavorable to violation of law.

7. Differential associations may vary in frequency, duration, priority, and intensity.
8. The process of learning criminal behavior by association with criminal and anticriminal behavior by association with criminal and anticriminal patterns involves all the mechanisms that are involved in any other learning.
9. While criminal behavior is an expression of general needs and values, it is not explained by those general needs and values since noncriminal behavior is an expression of the same needs and values.

Sutherland adds that, in a delinquency area, the "sociable, gregarious, active, and athletic" boy will likely "come in contact with the other boys in the neighborhood, learn delinquent behavior from them, and become a gangster." On the other hand, a boy in a different environment, with the same attributes, "may become a member of a scout troop and not become involved in delinquent behavior." However, Sutherland (1956) cautions that while differential association may be necessary for an individual to enter organized delinquency, it need not be sufficient to cause entry invariably. Cohen (1955), p. 148) adds: ". . . a subculture owes its existence to the fact that it provides a solution to certain problems of adjustment shared among a community of individuals. However, it does not follow . . . for every individual who participates that these problems provide the sole or sufficient source of motivation. Indeed, there may be some participants to whose motivation these problems contribute very little." Reasons for joining a particular subculture, feels Cohen (1955, p. 150), may be for no other reason than "the delinquent groups in his neighborhood happen to be of his own racial or ethnic in-group, whereas the nondelinquents are predominantly of an out-group from which he wishes to disaffiliate himself. . . . Another may join a gang as an alternative to being regularly beaten up by that gang."

Whatever the reason for joining a gang, gang membership is expected and accepted in the slums. Zorbaugh (1929) notes that in those areas where delinquency prevails, "highjacking" to achieve a decent living is looked upon appreciatively, just as the "higher" levels of society tend to overlook the means whereby some tycoons gain their fortunes. In *The Jack Roller* (Shaw,

1930), Stanley mentions that his stepmother would send him out "robbin."

That gang or group membership is important in the continuation of delinquency in specific areas was attested to by Shaw and his collaborators (1929, p. 186) when they discovered that ". . . the extent of recidivism is highest in the areas having the highest rate of delinquent gangs . . . This finding suggests that the factors contributing to delinquency in these areas of concentration tend also to give rise to recidivism by increasing both the proportion of delinquents who become recidivists and the number of times the recidivists appear in court."

But, not all deviants remain forever in the areas which fostered their delinquencies, nor do all remain deviants for life. Shaw (1930) noted how Stanley finally settled down after many years in various types of detention, got a job, married, and had a child. Cloward and Ohlin (1960, p. 198) state that "The successful racketeer or businessman generally takes up residence in the suburbs rather than continue to live in the slum of his youth. . . ." Thrasher (1927) mentions that "There has been a tendency for . . . the gang's members to be incorporated into the more conventional activities of society." "Members of the profession," says Sutherland's Thief (1937, p. 24), "make their exit from the profession in various ways. Some die, some get too old to work and wind up in a home for old people, some develop a habit (drug) and become too inefficient to be professional thieves, some violate the ethics of the profession and are kicked out, some . . . become big shots in gambling, vice, junk, or booze rackets, some get 'the big one' (extraordinarily large theft), and some settle down in legitimate occupations without getting the big one.'" He adds that detective agencies, cab companies, cigar stores, hotels, farming, manufacturing, and the movies are some of the legitimate pursuits entered by professional thieves. However delinquents choose to leave the slums, the area tends to degenerate still more. "What remains in the community is a residual of 'failures'—persons who have not succeeded in the search for higher socioeconomic status. The old forms of social organization begin to break down, and with them opportunities for upward mobility diminish" (Cloward & Ohlin, 1960, p. 199).

It is at such a time that new ethnic groups usually take over the neighborhood and find their routes to success and status hindered. It is in such a condition that Cloward and Ohlin predict the emergence of a *conflict subculture* (See Appendix).

CONCLUSION

There is often a tendency to look at the contributions of individual students and theorists of delinquency and attempt to rate the relative value of each. By so doing, however, one loses sight of the overall view. It is not what Durkheim theorized, not what Merton made out of it, nor is it what Shaw and Sutherland found, nor what Cloward, Ohlin, and Cohen have determined that is important, in-and-of itself. It is the compilation of all their works and those of many others that begin to tell the story.

Marx and Durkheim were among those theorists who provided a starting point. Sociologists such as Shaw, Sutherland, Zorbaugh, and Thrasher provided much of the "legwork." And criminologists like Cloward, Ohlin, and Cohen have attempted to put together and enlarge upon what has come before. Utilizing the earlier findings and tempering them with more modern determinations, scholars, of whom the latter three are representative, have gone far toward demonstrating the "why's" of delinquent subculture. Many social-work organizations in large cities are attempting to control those subcultures in existence, but it is now of utmost importance for academicians to seek answers on how to prevent them from being *necessary*.

A suggested approach is the combination of legislated opportunities, such as those set forth beginning with the 1964 Federal Civil Rights Act. Legislation has proven a useful method in combatting prejudice, when it is enforced, and superordinate goals are applied on a large scale which would allow slum dwellers to overcome various neighborhood problems. Whether such is feasible, or, if so, how it would be accomplished, will not be gone into here. Since the first is already being attempted, it might be well to first analyze the results to see how the second could be implemented.

SUMMARY

Delinquency has been explained by many theories, both simple and complex. However, the majority of these theories offers little in the way of useful material or simply does not go far enough to explain delinquency on a large scale. The purpose of this theme has been to bring together those singular theories which seem to offer the greatest possibilities of explanation of delinquent subcultures. An attempt has been made to demonstrate the need for anchorages to guide one toward success. It has been shown that slum youngsters, unable to utilize the greater society as their reference group, have been forced to band together in smaller groups which would allow them to achieve success, although illegitimately. For the most part, organized delinquency was treated as deriving in slum societies. While it is true that a certain amount of middle-class delinquency in groups has been known to occur, the reference group explanation would be equally valid in such situations. While middle-class delinquents are not denied pursuit of middle-class goals, they often are denied a feeling of belongingness which tends to make the banding together for "thrill purposes" necessary.

Using Marx's Alienation and Durkheim's Anomie to describe the lower-class plight, a direction was taken through youthful apprenticeship in crime to professional standing, all of which comprises the deviants' attempts to attain the success goals denied them by society. That societal success goals are the driving force behind much of organized delinquency may well be seen in the fact that many professional criminals, when successful, take their first opportunities to become a part of the normal society.

In conclusion, it was stated that a possible solution to organized delinquency in many areas might take the two-pronged form of legislation, and the development of superordinate goals which might encompass entire slum societies in our large cities.

REFERENCES

Allport, F. H.: *Theories of Perception and the Concept of Structure.* New York, Wiley, 1955.

Cartwright, D., and Zander, A.: *Group Dynamics: Research and Theory.* Evanston, Row, Peterson, 1960.

Cloward, R. A., and Ohlin, L. E.: *Delinquency and Opportunity.* Glencoe, Ill., Free Press, 1960.

Cohen, A. K.: *Delinquent Boys.* Glencoe, Ill., Free Press, 1955.

Durkheim, E.: *Suicide: A Study in Sociology.* Glencoe, Ill., Free Press, 1951.

Freud, S.: *Group Psychology and the Analysis of the Ego.* London, Hogarth, 1922.

Marx, K.: The notion of alienation. In Coser, L. A., and Rosenberg, B.: Macmillan, 1964.

Merton, R. K.: *Social Theory and Social Structure,* Glencoe: The Free Press, 1949.

Newcomb, T. N.: *Personality and Social Change.* New York, Dryden, 1943.

Parsons, T.: *The Social System.* Glencoe, Ill., Free Press, 1951.

Piaget, J.: *The Moral Judgment of the Child.* London, Kegan Paul, Trench, Trubner, 1932.

Seeman, M.: On the meaning of alienation. In Coser, L. A. and Rosenberg, B.: *Sociological Theory: A Book of Readings.* New York, Macmillan, 1964.

Shaw, C. R.: *The Jack Roller.* Chicago, University of Chicago Press, 1930.

Shaw, C. R.: *Delinquency Areas.* Chicago, University of Chicago Press, 1929.

Sherif, M. and Sherif, C. W.: *An Outline of Social Psychology.* New York, Harper and Row, 1956.

Sherif, M.; Harvey, O. J.; White, B. J.; Hood, W. R., and Sherif, C. W.: *Intergroup Conflict and Cooperation: The Robbers Cave Experiment.* Norman, Institute of Group Relations, University of Oklahoma, 1961.

Sutherland, E. H.: Critique of the theory. In Cohen, A.; Lindesmith, A. and Schuessler, K.: *The Sutherland Papers.* Bloomington, Indiana University Press, 1956.

Sutherland, E. H.: *The Professional Thief.* Chicago, University of Chicago Press, 1937.

Sykes, G. M., and Matza, D.: Techniques of neutralization: a theory of delinquency. In Wolfgang, M. Z., Savitz, L., and Johnston, N.: *The Sociology of Crime and Delinquency.* New York, Wiley, 1962.

Thrasher, F. M.: *The Gang.* Chicago, University of Chicago Press, 1927.

Whyte, W. F.: *Streetcorner Society.* Chicago, University of Chicago Press, 1943.

Zorbaugh, H. W.: *The Goldcoast and the Slum.* Chicago, University of Chicago Press, 1929.

APPENDIX

THREE TYPES OF DELINQUENT SUBCULTURE
(Cloward and Ohlin, 1960, pp. 161–186)

As a general rule, delinquency is treated as a singular phenomenon. Effort is not usually made to differentiate between various types of deviations. Whether one steals, fights, or partakes of some habit-forming concoction, he is merely "delinquent." Cloward and Ohlin, however, believe that "Delinquent responses vary from one neighborhood to another . . . according to the articulation of these structures in the neighborhood." The three subcultural differentiations that are made fall under the headings: Criminal Subculture; Conflict Subculture; Retreatist Subculture.

Criminal Subculture

In a way, the criminal subculture serves the purpose of a proving-ground for future "professionals." The neighborhood in which such a subculture evolves is usually highly integrated, with close bonds between the aspirants and the professionals. As a result of this relationship, the restrictions placed on the youngsters by the larger society is effectively bypassed as success is achieved, albeit illegitimately. That which is stolen by the young delinquents is not necessarily for use but may merely serve the purpose of developing skills. While under the tutelage of more experienced delinquents, "Social control over the conduct of the young are effectively exercised limiting expressive behavior and constraining the discontented to adopt instrumental, if criminalistic styles of life."

Conflict Subculture

In areas where both the conventional and the aforementioned criminal opportunities are limited, "frustrations and position discontent" are intensified. Lacking the integration noted in the criminal subcultural areas, there is a lack of social control. In such circumstances the adolescents who are no longer constrained by "the professionals" use violence to achieve status. Since criminal apprenticeship is unattainable, "Violence comes to be ascendent . . . under conditions of relative detachment from all institutionalized systems of opportunity and social control."

Retreatist Subculture

Up to this point, the discussion has centered on developments due to an inability to utilize legitimate means to achieve success. However, there are also those who find it impossible to achieve success even by illegitimate means, even when such means are available. ". . . adolescents who are double failures are more vulnerable than others to retreatist behaviors . . ." Of this group, some will become law-abiding lower-class citizens (Whyte's 'Corner Boys' (1943)). Others apparently do not find it possible to revise their "aspirations downward to correspond to reality." ". . . for those who continue to exhibit high aspirations under conditions of double failure retreatism is the expected result." Such activities take the form of addiction to alcohol or drugs.

Chapter 4

HUMAN PERSONALITY AND ITS ADAPTIVE AND DEFENSIVE DEVICES

M. M. VITOLS

Every man has three characters: that which he exhibits,
that which he has, and that which he thinks he has.
Alphonse Karr

- INFANCY
- EARLY CHILDHOOD
- SOCIAL DIFFERENTIATION
- MIDDLE CHILDHOOD
- PUBERTY AND ADOLESCENCE
- REFERENCES

THE HUMAN PERSONALITY is a complex of characteristics which distinguishes a particular individual in relation to others. The human personality not only denotes the functioning of the person but also distinguishes him from his fellowman. There are specific features in each individual personality, but on an average, the basic needs, drives, urges, and impulses are approximately the same in adulthood as is at birth. It also is true that there are individual differences in the degree of motility and activity of the newborn, as well as some inherited differences in temperament, and certainly some inherited differences in physique and body build. To understand the human personality it is essential to know how a particular person is expressing his needs and his relationship functions as a recognizable unity with distinctive traits, drives, attitudes and habits which enable or prevent him from attaining an adequate adjustment to himself, to other human beings, as well as to his environment.

Freud, when asked what was meant by "mental health," replied, "The capacity to work and love." The formulation of the nature of emotional maturity and wholesome personality is even better described by Saul (1958), who has expressed it as the capacity to enjoy loving and being loved and also the ability to maintain a proper balance between responsible working and harmless recreation. So, the well-adjusted, emotionally mature personality would be expected to have:

1. a sense of identity—the capacity to understand and respond to the needs of others, as well as awareness of the identity of others;
2. a sense of reality and a capacity to maintain contact with reality;
3. a capacity and ability to maintain control of one's drives;
4. an awareness not only about one's own capacity and the use of it, but also an awareness of one's handicaps;
5. a capacity and ability to delay action and assume responsibility for himself as well as for others;
6. considerable capacity to tolerate tension and discomfort.

These capacities should come about from a very complex development of biophysical and biopsychological processes which proceed in successive stages. The personality development is a genetic, dynamic, progressive, integrating, organizing, evolutional process that is biologically, culturally, and psychologically determined. From conception the human embryo develops from a single-cell to a multi-cell organism with genetic factors which play a significant role in the developing fetus. There is some inconclusive evidence that the mother's emotional state may influence the development of the future mental apparatus of the individual as far as cognitive functions are concerned. From birth the biophysical development continues with the mental apparatus emerging later as a personality. From birth, environmental factors (especially early childhood influences such as parents, culture, and society) exercise their influence and mold the personality. There is a continuity between the biological, psychological, and social evaluation in the development of the human personality. This evaluation proceeds in certain phases with each phase being characterized not only by biological development, but psychological development as well. This stage or phase is intimately coupled with biological growth and concomitant development of humans' adaption not only to deal with inner needs, but also with the world around him. Each stage of development might best be described by the most predominant developmental factor at that stage. Development really is a continuum; it often is divided into stages only for convenience of description and discussion.

The stages of development are: *Infancy*—the so-called oral stage referring to the fact that the infant gets the gratification of his needs mainly through his mouth as a part of his body around which sensations and activities are centered. This stage also might be called the stage of dependency.

Early childhood, the second through the fourth years, which includes the anal stage when toilet training is attempted and carried out, and in the third or fourth year, the phallic stage where some pleasurable interest is shifted from the anal to the genital region.

Middle childhood, fifth or sixth through ninth or eleventh year, is called the latency period, and is characterized by the development of social skills.

Puberty and ensuing adolescence, is characterized by striking bodily and psysiological changes, as well as sexual differentiation. Keep in mind that the sexual maturity in the biological sense is usually not coincidental with social.

INFANCY

Dependency Phase—Oral Stage

Prior to birth, one may say that the human fetus is living almost in a perfect condition. There is no need for the baby to breathe (the oxygen being provided by the mother's blood); he is fed through the mother's bloodstream; there is always a constant temperature maintained. The baby also floats in the amniotic fluid, which might be considered nature's best cushion and protection against any bumps or pressures. When suddenly it is born, not only the blood circulation changes, but there is an immediate need for oxygen, and in a short time a need for water and food. The basic biological needs of the human from birth are for oxygen, water, food, preservation of body temperature, and being sheltered. If some or all of these needs are not met, the biological development of the infant can be impaired and this would also produce impairment in the functioning of the organs or of the whole body. At the same time, if the infant's psychological needs are not met, the whole emotional growth and development of the human personality will be damaged. Except for the basically fundamental biological needs such as oxygen, water and food, in general the biological needs are converted to mental drives as we see in the total development of the human. Also in the development of the future psychic apparatus, which will form the human personality, we see that the psychological adaptive devices, also called defenses, actually stem from a biological derivation.

Each infant at birth resembles some other human infant in some ways, but also at the same time, each human infant resembles no other human infant in some ways, so we can see in the development that by the time the human reaches adulthood, each individual personality has distinct characteristics, giving not only individuality, but also personality characteristics resembling no other human adult.

At the birth of the infant, the central nervous system as well as the mental apparatus are underdeveloped. As we see at birth, the infant is helpless and, therefore, he needs somebody else to supply him with water, food, and shelter. This necessity brings him into an interaction with another adult, namely and preferably, the mother. In other words, the infant is in a stage of dependency and has to be cared for by another adult, namely his mother. This interaction and relationship also permits the growth and development of the human personality and its psychological adaptive devices. The human infant not only has the presence of the central nervous system, but also has a rather long period of dependency and nursing, and due to these two factors has a capacity to impose a delay between the internally arising instinctive forces which are present at birth and are of a biological nature and the final action to satisfy these drives. (These instinctive forces at birth are later expressed as mental needs or drives.) The presence of the central nervous system, really nature's computer, allows the possibility to sort and analyze any experiences and communicate these experiences to others through movement, action, symbols, and later by speech and writing. The infant's behavior at birth varies between tension (namely, a pure biological need for nourishment—food, water) and periods of relative quiescence. Through the instinctual needs for immediate satisfaction and with the development of the mental apparatus the human learns to delay immediate satisfaction. In a way, we are talking about omnipotence which could be expressed from the view that when baby cries, mother runs and satisfies his needs. This state of omnipotence to a certain degree, might be maintained through quite a few successive stages of human development. For example we are very familiar with the daydreaming of small children who picture themselves as omnipotent when they grow up, such as the small boy dreaming to be a policeman that with one gesture of the hand, he will stop all traffic and people have to obey him when he tells them what to do. But he later finds out, becoming more realistic, that his imaginary policeman has more responsibilities and duties but very few, if any, privileges.

There are variations in the initial emotional endowment in each baby, which stems from the intensity of the drives which vary from baby to baby. His future development depends also upon the maturity of the central nervous system and the presence or absence of birth defects or injuries. The infant at birth is unable to wait for immediate satisfaction and is very demanding. At the same time, both the infant and the mother are being involved in a relationship. The baby's behavior as well as the mother's responses play quite a crucial role and create the foundation of the personality characteristics to be seen in later life. A strong biological dependence and later a psychological dependence on the mother and/or parent result later in adults who need others to depend on and depend on others for emotional support. These persons are fairly characterized by being helpless, they are constantly asking for help, are ineffective in their lives, have little initiative and attempt to transfer their dependency needs from one person to another. In another person there are the same strong dependency needs. They are camouflaged and covert. The person will appear on the surface to be domineering, demanding, expecting that people owe him a living. This may occur when the mother, during infancy, has been over-protective, very indulgent, discouraging the infant from gaining emotional independence from her. Thus, the child becomes reluctant to give up a rather satisfying experience and to progress in emotional development. This same thing might happen when the baby has experienced a rather pronounced emotional deprivation from the mother. We see these people as immature, and sometimes trying to meet their emotional needs at the expense of others with no concern for them.

In normal development, the baby develops a confidence in the mother and when the need for food arises, he will develop the ability to wait. At the same time, he is developing a relationship with the mother, first actually recognizing the mother's face and later the mother as a whole. This is what we call the *Object Relationship*. This is also the first relationship with the outside world. This is also the basis for all other relationships to be developed in later life. An unsatisfactory relationship with the mother or her substitute can reflect in unsatisfactory relationships between the individual and other humans in later life. Some humans never develop the ability to impose a delay between a need and the satisfaction of that need, and, therefore, seek immediate gratification without respect or regard for other human beings. We see them in adult life as impulsive individuals who see the world only in the light of their own needs, not only having disregard for others, but also as self-centered, pleasure-seeking individuals.

Stimulation is also necessary for healthy physical and psychological development. The physical contact such as rocking, cuddling, and other warm gratifying responses from the mother provide the media for healthy development. The lack of adequate emotional responses, even with adequate water and food intake, may cause not only high tension states which form a biological foundation for future anxiety, but it actually also causes apathy and withdrawal, which is a biological foundation of depression. So the results not only physical or biological deprivation, but also emotional deprivation are seen in the personality characteristics of adolescents and adults coming not only from the lower socio-economic group but also from families with broken homes and homes with disturbed parent-relationships. At times these environmental factors have provided not only lack of physical stimulation but more important, lack of emotional stimulation. This lack of emotional as well as intellectual stimulation early in life affects the child's ability and preparedness to enter school and be successful. The program, Head Start, demonstrated rather clearly that this sort of stimulation should not start at the age of four or five, but preferably within the second year of the human life.

At this stage in development, in the beginning relationship with the mother, the baby not only starts a differentiation between himself and outside, but also begins to show the development of the first adaptive or defensive devices which is called Mental Mechanisms. These adaptive devices are necessary to the development of the personality and are in most successful adaptive mechanisms. There are also others which are rather unsuccessful adaptive devices. The first adaptive devices are *introjection* and *projection*. These mechanisms or devices have biological bases. Introjection (taking in) is represented on a biological basis (the good food is retained). Such biological needs are translated to mental needs. In the beginning good food is retained later on good images, good experiences, and good impressions are retained. This process also forms the first type of *identification* which is to be discussed later in this chapter. The conceptions of another person, the sentiments and effects are incorporated into the individual's own personality. At the same time, anger and hostility can be introjected creating anxiety and depression. The anger toward someone else might be retained within one's self, namely introjected, resulting not only in depression, but also in self-destruction, namely suicide.

The other mental mechanism, or adaptive device, *projection,* also first has a biological basis: what is bad, such as food or something else may be pushed away or spit out and later, translated psychologically, this becomes a mental device used against anxiety by which one's own disclaimed objectionable character traits, attitudes, motives, desires are directed outward and attributed to others. We use this device frequently by contributing our own guilt to somebody else. To a certain extent, it might be a reasonably successful device to prevent us from reasonable guilt or shame, but otherwise used, it might become an objectionable or unsuccessful defense mechanism. For example, the person acting out in a hostile or aggressive way or in a more extreme manner as we see in paranoid mental disorders. Projection is one of the most prominent mental mechanisms.

A controversy exists as to the source and development of Aggression. There is some thought that aggression is the result of frustration which every child undergoes to a certain degree, but one is also familiar with the infant's aggressive attitudes toward the food source, such as the mother's breast or the bottle of milk. The baby is not a passive recipient, there is a certain amount of aggression in all of us, for if an individual would not be aggressive he would not be able to satisfy some of his basic physical and emotional needs, nor could he pursue the goals of later life. One is very familiar with the so-called passive person and with persons who do not have sufficient aggressive drives. However, it should be pointed out that aggression should be constructive and channelized and not be destructive to ourselves or others. It has been pointed out by many authorities in recent writings that violence is not necessarily related to anger, hostility, or rage, and that violence can consist of acts carried out without ostensible emotion. Bettelheim (1969) for example, has described the violent acts of students as an expression of paranoid characters who deprived of parental warmth and affection are looking for an object on which to project and vent their rage.

Such statements tend to emphasize the effective component

of violence and overlook its instrumental nature. As recent research has shown (Blumenthal, 1972) the facts leading to violence are complex and include both affective-emotion as well as instrumental considerations. As it has been pointed out, in the actual process of executing an order to perform a violent action, emotions may play a considerable role. Resentment and suspicion alone, which might be regarded as measures of a tendency to feel paranoid and hostile, fail to account for a significant part of the variations and attitudes as to how much violence can be used to maintain or attain social control.

It should be emphasized that the child-mother unity is of extreme importance in the development of the first year of life, especially in the second half. The bodily needs, such as food, rest and feeling well are very closely connected to the child's need for affection for the mother, breakage of ties between the mother and child upsets the functioning of the bodily process to a much greater degree than the breakage of routine or external environment. In the close relationship to the parents, or better to say "to the mother" the child is able to develop functions such as speech, muscle control, and control of excretory functions. When the ties are disturbed or broken the newly acquired functions lose their value at least temporarily. Also, the future development of the moral values of the child depend upon the close relationship with the parent or parents' attitude. There again, when this relationship is disturbed or broken such as by death or separation, a child may regress to the developmental stages of the earlier time. Also, in this stage of development we can see the seeds of ambivalence, namely feeling two ways about the same thing or the same person. When the mother's attitude is somewhat inconsistent, the child develops an ambivalence towards the mother and later with people in general.

It should be brought up at this point that the original affection, namely relationship, between the child and the mother is also the first beginning of love. Of course, in the earlier years of the human development, the love would be better described as a positive feeling which makes the infant feel well. But concurrent with the object relationship the child develops a love; namely, the love of the child or infant for the mother. This is the only original love for all the other loves which a human will develop stem from this original love, as the son's love for the mother will be transferred to his wife, or the daughter's love for her mother transferred to the father and later to the husband of her choice. It is quite obvious that if the child has not been able to develop love—positive emotions—in the relationship with the mother, this will be reflected in future relationships with other people, as we can see in children who suffer severe emotional deprivations in early childhood. These people simply do not have the necessary emotions to give love to somebody, for unconsciously they are still looking to be loved on an infantile level.

EARLY CHILDHOOD

Mastery of Biological Skills—Toilet Training

Around the end of the first year or in the middle of the second year, the child not only becomes increasingly aware and responsive to his environment, but he also begins to discover parts of his body that distinguishes himself from the world outside. Also the motor functions become more active, more purposeful, and standing and walking increases. This is actually, in a way, a period of mastery of the biological skills. Now he has not only mastered muscle control to a great degree, especially starting to feed himself, but also with the maturation of the nerve fibres, the beginning of sphincter control begins to develop in the second year. The nerve fibres having matured usually around the eighteenth month of life. The child, in a way, becomes very interested in his excretory functions, but also the parent is very interested in controlling them. In a way, the child has to conform to the mother's demands and expectations or suffer the consequences. It is interesting to see that the mother's own feelings, conflicts originating in her own toilet training period, may influence to a very great degree how she deals with the child. Also, the speech and language, the human's distinctive property, develops in this time period providing a new level of communication as a human. Therefore, the mouth, which has been used not only for taking food but also to suck in order to provide a pleasurable sensation, loses some of its importance; the pleasurable sensations are continued, in a way, through the organs of elimination. The baby's own attitude toward its feces at first is that of disregard, but very soon from awareness and disinterest he starts to develop interest in his excreta. The mother had a "say so" about the feeding and sucking, but now with elimination the baby is more or less in control. The interaction between the child and the parent is in the bowel training. Not only is it important during the second and third years of life, but may also invoke a possible change in relationships.

The child may retain the bowels to defy the mother; so here begins the pattern of stubbornness, which might be reflected in later personality. He also can retain to please the mother; he denies the pleasure of defecation in order to please the mother. He also can move his bowels at his pleasure to defy the mother, but in a good relationship, he can also move them to please her, and there he has the ability to enlist his mastery of his motor system to establish a better relationship between him and the parent. It should be said that in this interaction between the mother and infant, there is a high potential for some future psychological conflicts to develop.

He is achieving more muscle control, so the baby starts to show more aggressive destructive behavior. Breaking and tearing up is prominent at that time. In case the mother or parents attempt the muscle control, not recognizing that somewhat pleasurable feelings with excretion, and before maturation of the nerve fibres, and also before the baby has developed some communication system, such as signs, later words, speech and language, any attempts to enforce toilet training by severe and punitive methods will produce emotional conflicts in the baby and so harmfully influence the developing personality. There is evidence that rather permanent scars in the personality, such as anger, hostility or resentment, as well as highly ambivalent attitudes toward parents may be created. These conflicts may have lasting impressions and under stress in later life show disorder of bowel functions, constipation, or diarrhea. The bowel disorders might persist in the early childhood or reoccur and so become a means of unconscious expression. There is a natural act between the biological status and the emotional development toward independence. As pointed out before, the child may stop in emotional development or regress to an earlier stage. The scars to a greater or lesser degree may reflect earlier unsolved conflicts and then we talk about so-called *Fixations,* which are a cessation of the process of development of the personality at a stage short of complete and uniform mature emotional development. In this particular stage, fixations will be reflected in the human personality as morbid stubbornness and obstinancy, as character traits, but also might be characterized by the mental mechanism of undoing or compensation. This is reflected in the character trait of over-cleanliness or meticulousness. Or in a pure form as a sloppiness or disorderliness, we also find roots of later adult compulsive neuroses and the ambivalence of personal attitudes.

SOCIAL DIFFERENTIATION

The Phallic Stage

By the third year, the horizons of the child are extended and his own individuality is more clearly asserted. There is a development of locomotion, motor skills, and speech. The child becomes more adventurous and so induces a change in his mother relationship. He becomes somewhat more independent and as a toddler explores the world around him. This may create a conflict in the mother, who in the infancy liked the infant and took complete care of him; however, now the mother starts to worry about the danger to which the child is exposed. Also, the toddler's disorderliness and destructiveness might provoke anger with her as well as helplessness. However, there are also mothers who welcome the toddler stage for there are many patterns of relationship between the mother and the child. The mother's personality, her own conflicts and needs have to be considered; therefore, the mother's capacity and effectiveness as a mother and the satisfaction of motherhood is not always the same at all points of the child's development.

The child now is able to make a distinction between himself and the external world. He also starts to learn the conditions under which his needs can be gratified. But more important, his pleasure-seeking intentions start to become much more defined by the demands of reality. He starts to realize and to know what mother likes and dislikes and the same extends to the father, the family, and people around him. With this, he is exposed to more people and objects and by the mental mechanism of introjection he internalizes them thereby providing himself with guides and models for his behaviors. (His identification increases rapidly at this stage, at times, by the means of imitation.) This process of identification continues and again will be quite pronounced during his development in the adolescent stage. A child at that age is unable really to exercise judgment and insight. Therefore, he is very much dependent on the feedback, namely, the emotional expressions, attitudes and behavior from the people around him. If the feedback is somewhat negative, the toddler might start to see himself as being bad by the same mechanism of introjection and might even have to a certain degree a self-depreciation. The result is that quite often, in spite of good accomplishments, he does not feel that he is good and therefore constantly devaluates himself, either on a conscious or unconscious level. This devaluation is usually referred to as feelings of inferiority and/or insecurity.

During the development in this stage, we see great attachments to inanimate things, such as an article of clothing, blankets, etc. They may become essential for comfort and sleep. There is also less inclination to use mouth and teeth aggressively and also there is less need for impulses to be immediately satisfied or immediately translated into behavior. However, we still see the remnants of the so-called oral stage, which actually will be retained in our adult life. These remnants include behavior such as smoking, chewing, kissing, and even in the use of language, using such terms as "I could eat you." Also, the oral aggression might be used in the term, "biting sarcasm," or "He has a sharp tongue." The child's curiosity increases about his own body, also about the bodies of the persons around him. His greatest discovery is the difference between the external genitalia of the boy and girl. He might perceive pleasurable sensations in genitalia and masturbation may occur at that age. However, it should be emphasized that the interest is not an essential one as in the adult sense of the term. There is some preoccupation and fantasy about ones' own external genitalia and the absence of the penis in the girl. A child might be either surprised, impressed, or frightened by the father's large penis or the mother's pubic hair. Curiosity about pregnancy and birth also arises at this time. This particular stage is a very turbulent one, for it is a period in which important differentiations between male and female are being made regarding self and figures in the environment. This stage also might be called the *STAGE OF THE PRIMARY SOCIAL DIFFERENTIATION*. It should be said that certain needs are universal. They receive different emphasis in different societies. Social and cultural factors play an important role in establishing the concepts of sexuality which are acceptable to the group. The societies are constantly perpetuating concepts. It must be granted that the human personality is a product of learning, and much of this learning is culturally determined and controlled. Human beings generally find it highly rewarding to behave like others who share the same culture. Also, during infancy and childhood, the child will in any event be developing certain "attitudes toward life," such as confidence, resignation, optimism, or pessimism. His attitudes will be determined largely by the kind and amount of "actual care given." Emotional patterns toward parents or brothers and sisters often will become the prototype of habitual reactions toward friends, associates, employees, and employers. Societies in which childhood experiences are typical of over-strong but unsatisfied dependency upon the father will create a fertile soil for the demigogue. On the other hand in cultures such as the Zuni Indians, the child's attachment is spread among many relatives and where the child's dependency is focused upon the group as a whole, rather than upon a particular individual, the child develops a resistance to a dictatorial type of leader. Also in cultures where the mother is a true center of family life, divinities are apt to be portrayed in a female form. In every culture, however, success or reward is essential to all learning. If a response is not rewarded, it will not be learned, so all responses will become habitual or "good" from the organism's point of view and will provide some sort of satisfaction. "Badness" of habits is a judgment that is attached to them by the other persons—a "habit" is bad if it annoys another person or persons. With the child being aware of the difference between the boy and the girl, between the father and the mother, the future development between the boy and girl start to differ. The culture, more and more plays a role not only determining the parents' attitudes and behavior, but also impinges directly upon the child, so what is masculine behavior in any society is determined both not only by a biological but also a cultural difference.

The Boy

Being aware of the anatomical differences the boy begins to associate more with his father and other male figures in the family. In the absence of male figures in his environment or even with the presence of a so-called weak father, the little boy might have difficulties in assuming a psychological masculine role in the overall process of identification. A boy taken care of only by females might have to identify with them, so he may develop feminine trends at the expense of a more masculine quality. We can see that the boy starts seeing himself as a little man and at the same time sees his father as a rival in competition for the mother. He feels more attraction to his mother, namely, the parent of the opposite sex, which at times is accompanied by jealousy, rivalry, and hostility toward the parent of the same sex, namely his own father. This situation between the father and mother and the son gave rise to the term *Oedipus Complex*. Quite a few anthropologists reject the presence of the Oedipus Complex and feel that this is a child's reaction toward one's own parents. This potentially emotionally changed relationship is usually resolved by the mechanism of *identification*, which in healthy situations, the boy identifies with his father and incorporates the father's drives, goals, and standards into his own behavior.

The Girl

During the development of the girl, she appears somewhat less aggressive, less defiant, but very often is precocious in her overall development. The girl, before she achieves the adult heterosexual status, must change her objects of love from mother to father, which is at times rather clearly seen in adolescent girls who have what is referred to as a "crush" on the father. The mother for the girl in a way becomes a rival and the girl might show some antagonism and anger or hostility towards her mother by constant complaining about her. If there happens to be a brother in the family and she envies him or feels that she might be better accepted by the father as a boy, the girl might pass through a period of masculine identification, namely, a "tomboy" phase.

The so-called Oedipus Complex, which develops in a boy generally between the ages of four and six is usually abandoned around the age of six as a result of excessive anxiety. However, in a girl, the Oedipal (Electra conflict) is continued, lasting until puberty or later.

The so-called Complex is in a way the inevitable outgrowth of the infant's dependence and need to be allowed to love and be loved, and the parents become the first love objects. As we can see from a cultural study, it appears that the successful evolution of the highly-developed Oedipal Complex and Electra Complex in our culture has greatly heightened the capacity to establish firm, lasting, and mature love relationships with the opposite sex, so giving a firm basis for later family formation.

The disturbance in relationships play a very important role if the child lacks parental relationships. For example, children living in institutions and foster homes can actually fail to develop to the point of the Oedipus Complex. The child, when he grows up, shows very infantile types of object relationships and aspirations. When the parent of the opposite sex has been removed from the scene or remains absent toward the beginning of this particular phase, the establishing of relationships with members of the opposite sex might prove difficult.

If the child has a parent of the opposite sex who unconsciously behaves in unduly seductive manner this will lead to a conflict which we can find in many neuroses, and if that child later marries, he or she might choose a marital partner who, more or less, would be the duplicate of that particular parent. A similar conflict and results may occur also if there are poor relationships between both parents. A harsh and punitive father makes the solution of conflicts difficult. Boys of such a father might not only give up the mother, but all women in general. He may assume a passive, compliant attitude toward the father and men in general. His personality will show an exaggerated trait of passivity, compliance and timidity, or he might develop more harsh or punitive than the father himself. Girls with such a harsh, punitive father may identify with same in an aggressive, masculine way, never achieving feminity. Or, she may assume a very passive masochistic attitude toward the father by assuming a martyr role, and being sexually frigid. If she marries, she marries a man who mistreats her but to whom she submits without complaint.

If the mother is somewhat aggressive with rather masculine identification and the father is passive, again difficulties are introduced. The boy in this case not only would have an inadequate father-figure with whom to identify, but also he would have to deal with a rather aggressive and punitive mother. The boy would either follow the father's footsteps and develop passive, feminine and a martyr-like character. Generally he would be shy and fearful of women and have a high probability of being sexually impotent. He might even turn toward homosexuality. In case he married, he most likely would look for a wife similar to his mother.

Girls in the same set-up would have difficulties. The aggressive, rather masculine mother would generally reject femininity as well as the maternal role; she would rebel against homemaking and maternal activities, including pregnancy and nursing. The girl might identify with the mother, thereby, developing aggressive, rather masculine identification and would regard passivity as dangerous; or, she may adopt a passive attitude toward the mother, holding the father in low appreciation and developing latent or overt homosexual relationships. In the same situation, the girl may assume a maternal, protective, understanding attitude toward the father and so establish a strong emotional relationship toward him which she is never able to break. However, many boys and girls successfully deal with difficult parent situations. The human not only has a great adaptive capacity, but additionally other figures such as teachers, counselors, members in the extended family, and church leaders may provide better objects of affection to the individuals. These other significant figures in the child's life also provide more adequate objects for identification. In this particular period, nightmares, fantasies and phobias are not uncommon. The children might make up stories and act out fantasies (killing the giant and marrying the princess, being the soldier and killing the big and hostile men). Also prevalent is the fantasy of being bigger than the parent. Interestingly, during this period, children move easily and quickly from fantasy to reality and back.

During this period there is a new facet in the developing mental apparatus, namely, the *Super-Ego*. The conscious representation of this is called *Conscience* or *Social Conscience*. The child in his natural development not only learns what gives him pleasure and pain, but also what kind of behavior gives mother pain or pleasure. Little by little, the image of the mother and later the father are built up by introjection within the child as a sort of guiding and controlling force which directs the impulses and activities of the child in such a way as to conform him to the parents' demands and needs. First, the child curtails activities only in response to direct threatening and harshness. But, after a while, the threat of punishment needs not be repeated and the child responds *if it were* by using the process of identification. The child consciously emulates and tries to be like the parent and sets up an ideal of what he would like to be or what he could be like. If he does not live up to the ideal, he might feel ashamed; when he does, he feels proud. So, the Super-Ego which contains as well as conscious elements, becomes an internalized representation of all the do's and don't's of (the representatives of the moral codes of the culture) the parents, later the family, teachers, counselors, and so on. In the successful development of the Super-Ego, the child makes his guide his own behavior without the actual physical presence of the parent. However, here again, many factors play a role. Many persons develop a rather excessive harsh and punitive conscience, so they exercise a guilty, disapproving and depreciative attitude toward themselves. There are persons who have very poorly developed conscience functions so their standards of living and approaches to life are guided only by their own needs with disregard for the needs of others.

Originally, the basic instincts of the human originate in the biological organization of the organism. However, little by little, psychological representations and other experiences become established in the mental apparatus and start to assume some measure of independence from the body itself, and may be referred to as *"Drives."* Drives are the psychic representations of the instinct, and drives have the effect of initiating, implementing, and modifying behavior and thought. Freud used a rather useful classification of the system of drives. In the structure of personality, they are described as three groups of forces and functions. They should be regarded as hypothetical and interacting psychic segments in the structure of the personality. They are usually referred to as *"Super-Ego"* described above, and *Id* and *Ego.*

The Id is actually a collective name for primitive biological and aggressive impulses and is also referred to as the unconscious part of the personality. It is a reservoir of drives for food, sexuality, aggressiveness, and drives to gain immediate satisfaction either for love or hate.

The Ego, or the reality-testing self, is a part of the personality which meets and establishes relationships with the world in which we live. It is an *Integrator* of the personality and is partly conscious and partly unconscious. The ego deals with the environment through conscious perception, thoughts and feelings and action, and, therefore, is the conscious-controlling part of the personality. It is an intermediary between the inner world and outer world. It might be regarded also as an integrative and executive agency of the personality. The function of the ego is to maintain an optimal, dynamic, and stable balance between the drives of the id and requirements of the external reality. The ego has so-called adaptive or defensive aspects that include prominent signals of warning functions, especially anxiety. It also has other signals such as depression, guilt, and shame. These danger signals of the ego serve to initiate our other defense and/or adaptive mechanisms and with these various adjustive techniques, the human tries to protect the personality as well as satisfy his emotional needs. Through physical and biochemical processes the body maintains a physiological equilibrium or homeostasis, so also the personality maintains an equilibrium or psychological homeostasis through automatic and unconscious psychological processes, called "adaptive" or "defensive" mechanisms. Every human personality continually make use of defense-adaptive mechanisms, which in themselves are not necessarily pathological. However, the type of defense mechanism unconsciously selected, the extent of its use and the degree to which it distorts one's personality and behavior and disturbs his relationships with others, actually determines the measure of an individual's mental health and the outstanding characteristics of the personality.

These adaptive-defensive devices are of two types:

Successful:

Ones which abolish the need for immediate gratification or ones which enable the individual to find substitute gratification. Some authorities use the term *sublimation* to apply to successful defenses.

Unsuccessful:

Defenses do not accomplish what the successful defenses do: therefore, they do not resolve the conflict and there is a continuing need for additional defenses.

The important early adaptive-defensive mechanisms are:

Denial

a mechanism by which consciously intolerable thoughts are disowned by an unconscious denial of their existence. The term *denial* when used in a psychiatric sense, does not include any conscious attempt to disown such as malingering or lying. It is the simplest form of the ego-defense, and it is closely related to rationalization. Examples include an alcoholic who refuses to admit that he cannot drink.

Repression

one of the commonest mental mechanisms in which instinctive drives are blocked from consciousness or are translated into corresponding behavior. It is the earliest type of defense developed by individuals. Repression is not only the principal defense in earlier years, but is best known and most commonly employed. However, unfortunately, repression is not without disadvantages, for the deep-seated drives and urges are unchanged in quality or intensity and they constantly seek satisfaction. Automatically, these drives are crushed and an attempt is made to reverse their effects by cultivation and promotion of characteristics sharply opposed in nature. These contrasting aims and efforts, designed to reinforce repression, lead to the formation of *prejudice* and a pronounced character defense is known as *Reaction Formation.* As a result we see character traits which are the exact opposite of those expected from the expression of the undisguised tendencies. Perfectionistic and rigid and uncompromising character traits often are reaction formations against forbidden tendencies to be sloppy, irresponsible, and uninhibited. Feelings of rejection or hostility may be disguised by scrupulous politeness or diffused expression of gratitude. The overtly aggressive person constantly demanding his rights and ready to fight at any provocation may be defending himself against deep-seated feelings of inferiority and insecurity. A facade of excessive amiability might be a disguise for unrecognized feelings of aggression and hostility. A great deal of expressed concern for a certain person might be a disguise of unrecognized feelings of hostility or jealousy or even a disguise of wishes for the person's death. Beneath the facade of devotion of a daughter there might be a concealed wish for the death of the father, for whom the spinster daughter has sacrificed herself and refused an offer of marriage in order to remain with him.

Displacement

a mental mechanism, in which an emotional feeling is transferred from its actual object to a substitute. Either the aim or the object of the drive might be changed, so an aggressive drive might be displaced from a dangerous object to a harmless object. A man who hates his mother "takes it out" on a person under him.

Substitution

an adaptive mechanism which is employed to reduce tension from frustration. This is done by replacement of an unattainable or an unacceptable activity by which one is attainable or acceptable. To be satisfactory, the substitutive activity must have a certain similarity to the original one. So motives or hostile impulses might be replaced by some impersonal destructive acts, such as punching a punching bag or shooting clay pigeons.

Reversal Into The Opposite:

The adaptive and defensive process whereby an unacceptable impulse might be turned into its opposite, such as love for hate and vice versa. So a child who is disturbed by having too many aggressive feelings towards his parents might talk and think mainly of the way in which he likes his parents. In a way, it is similar to the Reaction Formation discussed later.

Introjection

has been mentioned before, and is the first ego defense mechanism which serves the little infant to prevent or maintain an object relationship. With the little boy in a way saying, "I will prevent my mother from going away by keeping her inside me."

Identification

has been mentioned before, and is the first ego defense mechanism unconscious wishful adoption or interralization of the personality characteristics or identity of another. Generally, one possessing attributes which the subject envies or admires. Identification plays a major role in normal personality development, especially in the development of the Super-Ego. Normally, the boy identifies principally with his father and the girl with her mother, but a person may internalize certain undesirable personality traits of her parents or others, or even with the parent whom he hates. This is sometimes referred to as *Hostile Identification*. There is a second type of Identification. The image of one person is unconsciously identified with that of another. A person later in life representing authority might come to be identified with a harsh, punitive father and the hostility and anger felt for the father in childhood is directed toward the authority figure. So the hostility and other negative feelings have an origin in attitudes created during childhood but may be displaced or transferred to others in later life, thereby seriously distorting and interfering with human relationships.

Projection

a mental mechanism already discussed, whereby personally unacceptable impulses or drives are ascribed to another person or object. So they are ascribed to the outside rather than to oneself. In some respects, this is a form of displacement and is closely associated with the mechanism of *Denial*.

Compensation

is an unconscious attempt to overcome real or fancied inferiorities. In biology and physiology the heart muscle hypertrophies so that additional force might be able to compensate for an impairment of circulation. We also see compensation in a psychological sense. The compensation might be socially acceptable, such as a blind person becoming excellent in music or it might be socially unacceptable, such as a physically handicapped person becoming a bully, or the short person becoming aggressive and domineering with the so-called "small man's syndrome," demonstrating a good example of "over-compensation" familiar to us all. The guy in the bar telling about all his sexual conquests often is showing an overcompensation verbally to hide his sexual inferiority and lack of experience.

Sublimation

is considered one of the most successful adaptive-defensive mechanisms and effective use of this device may present a well-rounded personality. By using this device unacceptable, instinctual drives are channelized into socially-sanctioned channels. This is actually a socialization of emotion, so by this mechanism the energy is transformed and diverted to socially-acceptable goals. Aggressive impulses might be sublimated through sports, games, and other socially-acceptable channels. Vocational choice for many people may in part represent a sublimation of some underlying unacceptable impulse. It is difficult at times to see that one's activities which serve the material, mental, as well as the cultural welfare of himself and his fellows derive energy from impulses originally stemming from biological and selfish needs. In repeated sublimation, impulses are gratified at progressive higher levels, resulting in constant cultural advance. Successful sublimation is one of the most important adaptive mechanisms in the formation of sound character.

Rationalization

is one of the common mental devices used to maintain self-respect and prevent feelings of guilt to a large degree. Our behavior is the product of unconscious motives. Our real desires and attitudes remain concealed and disguised, so in this way, "Our thinking defends our feeling." This mechanism rationalization provides rational and intellectual explanations for behavior which has been prompted by our unrecognized motives. A type of rationalization which helps us to maintain self-esteem in the fact of inadequacy is the so-called "sour grapes" mechanism. By this mechanism, the individual depreciates some particular goal, which he would like to attain, but can not reach due to some obstacle, usually some personal inadequacy. Quite related is blasé indifference in the face of circumstances that would naturally offend our self-esteem.

Regression

is actually a regressive phenomena and describes a return to an earlier level of emotional adjustment or development. The regression is not a desirable adaption since in the process some developmental maturity is lost. An example could be that of a man promoted to a higher position with increasing duties and responsibility. As a result of an underlying insecurity, which is being stimulated due to pressures of the new job he reacts by wanting to return to his old job which was more secure.

Suppression

is actually a voluntary relegation of unacceptable ideas or ideas out of the mind and so constitutes a *conscious* forgetting. Therefore, it is not considered a true defense mechanism. A person who has behaved somewhat unacceptably at parties the previous evening consciously tries to forget about his behavior the following day.

MIDDLE CHILDHOOD

Latency Period

This is a period approximately between the sixth or about the eleventh or twelfth year and is latent only in a relative sense. It is a period of communal socialization, steering away from the restricted family constellation toward other outside relationships. It is characterized by intellectual growth, for it is also the beginning of schooling for the child. The child's interests outside the family rapidly expand. He is able now to think out problems and make judgments as to the meaning of his behavior. His understanding of reality is developing rapidly. The developing Super-Ego function is rather important. This is a period for the boys to be with the boys. Children in this developmental period react with some hostility toward the opposite sex. This reaction to the opposite sex facilitates the child identifying more strongly than before with the parent of the same sex. At the same time, the child's return to cruelty, sadism is rather striking. In spite of all attempts to break away from the parents, the dependency needs remain rather strong. The youngster strongly needs his parents' encouragement, advice, and approval, and they suffer when it is absent. The boy gains self-adequacy rather through group identification. This is the age of boys' clubs or boys' gangs, with the girls being excluded. There is intense group loyalty within the club. Girls on an average in this period do not show very strong interests in clubs or gang participation, except for girls who have a somewhat masculine identification. Daydreaming is a prominent activity and the child shows habitual ways of reacting to external as well as internal demands. We see the development of the adaptive defense mechanism.

Reaction Formation

Excessive cleanliness, orderliness may be a reaction formation defense against an impulse to be dirty. Excessive kindness and compassion might be a reaction formation defense against cruelty, and so excessive need to give might be a similar defense against a wish to take. This is also the time for the expression of the defense mechanism of *Undoing,* which is a mechanism in which something positive is done which actually or magically is the opposite of the forbidden impulse. Some unacceptable behavior is symbolically acted out in the reverse, usually repetitiously.

The middle childhood or latency period is only relatively latent in contrast to the more turbulous early childhood and adolescence.

PUBERTY AND ADOLESCENCE

The latency period is brought to a close with appearance of the change of puberty. This is a very stormy period of development during which youngsters struggle with the great intensification of the instinctual drives. Actually, the adolescence is a revival in which many of the old problems emerge in a different context. The onset of puberty is much more abrupt and earlier in the girl than it is in the boy. In the girl, it is heralded by two physical-biological changes; namely, the beginning of menstruation and development of the breasts. There appear to be some relationship between the intensification of the biological-functioning of the sex glands and the psychological drives. It is further complicated by the fact that the adolescent now has at his disposal the necessary apparatus for initiating and completing the sexual act, combined with a strong biological and psychological sexual drive. The parents are no longer the objects of affection and new objects must be found, not only to satisfy the dependency needs, but also the sexual needs. This is more complicated by the drive to gain more independence from the parent. The adolescent must rely to a much greater degree now on the internal controls developed previously. The dependence now becomes quite threatening and a great deal of overt hostility toward the parents now referred to as "the generation gap" appears. The boys in groups and clubs develop some interest in the girls. The first signs of a boy's interest in girls is through kidding and taunting the girls. The kidding not only represents a hidden wish, but also a way of dealing with anxiety. The girls start to band together and the boys "run in packs." Curiosity and exhibitionist behavior is rampant and the need to get away from the parents' supervision and scrutiny is quite evident. They are described by Anna Freud as *Excessively Egoistic* by regarding themselves as the center of the universe and the sole object of interest, and yet at no other time in life are they capable of so much self-sacrifice and devotion. They form the most passionate love relationships only to break them off as abruptly as they began. On the one hand, they throw themselves enthusiastically into the life of the community and, on the other hand, they have an overpowering longing for solitude. They oscillate between blind submission to some self-chosen leader and defiant rebellion against any and every authority. They are selfish and materially minded, and at the same time full of lofty idealism. At times their behavior in regard to others is rough and inconsiderate, yet they themselves are extremely touchy.

Two extreme reactions in adolescence can be seen. The unconscious striving, now very strong, may overcome the previous character traits and a riot of uninhibited gratification of the primitive instincts takes place. This may be seen in the unruly, uncontrolled behavior of the teen-age gangs. Or, the conscious personality may overcome all the upsurge of the unconscious strivings and cling to the same values and defenses that were satisfactory in the earlier developmental stages, especially, during the latency period. This is represented in the shy and childish adolescents who avoid the situations and relationships in which peers plunge.

There are two characteristic behavior patterns; Ascerticism in which the adolescent may renounce any impulse connected with sexuality. This adolescents will avoid adolescents of their own age, shun dancing, restrict food, drink and sleep seeking solitude and avoiding society. In the other behavior pattern there is a great deal of intellectualization, with an insatiable interest in abstract subjects. However, interestingly enough, there is a gross disparity between the idealistic views expressed by the adolescents and their actual behavior.

Adolescence is important in the development of identity. Many of the characteristics of adolescent behavior are understandable from the view that there is an attempt to establish an identity that is not to be dependent on earlier identifications. There is a great need to break away from the parents and other family figures; therefore the adolescents go through a great amount of confusion about identity, with great preoccupation in introspective meditation and discussion about their role identity, about life goals. The questions always asked are "Why are we here? Who are we?" They complain, and many times realistically, about the lack of care and understanding of their parents during the early years of development. There is a great deal of ambivalence about people. With this confused identity and the ambivalence, it is not unusual for the adolescent to develop tremendous admiration and want nothing more than to be "like him" only to acquire an entirely different idol and assume a completely different or even opposite role a little later. Eventually, and hopefully, as the adolescent has some successes of his own in school, in work, and in interpersonal relationships, his own identity starts to emerge, and the young adult finds some place in society. In so doing Erikson feels the adolescent, "Achieves a sense of inner continuity and social sameness which will breach what he was as a child and what he is about to become and will reconcile the conception of himself and his community's recognition of him. By spanning this breach the adolescent will bring himself to adulthood and mature in personality with the attainment of full growth and development.

In the development of the personality, we see that the success or failure of an adult to establish satisfactory and rewarding relationships with his fellowman depend upon his childhood experiences. The early childhood experiences and specific adaptive-defensive mechanisms used lead to the formation of either positive or negative attitudes toward fellow beings. All the earlier relationships with the parents determine the character of all later attachments, affections, or animosities. In a way the figures who are of importance in adult life represent for that particular individual all the important people of his early childhood. Aggression is an integral part of human nature and enters into every human relationship, but the manner in which a child learns to handle his aggressive feelings toward the parents are responsible for many of his hostile, or intolerant attitudes toward his fellow beings in adult life. We see an example of this development in a displacement of hate onto strangers and the projection of aggression to others.

The attitudes which are responsible for tensions, conflicts, and hostilities between individuals and groups actually are established in childhood. They can be influenced more effectively in childhood therefore it is important for us to recognize these attitudes early and deal with them.

The human in his physical, biological and psychological development repeats and duplicates what all other humans do and have done before. He repeats and perpetuates not only the genetic aspects brought forward by his ancestors, but he also develops in a family setting predetermined not only by the personalities of his parents but also by the society and culture in which he lives. There are genetic and biological as well as environmental factors which are different in each child. Due to many circumstances, the adaptive-defensive mechanisms are common to all human beings, but the use of them is quite different in each individual. These factors are basic in molding the personality and consequently, makes each of us, to some extent, like others but at the same time, quite distinctly different from others. These facts bear out the truth of the old Chinese saying "that the hand has five fingers but each of them is different."

REFERENCES

Bettelheim, Bruno, In Spiegel, J. P.: *Campus conflict and professional egos. Transaction, 6 (11)*, 1969.

Blumentahl, Monica D.; Kahn, Robert L., et al.: *Justifying Violence.* Institute for Social Research, University of Michigan, Ann Arbor, Michigan, 1972.

Engel, George L.: *Homeostasis, behavioral adjustment and the concept of health and disease.* In Grinker, Roy R.: *Mid-Century Psychiatry.* Springfield, Ill., Charles C Thomas, 1953.

Engel, George L.: *Psychological Development in Health and Disease.* Philadelphia, W. B. Saunders, 1962.

Erikson, E. H.: *The problem of ego identity. J Am Psychoanal Assoc, 4:* 56, 1956.

Freud, Anna: The bearing of the psychoanalytic theory of instinctual drives on certain aspects of human behavior. In *Drives, Affects and Behavior,* Loewenstein, R., Editor. International University Press, 1953, pp. 259–277.

Freud, Anna: *Ego and Mechanisms of Defense.* International University Press, 1940, Chap. XII.

Fries, M., and Woolf, P. J.: *Psychoanalytic Study of The Child.* New York, International University Press, 1953, vol. 3, p. 48.

Kluckhorn, Clyde: *Mirror For The Man,* McGraw-Hill Book Company, Inc.

Noyes, Arthur P., and Kulb, Lawrence C.: *Modern Clinical Psychiatry,* 5th ed. Philadelphia, W. B. Saunders Company, 1958.

Rowe, Clarence J.: *An Outline of Psychiatry,* 4th ed. Dubuque, Iowa, William C. Brown Company, 1965.

Saul, Leon J.: *Techniques and Practice of Psychoanalysis.* Philadelphia, J. B. Lippincott Company, 1958.

Sheldon, W., and Stevens, S.: *Varieties of Temperament.* New York, Harper, 1942.

SPECIAL PROBLEMS IN POLICE WORK AND CORRECTIONS

PART II

- ■ CRIME AND NARCOTIC ADDICTION
- ■ LAW ENFORCEMENT IN INEBRIETY CASES
- ■ LAW ENFORCEMENT AND PHYSICAL DISABILITIES

Chapter 5

CRIME AND NARCOTIC ADDICTION

RICHARD C. STEPHENS AND STEPHEN LEVINE

NARCOTIC ADDICTION has become a major political, moral, and public health issue in the United States. Not a small part of this notoriety is due to the large amount of criminal activity which is associated with the abuse of narcotic analgesics. In this chapter we hope to further explore this relationship. Over the years, the debate surrounding the association of crime and addiction has revealed several important issues. The literature discussed in this chapter will be organized around the issues.

Before we begin discussion of these issues, however, we should like to draw the reader's attention to two important points. First, we have chosen to largely review in this chapter some of the more recent empirical studies of the relationship between crime and addiction. We do this for a couple of reasons, one of which is that many of the findings of the earlier studies are generally supported by those of more recent studies. However, more importantly, we feel that within the last decade there appears to have been an almost cataclysmic increase in narcotics abuse. Accordingly, there may well have been significant social and demographic changes in the addict population which might have affected the nature of the relationship between crime and addiction. Because of these reasons, we have restricted our detailed review of the literature to that published since the late fifties.* Second, it should be emphasized that this discussion is limited almost entirely to narcotic addiction. Studies of other important psychoactive drugs, including marijuana, hallucinogens (LSD, mescaline, peyote, etc.), stimulants (amphetamines, ritalin, etc.), tranquilizers, and barbiturates reveal no evidence of any cause and effect relationship between drug abuse or addiction and criminal activity (see Blum, 1967a, 1967b, for a comprehensive review of this subject). With narcotics, however, because of their expense, addiction liability, and wide prevalence of abuse, the relationship between their abuse and criminality has become a much debated topic.

THE TEMPORAL RELATIONSHIP OF CRIME TO ADDICTION

It would appear that all studies which have been done have found a strong association between crime and addiction. However, studies are not clear as to the temporal sequence of the relationship. Dai (1937) found in a 1937 study of Chicago addicts that 81 percent had no criminal records prior to addiction and most of the offenses of this group were limited to narcotic offenses, *per se.* In the same year Pescor (1938) found at Lexington

* An annotated bibliography of many of the earlier studies can be found in Kavaler (1968).

that 75 percent had no criminal records prior to addiction while 82 percent did have records after becoming addicted. A study by Vaillant (1966) of New York addicts found 57 percent of the sample who were treated at Lexington had criminal records prior to addiction with 46 percent having served time. After treatment the percentage eventually serving time rose to 92 percent. Chein et al. (Chein, Gerard, Lee, and Rosenfeld, 1964) report changing delinquency rates prior to addiction.

In 1969 John A. O'Donnell published a follow-up study which in part analyzed the criminality of a sample of 266 white Kentucky addicts. He found that one-third of the men and less than 10 percent of the women had criminal records prior to their addiction. Further he found that the proportion of those addicts with prior criminal records increased with the recency of their addiction; this finding supports those of others that the degree to which addicts are recruited from the ranks of those with criminal records has been increasing. O'Donnell's study also supported the general finding that more criminal acts were committed by individuals after addiction than before. In fact, O'Donnell feels that addiction was followed by more crimes than the addicts would have been expected to commit had they not become addicted.

Voss and Stephens (1972) have also recently explored the criminal history of narcotic addicts. Studying a sample of 1096 patients committed to the NIMH Clinical Research Center at Lexington, Kentucky they presented a variety of findings. Most of these findings support those of prior studies. For instance, they found that involvement in criminal activity prior to the subjects' first use of drugs (alcohol was included in the definition of drugs) was minimal. However, the subjects have been extensively involved in crime—three-fourths were involved in some form of theft (other than burglary or armed robbery), three-fifths had sold drugs, one-half had committed burglaries, and two-fifths admitted forgery. The range of this illegal behavior broadened following drug use. Voss and Stephens (1972) note that in terms of arrests 20 percent of the addicts admitted arrest before the use of any drug including alcohol. With alcohol excluded from the definition of drugs, 44 percent of the sample had been arrested before any other drug use; when use of alcohol and marijuana are excluded, 53 percent of the sample reported an arrest before they used any other drug. Fifty-seven percent of the sample were arrested before they used any narcotic including heroin. The investigators conclude that "the relationship between drug use and crime is not simple or unidirectional; some addicts were involved in crime prior to drug use while others turned to crime after they began their involvement with drugs."

In 1965 a study of addicts admitted to the California Rehabilitation Center revealed that only 5 percent had no prior criminal records and that a majority had previous offenses for crimes other than drug violations. In the same year Morgan (1965) reported that a majority of New York addicts had criminal records prior to identification as opiate users. After they were identified as opiate users, those without prior records limited their criminal activity, for the most part, to narcotic offenses. He concluded that addiction was not a cause of, but rather a product of delinquent lives.

Chambers and Inciardi (1971) studied the criminality of fifty-two New York female addicts. They discovered that about 65 percent of the women have known arrest records of which 40 percent have juvenile arrest records, and 60 percent have been arrested for specific narcotic offenses. Ten percent of the sample have arrest records which predate their drug use.

These findings spotlight some of the problems in determining the temporal relationship between crime and addiction. It would appear that although addicts in the thirties and forties frequently did not have criminal records prior to their addiction, the current picture is considerably different. Increasingly, larger and larger percentages of younger addicts with prior criminal records (or self admitted criminal) are being observed. It would appear, then, that addicts today frequently have pre-addiction criminal records.

THE TIME FACTOR

This general conclusion must be further elaborated however on several accounts. One reason for this is the time factor. Most addicts become addicted at a fairly young age, and thus they have a much greater time in which to commit criminal acts after their addiction than before. An example will make this point clearer. Let us take the case of a twenty-seven-year-old addict who first became addicted at age nineteen. Assuming his delinquent career may potentially start at age fourteen, he had about five years before and eight years after addiction to commit his first criminal act. Thus, his "at risk" time was greater after addiction than before. Similarly, in terms of the potential volume of crime committed, he would have had more time after addiction to commit more criminal acts than before. Consequently, the fact that even larger percentages of addicts are not found with pre-addiction criminal records may be due to this artifact of "at risk" time.

UNRELIABILITY OF CRIMINAL RECORDS

Another factor which must be taken into account is the source of the data used in studies of the relationship between crime and addiction. Many of these studies use official arrest records. These statistics have been roundly criticized by many criminologists as being unreliable indices of the individual's criminal involvement. Specifically in regard to narcotic addicts, Inciardi and Chambers (1972) conducted a research study whose principal conclusion was:

"As noted earlier in this paper, the quality of reporting mechanisms for the accumulation of criminal and social statistics in the United States is extremely poor, and the extent of our present state of knowledge regarding volume and trends is at best, insignificant. The data of this study tend to dramatize this notion. Of some 13,181 specific crimes against person and property reported by this survey sample, it is not known how many became part of official enumerations, yet nevertheless, some tentative and arbitrary estimations can be had. Using the recent FBI ratios of 'crimes known to the police' and 'crimes cleared by arrest' and applying them to the present data, it would seem that only 4% of the property crimes and 5% of the personal crimes reported here eventually appeared in our national statistics."

Also, closely related to the above point is the observation that when a person becomes addicted, he becomes more known to the police. He is in all likelihood more closely scrutinized and hence more liable to arrest. Consequently, those studies which utilize arrest statistics may have this additional built in bias.

THE EFFECT OF ARREST PROCEDURES AND INSTITUTIONALIZATION

Still another complicating factor is the unknown effect of arrest procedures and institutionalization. A whole school of sociological thought is built around the idea that once a person is publicly acknowledged to be a deviant, he has a tendency to assume this deviant role and in effect becomes more deviant. Thus, the very mechanisms which society has created to control addiction may be perpetuating and enlarging addiction and criminal patterns *after* the person is labeled an addict.

Not only is the addict labeled by institutionalization, he also has greater opportunities to learn addict skills. When a person is imprisoned or hospitalized with other addicts he is in effect further schooled in the addict life. He fills the many empty hours talking with other addicts, learning about new drugs or different ways of using familiar ones and discussing different illegal methods of obtaining the large sums of money necessary for a "habit." He becomes a better addict through institutionalization. In short, the criminalization of addiction, designed to control drug abuse, may actually create further drug abuse.

ADDICTION AS CRIME

This raises still another technical issue; namely, what is crime? Presently any non-medical use of opiates is defined as illegal and therefore any person using these drugs in such a context is a criminal. It would be illogical, however, to argue that such crime was caused by the drug. Some authors have argued, in fact, that society's present attitude toward opiate use is responsible for much of the criminal activity of addicts who are forced to resort to illegal means to support their dependence. Furthermore, by restricting legal sources of opiates, addicts are forced to acquire their drugs illegally and in the process associate with more strictly criminal elements. Scher (1961) for example, compares society's present position with respect to narcotics with prohibition and argues that "the larger the structure developed to suppress narcotic trade, the larger the population needed to support it."

TYPES OF ADDICTS

Almost all studies of crime and addiction which have been conducted place all addicts into one category. However, it is becoming increasingly apparent that there are many different types of narcotic addicts and that generalizations about one type may not be necessarily true of another. Levine and Stephens (1972) have described some types of narcotic abusers—the pain-prone, Southern, medical profession, and Chinese addicts—who do not belong to addict subcultures and do not engage in criminality to support their habit. However, the subcultural addicts—the "hippie" and street addicts—are much more likely to turn to crime as a means of supporting their habits. Generalizations which apply equally as well to all these different types of addicts are difficult to make.

THE CRIMINOGENIC EFFECTS OF NARCOTICS

The final issue to be discussed is the potential criminogenic effects of narcotics.

In general the pharmacological and psychological effects of narcotic analgesics are such that they do not foster or release criminal tendencies in individuals. As Maurer and Vogel (1967) point out, narcotics are depressants and tend to allay aggression in violent psychopaths. They also note that narcotics inhibit the sexual drive and may actually make addicts less susceptible to committing sexual offenses. Although narcotics do inflate the ego through their euphorigenic properties, at the same time they create a sereneness (the "nod") which lessens the tendency for actions. Wikler (1967) has corroborative evidence which substantiates the claim that opiates reduce drives generated by sex, hunger, and pain. And as noted, a number of studies indicate that addicts do not engage in non-income producing criminal acts.

There has also been no evidence which indicates that narcotics lead to a deterioration of personality. Although there are data which demonstrate that addicts are psychologically different (e.g. perform differently on certain personality inventories), these findings cannot be used to document the case that the personality changed after addiction. In fact, some studies using the Minnesota Multiphasic Personality Inventory (Berzins, Ross, and Monroe, 1971; Wikler, 1967) reveal similar profiles for addicts, alcoholics, and non-addicted criminals. Furthermore, no studies have demonstrated that there is a characteristic or definitive personality profile for narcotic addicts (Levine and Stephens, 1972).

It is true that narcotics create physical dependence such that if the addict does not take narcotics he will become quite ill. This factor, along with the "craving" phenomenon, may create such a desire for drugs that addicts will commit crimes in order to have money to purchase their needed drugs. However, O'Donnell's (1966) data indicate that narcotics *per se* are not directly responsible for this criminality. He showed that addicts who received their narcotics from legitimate sources, and thus did not have to pay exorbitantly inflated prices for illicit drugs, generally were not criminals. Thus, although these individuals were constantly receiving narcotics and accordingly should have been subject to any pharmacological or psychological effects, few engaged in criminal acts. Thus, these data, combined with findings of other studies that addicts do not engage in violent, non-income producing crime, support the view that crime is not directly a product of either the psychological or physiological effects of narcotics.

In effect, then, the whole unresolved debate centers on whether there is any causal connection between addiction and crime. It may very well be in the case of the vast majority of narcotic addicts that addiction and crime co-appear with little causality between the two. That is, addicts may grow up in an environment that is conducive to both addiction and crime. As Joel Fort (1969) says:

"A number of chicken and egg studies have been done as to whether addicts were criminal before or after becoming addicted. The overall results appear to indicate that most illegal narcotic addicts in the United States have grown up in environments generally conducive to delinquency and crime, and the drug subculture can become for some a part of a broader criminal life style [p. 115]."

What Fort (1969) is saying is that addicts grow up in a ghetto subculture which is deviant by middle-class standards. This subculture is such that both criminal and addict life styles are available to the ghetto youth. In fact, crime and addiction may be two sides of the same coin.

At any rate, the youth does appear to grow up in a world apart from that which most Americans experience. This world is enough apart that it ill prepares them for any kind of nondeviant interaction with middle-class America. As Finestone (1966) notes: "These young addicts have come increasingly to live in a world apart, and all their experiences are such as to make them, realistically, increasingly unemployable as time goes on [p. 154]." It is this deviant way of life—this world of the street addict—which will be discussed in the remainder of this chapter.

THE STREET ADDICT

Studies by O'Donnell (1966), Ball (1968), and others (Freedman, 1966; Rubington, 1968; Preble and Casey, 1969) have all revealed a significant trend in recent decades toward an increasing association of narcotic addiction with criminal behavior. The street addict pattern reflects this trend. Such findings prompted observers, such as Bejerot (1969), to investigate epidemiological aspects of addiction. He quotes a 1964 WHO report of "an epidemic-like outbreak of abuse of hypnotic drugs in a particular region . . ." which in the committee's view pointed to "the relevance of sociologic and environmental factors, as distinct from individual motives, in the etiology of drug abuse."

The single most important sociologic and environmental factor, we believe, is the street addict subculture. It is our belief that street addicts belong to a well-developed subculture which provides the addict with:

". . . all that is necessary to be a 'good addict.' First, the subculture is the source of both the heroin and the related knowledge of how to administer and evaluate the drug. The subculture also provides the addict with knowledge of how to obtain the drug and how to obtain money for drugs. Other members of the subculture frequently teach the addict criminal skills or act as partners in his criminal enterprises. In addition, the subculture provides the addict with a set of values and a set of norms and gives respect and admiration to those who adhere to these behavioral prescriptions. In short, the subculture provides the addict with a way of life [Stephens and Levine, 1971, p. 351]."

The typical street addict is a heroin-using, slum-dwelling minority group member. As such, he grows up in an atmosphere and environment that is conducive not only to drug abuse but to crime as well. The black street youth finds himself in a milieu where the available role models are con men, hustlers, addicts, and others involved in the criminal underworld. The street addict role reflects the ethics of these various groups. Essentially, the role consists of three interrelated aspects (Stephens and Levine, 1971): (1) The "cool cat." This aspect of the street addict reflects his emotional neutrality. He does not allow others to glimpse his feelings. He must always appear "together," calm, unperturbed, in a word "cool." Display of emotion is a weakness and invites others to take advantage of you. The "cool cat" makes plenty of money effortlessly, has fine clothes, a big car, and plenty of women. He is free to gratify his senses and need never make sacrifices or deprive himself. (2) The "con-man." The street addict lives by his wits. His view of the world is one in which everybody is out for himself. If you don't get them first, they'll get you. A smart man, then, is one who learns a successful "game" which allows him to "get over" on others. Wealth, power, and influence are what really matter; these ends justify any means (Levine and Stephens, 1972). (3) The antisocial man. Street addicts are not rebels because they are not trying to reform society. However, they are antisocial. They hate established society and its authority, which they feel has suppressed them. The street addict role provides these people with a means of attacking society and gaining revenge.

It can be seen that this role combines elements of the non-addict criminal and ghetto life styles. The role may well be a mirror of the aspirations of many ghetto youth. As such, it may be very easy for ghetto youth, both delinquent and nondelinquent, to make the transition to becoming a street addict.

In summary, while narcotic addiction and crime do seem to be related significantly, the relationship does not appear to be one of cause and effect. Neither does crime inevitably lead to narcotic addiction, nor does addiction *per se,* create criminals. Narcotic addiction and crime, rather, are common ingredients in the genesis of a growing and deviant subculture of alienated, deprived, antisocial, ghetto youths.

REFERENCES

Ball, J. C.: Two patterns of narcotic drug addiction in the United States. *J Crim Law, Criminol Pol Sci, 59:*171–182, 1968.

Bejerot, N.: Social medical classifications of addictions. *Internat J Addictions, 4:*391–405, 1969.

Berzins, J. I.; Ross, W. F., and Monroe, J. J.: A multivariate study of the personality characteristics of hospitalized narcotic addicts on the MMPI. *J Clin Psychol, 27:*174–189, 1971.

Blum, R. H.: Mind-altering drugs and dangerous behavior: Dangerous drugs. In President's Commission on Law Enforcement and Administration of Justice (Ed.), *Narcotics and Drug Abuse.* Washington, D.C.: USGPO, 1967, pp. 21–39 (a).

Blum, R. H.: Mind-altering drugs and dangerous behavior: Narcotics. In President's Commission on Law Enforcement and Administration of Justice (Ed.), *Narcotics and Drug Abuse.* Washington, D.C.: USGPO, 1967, pp. 40–63 (b).

Chambers, C. D., and Inciardi, J. A.: Some aspects of the criminal careers of female narcotic addicts. Paper presented at the meeting of the Southern Sociological Society, Miami Beach, May, 1971.

Chein, I.; Gerard, D. L.; Lee, R. S., and Rosenfeld, E.: *The Road to H.* New York, Basic Books, 1964.

Dai, B.: *Opium Addiction in Chicago.* Shanghai, China, The Commercial Press, 1937.

Finestone, H.: Narcotics and criminality. In O'Donnell, J. A., and Ball, J. C. (Eds.): *Narcotic Addiction.* New York, Harper and Row, 1966.

Fort, J.: *The Pleasure Seekers.* New York, Bobbs-Merrill Co., 1969.

Freedman, A. M.: Drug addiction: An eclectic view. *JAMA, 197:*156–160, 1966.

Inciardi, J. A., and Chambers, C. D.: Criminal involvement of narcotic addicts. *J Drug Issues, 2:*57–64, 1972.

Kavaler, F.; Krug, D. C.; Amsel, Z., and Robbins, R.: A commentary and annotated bibliography on the relationship between narcotics addiction and criminality. *Municipal Reference Library Notes,* New York Public Library, 1968, vol. 42, pp. 45–63.

Levine, S., and Stephens, R.: Types of narcotic addicts. In Hardy, R. E., and Cull, J. G. (Eds.): *Drug Addiction and Rehabilitation.* Springfield, Ill., Charles C Thomas, 1972.

Maurer, D. W., and Vogel, V. H.: *Narcotics and Narcotic Addiction.* Springfield, Ill., Charles C Thomas, 1967.

Morgan, J.: Drug addiction: Criminal or medical problem? *Police, 9,* 1965.

O'Donnell, J. A.: Narcotic addiction and crime. *Soc Prob, 13:*374–385, 1966.

O'Donnell, J. A.: *Narcotic Addicts in Kentucky.* Washington, D.C., USGPO, 1969.

Pescor, M. J.: A statistical analysis of the clinical records of hospitalized drug addicts. *Public Health Reports,* 1938, Supplement No. 143, pp. 1–30.

Preble, E., and Casey, J. J., Jr.: Taking care of business—the heroin user's life on the streets. *Internat J Addictions, 4:*1–24, 1969.

Rubington, E.: Two types of drug use. *Internat J Addictions, 3:*301–317, 1968.

Scher, J. M.: Group structure and narcotic addiction: Notes for a natural history. *Internat J Group Psychother, 11:*88–93, 1961.

State of California, Department of Corrections. *Characteristics of narcotic addicts in California Rehabilitation Center Institution, June 30, 1965.* (Mimeo.)

Stephens, R., and Levine, S.: The "street addict role": Implications for treatment. *Psychiatry, 34:*351–357, 1971.

Vaillant, G.: A twelve year follow-up of New York narcotic addicts: I. The relation of treatment to outcome. *Am J Psychiat, 122:*727–737, 1966.

Voss, H. L., and Stephens, R. C.: The relationship between drug abuse and crime. *Drug Forum: J Human Issues, 2,* 1972.

Wikler, A.: Personality disorders. III. Sociopathic type: The addictions. In Freedman, A. M., and Kaplan, H. I. (Eds.): *Comprehensive Textbook of Psychiatry.* Baltimore, Williams and Wilkins, 1967, pp. 989–1003.

Chapter 6

LAW ENFORCEMENT IN INEBRIETY CASES

David B. Coffler

- ■ Scope of the Alcoholism Problem
- ■ The Disease Concept of Alcoholism
- ■ Public Intoxication and the Disease Concept
- ■ Alternative to Arrest
- ■ Treatment for and Levels of Intoxication
- ■ Causes of and Specific Treatments for Alcoholism
- ■ Criteria and Goals for Treatment Success
- ■ References

A LCOHOLICS CAN BE HELPED. How many alcoholics can recover and maintain their sobriety depends on the repairing of the other areas of their lives that have been damaged as well as the treating of their excessive drinking.

No one is immune from the disease of alcoholism. It crosses

most age categories, as well as social, occupational, economic, and cultural spheres in varying degrees and can be found in virtually every nation in the world.

Alcoholism is a chronic disease with a tendency for its victims to relapse. The frequent return to drinking following treatment and "drying out" is similar to the repeated failures people experience when they try to stop smoking or overeating. One result of the repeated alcoholic relapses is that treatment may focus more on punitive control than on rehabilitation.

One attitude toward alcoholics is that they cannot be helped until they actually want help. Everyone would probably feel better working with alcoholics who were motivated and would abstain. But would they need us (Einstein, 1970)?

SCOPE OF THE ALCOHOLISM PROBLEM

Drinking beverage alcohol is typical behavior among 68 percent of the adult population in the United States, leaving only 32 percent of the population abstaining (Keller, 1971). The average consumption of "hard" liquor increased from 1¼ gallons per year per person to 1⅝ gallons between 1950 and 1969 (Erskine, 1972).

More men than women use alcohol although the number of women drinking has increased since World War II (Keller, 1971). Most people who do drink, about 82 percent of them, are considered light or moderate drinkers (Dorris, 1968). Light and moderate drinkers drink at least once a month, consuming from one to four drinks per occasion. Approximately 12 percent of the total population of consumers have been classed as heavy drinkers (Task Force, 1967). Heavy drinkers imbibe nearly every day, usually five drinks per occasion (Keller, 1971). Alcoholism afflicts one out of fifteen Americans or between nine and twenty-seven million people in the United States (Coburn, 1967; Task Force, 1967). The rate of alcoholism in the United States is second in the world; France is number one (Erskine, 1972).

There is a relationship between the use of alcohol and the incidence of crime. In one report alcohol was involved in 64 percent of the homicide cases and over 43 percent of another sample of homicide *victims* had blood alcohol levels over 0.15 percent (Task Force, 1967). Problem drinking is associated more frequently with crimes of aggression against persons and property than with other types of offenses. One investigator found ". . . that alcohol was present more often in crimes of violence (e.g. 92 percent of the cuttings' and concealed weapons) and less often during more skilled offenses against property; 60 percent in forgery," (Task Force, 1967).

Billions of dollars are spent by governments and the private sectors to treat alcoholism and combat the financial disasters it inflicts. The National Council on Alcoholism indicates 6.5 million employed workers are alcoholics and as a result, the loss of productivity costs industry $10 billion annually (National Council, 1971). "A bill of at least $2 billion is run up each year for medical payments and for welfare benefits to alcoholic individuals who are physically or emotionally incapacitated," (Keller, 1971). Alcohol-related traffic accidents also cause injuries annually to half-a-million people, result in several hundred thousand arrests, and carry a price tag of more than $1 billion for property damage, insurance costs, and medical services (Keller, 1971). Fifty percent of all fatal accidents occurring on the roads today involve alcohol, and 50 percent of these fatal accidents involve an alcoholic (National Council, 1971). A surprise to many is that less than 5 percent of the alcoholics are located on skid row. The average alcoholic is a man or woman in his or her thirty's with a job, home, and family.

THE DISEASE CONCEPT OF ALCOHOLISM

No one knows for sure how an individual becomes an alcoholic. Dr. E. M. Jellinek described four phases of alcoholism development and labeled them alpha, beta, gamma, and delta (Jellinek, 1960).

Alpha alcoholism is characterized by drinking for relief and rarely getting drunk. Whereas alcoholics at the beta phase will develop an increased tolerance for alcohol and can drink more without signs of intoxication. Beta alcoholics often develop serious physical complications as a result of their drinking and their usual poor eating habits. It is usually at the beta stage of alcoholism that the alcoholic begins to drink surreptitiously. Craving for alcohol and a loss of control over when and how much to drink is characteristic of gamma alcoholism. Gamma alcoholism often results in losing a job and friends as the individual becomes trapped in going back and forth from guilt and remorse over his actions to open resentment and hostility toward others (Dorris, 1968). The gamma phase is further characterized by tremors and shakes that are "cured" by taking a drink first thing in the morning. However, the gamma alcoholic retains a capability of abstaining for periods. Delta alcoholism is characterized by an obsession to drink and an inability to abstain. Delta alcoholics drink for days or weeks, as long as their bodies can tolerate, even though their tolerance for alcohol has reduced (now one-half of their prior intake is sufficient to cause oblivion) (Dorris, 1968). It is important to realize that these classifications are not explanations but descriptions.

In 1951 the World Health Organization defined alcoholism as the ". . . use of alcoholic beverages to the extent that health or economic or social functioning is substantially impaired" (Keller, 1971).

The American Medical Association followed suit in 1956:

"Alcoholism is an illness characterized by preoccupation with alcohol and loss of control over its consumption such as to lead usually to intoxication if drinking is begun; by chronicity; by progression; and by tendency toward relapse. It is typically associated with physical disability and impaired emotional, occupational, and/or social adjustments as a direct consequence of persistent and excessive use of alcohol." (AMA, 1968).

Although the disease concept may have gained wide acceptance in present day thinking the corollary that alcoholic behavior is involuntary, has not. Survey samples suggest that alcoholics are still perceived as "morally weak" or "weakwilled," or both (Room, 1970).

People belonging to temperance groups believed that one way of stopping the drunken behavior of which they disapproved was to prohibit the sale and distribution of the beverage. The outcome of the temperance movement resulted in Congress passing the 18th Amendment (Prohibition) to the Constitution that forbid the sale and distribution of alcoholic beverages. A primary objective was to control the excessive drinking behavior with the result that the substance itself, alcohol, was perceived as the villain. In this case, the law did effect behavior as prohibition was not altogether a failure. "For one thing, total consumption was actually lower during prohibition than before or after (Room, 1970). Prohibition was later repealed in 1933 by the 21st Amendment.

The intention of the temperance movement was to moderate or reduce to a level of moderation, people's drinking. Logically, the argument went something like this: ". . . many felt that the problem was that people drank too much and the answer was that they should drink less. For many years the Temperance Societies preached temperance and to their disappointment and frustration it didn't work, it didn't help these people. They went right on drinking too much" (Utah, 1968). With Prohibition, the excessive drinking objected to became more prevalent even though the rate of total consumption reduced. Attempts to control behavior by changing the law produced an increase in the very behavior the change sought to reverse (Room, 1971). This lack of change in drinking behavior probably resulted in the perceived evil possessed in alcohol being transferred from the substances to the individual so that he became evil and morally a sinner.

At the center of such a restrictive measure is the concept of voluntary behavior. For example, a basic assumption of the temperance preachings was that the drinker had within his own power the ability to change if he really wanted to. Since excessive drinking continued, and perhaps even increased, the next logical step was to *force* a change. The concept of force resulted in a present day practice of incarcerating public drunkards more than before. This approach burdens our criminal justice systems from the standpoints of law enforcement time and expense. The influences of these practices on the drinking behavior of chronic alcoholic offenders have yet to produce fruitful results. Drunken behavior hasn't decreased overall, it has increased (Task Force,

1967). "When drinking by legalized channels is made too difficult, recourse is had to illegal ones, and the practice tends to
spread with disastrous effects . . ." (Room, 1971).

Among the many advantages of defining alcoholism an illness
the major one is social. "It legitimates social support for rehabilitation of the alcoholic instead of punishment" (Room, 1970).

PUBLIC INTOXICATION AND THE DISEASE CONCEPT

Public intoxication has been a crime in the United States for
over three-hundred years. In 1606 England made public intoxication a crime, a practice that was later carried over to the
colonies in America. That 1606 approach didn't change in this
country until three-hundred-and-sixty years later.

"In 1966 the Circuit Courts of Appeal of North Carolina and
District of Columbia handed down their landmark decisions, in
the *Driver* and *Easter* cases, that a chronic drunkenness offender
who was an alcoholic could not be criminally convicted of public
intoxication" (Driver, 1969). Driver had been convicted of public intoxication more than two hundred times up to the time of
his trial. His numerous drunk arrests took place over a period of
thirty-five years. The court, in his case, concluded that his drinking was not "voluntary" because he was a chronic alcoholic.
Easter had been arrested for public intoxication more than
seventy times, and the court also held his intoxication to be a defense against criminal punishment because he was a chronic
alcoholic (Coburn, 1967).

Forming the basis for both these court decisions is the concept of involuntary versus voluntary behavior.

> "The theory of the common law was that a person presumably
> had capacity to control his behavior and to choose between alterna-
> tive courses of conduct. If it could be proven that the person had
> lost his power of self control then the essential element of *mens rea*
> was lacking and the law absolved him of criminal responsibility for
> his conduct which was considered 'involuntary,' i.e., lacking a free
> mind involuntarily choosing evil rather than good" (Coburn, 1967).

It was on that common law basis that the court based its decision in the Easter case. In the action against Driver, the court

held that to ". . . ignore the common law principle followed in the Easter decision, violates the prohibition against cruel and unusual punishment contained in the 8th Amendment to the United States Constitution" (Task Force, 1967). In essence, these court decisions have recognized that chronic alcoholism results in involuntary drinking rather than voluntary.

"In the case of drunken driving, it would appear that this defense could seldom be sustained. A defendant would have difficulty proving that he was so intoxicated that he could not control his impulse to drive a car, yet he was sufficiently in control of himself to get into the car, start it, and drive it for at least some distance" (Hutt, 1966). Concern continues that chronic alcoholism will be construed as a defense against any criminal punishment, for example, murder. The results have been that most changes in statutes have emphasized that alcoholism is a defense against punishment for simple drunkenness and not available as a defense when another crime has been committed.

Prior to the Driver and Easter decisions, the traditional attitude was that all drinking by a chronic alcoholic was voluntary because the alcoholic had to have gone through an initial period of voluntary drinking before he became an alcoholic. Therefore, he should be held accountable for all subsequent behavior unless he was insane (Hutt, 1966).

The significant factor that resulted in changing this traditional attitude came from medicine, not law. That is, judicial notice of medical authority recognizing alcoholism as a disease ". . . requiring social help rather than penal consequences . . ." precipitated the change (Coburn, 1967). Thus we see the tremendous impact the disease concept of alcoholism has had on legal systems.

A later judicial event worth noting occurred in October, 1967, when the United States Supreme Court agreed to hear the case of Powell versus Texas and whether or not alcoholism protected him from being punished for public intoxication under Texan law (Coburn, 1967). If the Supreme Court's decision had been in favor of Powell, ". . . overnight the traditional practice of committing skid row alcoholics to local jails on short term sentences (would) no longer (have been) legal" (Goff, May,

1968). But on June 17, 1968, the U.S. Supreme Court ruled, by a margin of 5 to 4, that a ". . . chronic alcoholic with a wife, family, and home in which 'to stay off the streets while drunk' could be convicted under a state law against public drunkenness" (Coburn, 1967). Opinions regarding the court's decision have generally cited three reasons why the court ruled as it did: (1) ". . . the development of common law principles of criminal responsibility, and their application to new medical knowledge, should be left to the States and should not be hardened into rigid constitutional principles."; (2) Powell had a home and could have avoided being arrested in public; (3) to rule in agreement with the Easter and Driver decisions would have released thousands of alcoholics from the criminal justice system and directed them to a health system that lacks adequate resources to deal with a problem of this magnitude (Task Force, 1967). In essence the U.S. Supreme Court agreed that alcoholism should be treated and not punished, however, the paucity of treatment facilities in this country influenced their decision.

Legislative and judicial changes proceed as pressure for reform continues. To date, among the State legislatures that have modified or abolished their statutes defining public intoxication as a crime are: Hawaii, Maryland, North Dakota, Connecticut, Florida, Massachusetts, and California (Keller, 1971). Alternatives to arresting alcoholics are sought in hopes of relieving the human suffering and reducing the burdens on criminal justice systems. Jail is supposed to protect the community, punish the offender, deter him from future offenses, and resocialize him. Experts agree that jail does not do this with the alcoholic (Rubington, 1965). A disease cannot be punished away; yet millions of arrests continue to occur in the wake of reform.

"Public intoxication alone accounts for one-third of all arrests reported annually" (Keller, 1971). If reported arrests for vagrancy, driving while under the influence, and disorderly conduct were added, the arrest figures jump to 40 and 49 percent (Keller, 1971). About 50 percent of all arrests are directly associated with alcohol when alcohol-related felonies are added to the above total. In other words, out of 5,922,688 reported arrests for 1970, 2,830,392 were directly associated with alcohol (Erskine, 1972). These figures do not represent total numbers of different individuals arrested because the chronic drunkenness offender is a repeater. He is a victim of the revolving door; arrest-imprisonment-release-rearrest. "Some (chronic drunkenness offenders) have been arrested 100 to 200 times and have served 10 to 20 years in jail on short-term sentences" (Task Force, 1967). The jail recidivism of the chronic drunkenness offender (CDO) has been referred to as a life sentence on the installment plan. These arrest and incarceration procedures result in over $100 million annual costs to the criminal justice system. Compounding the expenditures is the fact that at least 50 percent of the prison population in the U.S. have histories of alcohol use (Erskine 1972).

ALTERNATIVE TO ARREST

The alcoholic can be helped. Even the skid row and chronic drunkenness offenders can be helped out of the criminal justice system revolving door and assisted in shaping a new way of life for themselves. There have been three major projects in the U.S. which have utilized more of a medical-rehabilitation approach, than one of punitive control, as an alternative to arrests in dealing with alcoholism and CDOs. All three projects emphasized detoxification as a primary treatment approach with continuing care to maintain sobriety secondary.

The first of these was the St. Louis detoxification program which is considered the first detoxification system in the United States. The St. Louis project started in late 1966 and is currently budgeted for over $200,000 per year receiving approximately 1600 cases annually. Persons arrested for public drunkenness were offered the choice of jail or the detox center. If they chose the detox center charges were dropped provided the individual agreed to stay for a minimum of seven days (Nimmer, 1971). The center provides short-term medical care, referring acute cases to hospitals, combined with rehabilitative therapy designed to motivate the individual to continue treatment when he's discharged. Disappointedly, only 15 to 20 percent of center referrals accepted aid in housing or employment after discharge from the center (St. Louis, 1970).

Generally, center referrals experienced improvement in their drinking (47 percent); employment (18 percent); income (16 percent); health (49 percent); and housing (15 percent). However, in the same areas, 50 percent experienced no change in drinking behaviors, (3 percent deteriorated); 76 percent no change in employment, (6 percent deteriorated); 71 percent, 42 percent, and 82 percent, no changes in income, health or housing with 13 percent, 9 percent, 3 percent experiencing deterioration in these latter three areas (Nimmer, 1971). Overall, the center was effective in reaching the public inebriate and providing short-term treatment.

The roles of law enforcement in relation to the effectiveness of the St. Louis project are important. All referrals to the detox center were made by police officers. Police became discouraged after returning many of the same persons again and again for detoxification and eventually reduced the number of referals as a result. The readmission rate was 40 percent (St. Louis, 1970). In fact, ". . . during one two-day period, no men were brought to the center" (Nimmer, 1971). In addition to providing short-term treatment for alcoholics the center also sought to reduce the amount of time required by police officers in handling drunkenness offenders. The result was a 50 percent decrease in the time usually expended by an arresting officer.

The reported monetary savings to the police department as a result of referring public intoxicants to the center rather than jail may have been offset by the high treatment costs of $41 per person per day (Nimmer, 1971). In essence, the St. Louis project did demonstrate that alcoholics could be helped by detoxification measures, and many lessons in approaching reform in this manner were also learned.

The second plan for alternatives to the arrest of alcoholics is the District of Columbia detoxification program. The basis for development of the District of Columbia program was the Easter decision cited earlier, i.e. chronic alcoholism was a defense against punishment for public intoxication. The reaction of District of Columbia Police to the Easter ruling is important because it set the stage for their roles in the program.

The general attitude of the police toward skid row alcoholics prior to the Easter ruling was protective. The District of Columbia Police tended to perceive the alcoholics as coming to rely on arrest for protection, with the primary resource for recovery being the jail sentence. "The Easter decision took away the availability of the long sentences, but did not remove the officer's conception of his responsibility" (Nimmer, 1971).

The Washington D.C. program differed from the St. Louis program in three important areas: (1) District of Columbia emphasized nursing care and relied on outside sources for rehabilitative therapy to motivate patients for continued treatment (the low acceptance of referrals by District of Columbia alcoholics were similar to the low rates experienced in St. Louis), (2) Most of the District of Columbia detox patients (55 percent) were released after one day and the remainder after three days, (3) the District of Columbia program admitted self-referrals in addition to police referrals, and the rates of self-referrals were highest for the first year (Nimmer, 1971). The restricted use of the District of Columbia program by police seemed based more on confusion about the legality of escorting inebriates to the center in face of the Easter decision and consequent rumors of law suits for false arrests than on disappointment. Similar to the overpromise-underperformance situation experienced by St. Louis Police, the District of Columbia Police also observed, derisively, that inebriates were back on the streets the next day (Nimmer, 1971). The criminal justice system's revolving door, arrest-imprison-release-rearrest, for which they had received criticism for lack of fruitfulness in deterring drunken behavior, was seemingly being replaced by a health services revolving door: detoxify-release-redetoxify, with similar poor results.

"The (D.C.) evaluation study concluded that the center was 'ineffective as a link in the chain of treatment events leading to lower relapse rates'" (Nimmer, 1971). Although the results of the project were not entirely positive, there were at least three useful lessons: (1) limiting treatment for public intoxication to nursing care and detoxification can create a health services "revolving door," (2) voluntary acceptance of a program does not guarantee staying in the program long enough to maximize the possible benefits, (3) the 50 percent reduction in financial expenditures for alcoholism and the subsequent savings to the criminal justice system were more a function of reduced police activity in making arrests than detoxification services *per se* (Nimmer, 1971).

The last alternative to arrest to be considered is the Vera Institute program in the Bowery of New York. The Vera Institute services consist of a detoxification center, an out-patient clinic, and an emergency medical clinic that provides services to people regardless of whether they're intoxicated or not. Admissions are voluntary with about 25 percent accounted for by self-referrals. The remaining 75 percent of the admissions are from civilian rescue teams which emphasize voluntary acceptance of the program. There are no police escorts, *per se,* although one member of the rescue team is a plainclothes police officer and the other, a recovered alcoholic (Nimmer, 1971).

In particular contrast to St. Louis and the District of Columbia the Vera program reports a 60 to 70 percent acceptance of referrals to continuing care services after detoxification. Readmission is also very high among Vera patients, however, the rates averaging about 51 percent (Nimmer, 1971). Finally, less than 10 percent of the police referrals to St. Louis refused detox services choosing jail instead. The Vera program experienced a 33 percent refusal rate of services. The contrasts between detoxification centers in percentages of patients refusing to accept further service after discharge may be based on the difference that police versus civilian referrals to the centers have on alcoholics' willingness to accept further treatment.

In general all three alternatives to arrest represent high costs and high rates of recidivism. The most frustrating, and yet critical, aspect for accepting and understanding alcoholism is the complexity and chronicity of the disease. The frequently encountered relapse rates continue to be of concern not only to professional law enforcement but to professional medical helpers as well.

TREATMENT FOR AND LEVELS OF INTOXICATION

There is no single agreed upon treatment for all alcoholics. The disease is generally seen as a multi-faceted problem requiring medical, psychological, and social services. Often what dictates the specific treatment are the varying needs of the individual patients.

Stages of intoxication differ from person to person due to the variability among people in body weight, build, amount of alcohol consumed, amount of food in the stomach, etc. Generally speaking, the body takes about one hour to metabolize one ounce of alcohol. This metabolism rate is based on a man of average build weighing 150 pounds. A .05 blood alcohol level (2 ounces of 90 proof whiskey or 2 twelve-ounce bottles of beer) is considered "alcohol affected" (Alcohol & Alcoholism, 1971). An average person with .05 percent alcohol concentration in his blood would probably feel less inhibited and more relaxed. After four to six ounces of 90 proof whiskey or four to six 12 ounce bottles of beer the alcohol blood concentration rises to .10 or .15 percent level as "legally drunk" (Alcohol Abuse, 1972). Higher levels of alcohol blood concentration produce stupors and comas and often death follows due to the lowest part of the brain being put to sleep because this is the area that controls the heart and breathing.

Detoxification procedures differ depending on the stage of intoxication. For example, mild to moderate intoxication often requires only time for recovery, sleep it off so to speak, provided the individual is a nonaddictive drinker and has been drinking for less than a week. If he is an addict and has drunk a quart of whiskey daily for a week or more, withdrawal in an institution is required. Hospitalization is generally needed for a person drinking more than a quart of whiskey, 3 to 4 quarts of wine, or 10 quarts of beer, per day, for a week or more (Picken, 1970). Abstaining from alcohol after drinking excessive amounts or reducing the usual intake may develop abstinence symptoms (changes that occur after alcohol intake is discontinued or reduced abruptly) such as tremulousness, alcoholic hallucinosis, alcoholic epilepsy, and delirium tremens.

After sobering up the alcoholic is alert, startles easily, loses his appetite, is weak, and experiences rapid heart actions and trembling. Trembling may be the only observable symptom and may clear in a few days without treatment (Picken, 1970).

Alcoholic hallucinosis (seeing and/or hearing things that are not real), includes nightmares, hearing accusing voices, and mis-interpreting sounds and shadows. The individual generally reacts to hallucinosis by barricading himself, calling the police and telling them about the accusing voices, or suicide. Usually he recovers within days but some may hear the voices for months or years.

Alcoholic epilepsy, or the "rum fits," occur in the first forty-eight hours after alcohol intake is stopped or reduced. These seizures precede the most dramatic and dangerous withdrawal reaction—delirium tremens (D.T.'s).

D.T.'s generally begin on the third or fourth day after withdrawal following a seizure and can last eighteen hours to six days (Picken, 1970). Usually the alcoholic mutters or screams, wanders around aimlessly and is in constant motion. He is disoriented to time, misidentifies people, and has terrifying and vivid hallucinations of insects or animals. In three to five days, following a sudden sleep, the D.T.'s stop and he awakens clear and lucid remembering only part of the episode. D.T.'s are frequently precipitated by head injuries, infections, or surgical operations and result in a 20 percent mortality rate (Taber, 1965 and Picken, 1970).

Most of the symptoms characteristic of levels of intoxication can also be caused by other conditions besides excessive drinking, e.g. diabetic coma, epileptic seizures, barbiturate withdrawal, etc. The best guide in these cases is to get the individual to medical attention where appropriate diagnosis and treatment can be instigated.

Many alcoholics suffer severe physical disabilities because of their excessive drinking and poor nutrition that has continued over long periods of time. The brain, stomach and intestines, liver, bone tissue, and pancreas are among the more common targets for damage (Alcohol Abuse, 1972). For these reasons medical services including proper nutrition are often required. Restoring an alcoholic to good physical health can require long periods of time and in some cases he is left permanently disabled and suffers an early death.

In addition to the physical damage, the alcoholic suffers personality damage as well. The result is often broken homes, loss of jobs, abandoned children, crime, violence, and psychiatric hospitalization. Recovery from these problems can often take a long time and, in some cases will not be complete; e.g. some families totally reject the alcoholic and disown his existence.

Detoxification is one aspect of treatment and is usually successful insofar as "sobering up" the individual. In order to stay sober or abstain from alcohol use altogether, the alcoholic may require a period of inpatient hospitalization where his physical and emotional recovery can be emphasized simultaneously. Once back on his feet, he can be discharged to outpatient services where he can begin to rebuild his life in the community. There are a variety of therapeutic approaches used to help the alcoholic return to the community and improve his ability to cope successfully with everyday living without relying on alcohol.

CAUSES OF AND SPECIFIC TREATMENTS FOR ALCOHOLISM

Almost everyone agrees there is no unitary and distinct cause for alcoholism. The American Medical Association states, ". . . there is no single cause, but rather a complicated interplay of physiological, sociological, and psychological factors which leads to the origin and development of alcoholism (AMA, 1968).

Biochemical or physiological explanations for alcoholism involve such concepts as addiction, tolerance, loss of control, and a craving for alcohol.

Addiction is a term that includes many social and medical meanings. Generally, addiction refers to both physical and psychic dependency wherein the individual's behavior is deeply involved in obtaining alcohol. The high tendency to return to drinking after withdrawing is also characteristic of alcohol addiction. Alcohol addicts often cannot go one day without drinking, or they continue to drink for three months or more. As the alcoholic continues to drink, he can develop a tolerance for increased amounts of alcohol; subsequently, he will need to increase his intake more and more to obtain the desired effects. Tolerance can lead to a loss of control wherein the individual drinks himself into oblivion and awakens craving more alcohol.

Among the biochemical theories that attempt to explain the causes for the addiction concepts are: vitamin deficiency theory, glandular dysfunction theory, and the contention that alcoholism is inherited.

Alcoholics frequently suffer from nutritional disorders that create a need for unusual amounts of some vitamins. It is held that an individual may inherit a defective metabolism that results in a higher-than-average requirement of essential vitamins. For those persons who become acquainted with alcohol, the result can be an abnormal craving for the substance. Experiments with animals that were fed deficient diets and then presented with both water and alcohol showed that those on deficient diets tended to drink more alcohol than animals who received an adequate diet (Keller, 1971).

Our glands help maintain a balance of our body's functions. Excessive alcohol intake could upset and cause a breakdown of some of these glandular functions, such as a hormonal imbalance. Evidence gathered so far, however, suggests that glandular involvement may be more the result of drinking than the cause for drinking.

Alcoholism has been found to run in families and therefore may be inheritable. Several studies involving families, twins, and animals have, in general, been unsatisfactory and fail to support adequately the inheritable concept.

Sociological explanations for alcoholism emphasize the varying rates of alcoholism found among different cultural and national groups. For example, high incidences of alcoholism have been reported in the United States, France, and Poland; whereas, China, Greece, and Spain report lower incidences (Keller, 1971). Sociologists atempt to explain alcoholism by examining the differing values and attitudes of these cultures and groups of people.

Some religious groups require total abstinence while others include alcohol in their rituals. Drunken behavior is also subject to varying degrees of tolerance from differing groups. Legislative differences with respect to minimum age for permissible drinking also differ among cultures. Lastly, the availability of alcohol as compared with other liquids can also be a determining factor in the incidence of alcohol use and abuse. For instance, there is a drinking water shortage in France and wine has become the traditional beverage.

Sociological explanations for the etiology of alcoholism have definitely identified evidence linking cultural factors and patterns of drinking and the consequent behavior.

It is generally agreed that psychopathology is involved in the development of alcoholism. Psychological theories regarding the etiology of alcoholism assume the alcoholic has an underlying personality or emotional disorder that causes the individual to use alcohol in attempting to deal with the problem. Two prevailing psychological theories offering explanations for the causes of alcoholism are psychoanalytic theory and learning theory.

A basic foundation for psychoanalytic theory is that alcoholism is a symptom of an underlying emotional disturbance (Yates, 1970). Forming the basis for the psychoanalytic approach is the belief that alcohol relieves a continual internal discomfort by the alcoholic. Furthermore, alcoholism is often an expression of destructive behavior.

Anxiety, hostility, and inferiority are among the feelings that are relieved by the effects of drinking alcohol, a practice that becomes habitual because of the continual seeking for relief. Alcohol can be used against the self in a destructive manner as well as against others. Many alcoholics appear to drink themselves to death. Using alcohol to express hostility toward others is illustrated by the individual who continually drinks to the disappointment of family and loved ones.

Learning theorists consider alcoholism to be the result of learned behavior patterns that are reinforced and subsequently repeated. For example, an individual learns to reduce the tension he feels by having a drink. Later on he begins to rely on drinking to reduce additional tensions that occur in other areas of his life. His reliance on drinking becomes strengthened through the reinforcement of reduced tensions and the increase of his tolerance for tension, so that drinking begins to dominate other behavior patterns as well. The pain and discomfort that come with prolonged drinking would at first seem to deter excessive drinking rather than reinforce it. The problem is that alcohol has the immediate effect of reducing tension while the unpleasant consequences of drunkenness occur later. Therefore, the learning pattern encourages the resort to alcohol for immediate relief.

There may or may not be a distinct treatment approach for each of these theories. In most cases, the treatment of choice is based on more than one theoretical orientation. For example, one therapeutic approach might incorporate vitamin supplements as well as group psychotherapy and AA. Finally, more than one treatment approach may develop from one theoretical orientation.

In a very broad sense the treatment and rehabilitative therapy for alcoholism, in addition to medical services, emphasize a new way of life for the alcoholic. A variety of treatment methods are used to accomplish this, e.g. individual and/or group therapy, psychotropic drugs, and behavior therapy. The alcoholic will require understanding, acceptance, and encouragement in order to recover and, later on, maintain his recovery. Most therapists agree that a vital part of any treatment program is the opportunity offered the alcoholic person to develop trust in someone (Keller, 1971).

Individual and group therapy can take many directions, but basically each attempts to develop close interpersonal relationships designed so the alcoholic can gain greater self-understanding. The group process is often preferred in treatment and is perceived as the more logical and effective in helping alcoholics solve interpersonal problems. One major crippling aspect of alcoholism is denial of having an alcohol problem. That is, the individual denies being an alcoholic even in the face of evidence. Although difficult to believe, and even harder to accept, the alcoholic is often unable to link his abuse of alcohol to the other areas of his life that are suffering. He genuinely may feel that he does not have a drinking problem and that his family and job problems, failing health, etc., are due to other causes, not to alcohol. In this event, which is a common one in therapy, the denial becomes a strong barrier to treatment. One group approach which attempts to remove this barrier and that is gaining wider acceptance is the confrontation process. Similarly afflicted people confront one another about their denials. The result can often be greater insights into one's drinking as well as an understanding of the rationalizations for denying the problem.

An inherent danger in providing psychotropic drugs to alcoholics is that they can transfer their dependency from alcohol to the drugs. Most of the drugs used fall into one of two categories: tranquilizers and antidepressants. Tranquilizers are used to calm the excited or anxious alcoholic without making him unduly drowsy or euphoric and without interfering with his ability to move about (AMA, 1968). Antidepressants are used, although not routinely any more, to raise the mood of the alcoholic; e.g. relieve his depression. One other type of drug is frequently used, a deterrent drug, called antabuse. An individual taking antabuse who drinks any alcohol will experience some very uncomfortable reactions. His skin will flush, his heart begin to race; he will have nausea and vomiting, and even difficulty in breathing. The alcoholic on antabuse takes his pill each day and often believes that the decision whether or not to drink, for that day, has already been made for him.

An additional treatment approach which is gaining wider acceptance is behavior therapy (Lunde, 1970). The techniques utilized in behavior therapy are based on established principles of conditioning. The major technique in the treatment of alcoholics has been the use of aversive conditioning. Essentially this involves conditioning an aversion, by various means, to the sight, taste, and smell of alcohol. This is done by inducing vomiting (through an emetic) or by administering electric shock immediately after the individual has ingested alcohol. Hopefully, the sight, taste, and smell of alcohol will subsequently evoke nausea (induced by the emetic) or fear (induced by the shock), thereby preventing the individual from drinking. It is hoped that after the treatment the conditioned aversion to alcohol will last indefinitely. The effectiveness of antabuse is also based on similar principles as the aversion techniques just mentioned.

Treatment often breaks down, and the alcoholic begins to drink, when he leaves the treatment facility. One useful means frequently employed to combat this relapse is based on the sociological aspects of treatment, namely, group support.

Alcoholics Anonymous is one example of the group concept and a very effective one. "The aim of Alcoholics Anonymous members is to help each other maintain their sobriety, and to share their recovery experience freely with anyone who may have an alcohol related problem" (Keller, 1971). "AA began in 1935 in Akron, Ohio as the outcome of a meeting between a well-known surgeon and a New York businessman. Both were alcoholics" (Dorris, 1968). Each one helped the other to gain his sobriety; and later on, both began to help others and AA was born. ". . . the fellowship has grown to approximately 400,000 people in 14,000 groups in ninety countries" (Dorris, 1968). Alcoholics Anonymous concerns itself with the personal and continued recovery of the individual. Guiding the personal recovery are the 12 Steps of AA ranging from admission to being powerless over alcohol to carrying the message of the 12 Steps to other alcoholics. Alcoholics Anonymous emphasizes sobriety one day at a time. It is difficult to know exactly how many alcoholics have gained their sobriety in AA because the fellowship does not keep membership records. Nevertheless, AA is credited with helping more alcoholics than any other single effort (Dorris, 1968 and Keller, 1971). Alcoholics Anonymous can be found among many multifaceted treatment groups and programs, both inpatient and outpatient, government sponsored and private.

As parents, children, and others began to accompany alcoholics in their families to AA meetings, Al-Anon and Alateen came into being. Al-Anon seeks to help nonalcoholic relatives who have a family member who is a practicing alcoholic. Alateen is a further specialized group for nonalcoholic teenagers whose parent(s) are practicing alcoholics.

Halfway houses are also used to help the alcoholic re-enter the community after release from a hospital or rehabilitation facility. The halfway house approach attempts to ease the alcoholics re-entry to the community by providing a supportive environment for him to live in before going on his own. Many alcoholics have no place to go after inpatient treatment (detoxification and rehabilitative therapy). The halfway house provides a place to live halfway between the inpatient facility and the mainstreams of life. There are halfway houses for men and women, and most are small, usually fifteen to thirty beds. Churches, civic groups, private individuals, AA members, and some local governments have operated halfway houses. Most houses, however, face financial crises daily and many are forced to close because of delayed payments from welfare and/or private sources. Residents are expected to accept employment once they are able to work, at which time they begin to pay their own board and room.

The average time a person may spend in a halfway house ranges from thirty days to six months. During this time the resident may participate in AA meetings and group therapy conducted in the house while receiving outpatient services from a nearby clinic, e.g. medication, vocational rehabilitation. In almost all cases the major obligation of a resident is abstinence. Failure to abstain results in expulsion.

The causes of alcoholism appear to be many and varied. Subsequently, treatment must also meet these variations. There is some agreement that there are several different types of alcoholics and no single treatment that results in "curing" all of them.

CRITERIA AND GOALS FOR TREATMENT SUCCESS

The interaction of various theories regarding the causes of alcoholism is evident in the multifaceted treatment approaches frequently adopted. For example, we have already seen that a cessation of drinking and restoration of diet can be offered in a detoxification center in a few days. However, since many alcoholics suffer from additional physical and psychological side effects, continued abstinence and proper nutrition as well as repair and reversal or arrest of further deterioration is also required.

A strictly medical approach, one that does not allow for consideration of psychological or social problems, would undoubtedly be doomed to failure. Separating an alcoholic from alcohol and building him up physically has been tried by criminal justice systems for years with the result being that he continues to drink after release from jail.

Concentrating on just the consequences of alcoholism or on a single cause can only result in disappointment for the individuals attempting to help the alcoholic as well as initiate relapse and/or further deterioration of the neglected areas for the alcoholic.

Success is best accomplished and realized when the objectives are clear and distinct. Alcoholism is a very complicated disease that affects the victim's health and his vocational, social, psychological, and family life. Improvement in any of these areas can be interpreted as success. However, the central frustration or difficulty in defining success appears to be the chronicity of alcoholism; that is, the repeated failure of treatment and the resultant (alcoholic's) return to drinking. Staff treating alcoholics can expect relapse, and those staff members who continue to work with alcoholics may have to accept incomplete success. Concentrating on abstinence at the expense of other important features in the alcoholic's recovery can be self-defeating. The result can be reinstigation of drinking because of a stressful social situation or unresolved psychological conflict that has been ignored. However, adjustment in all areas of life adaptation may be idealistic (Saslow, 1969).

Some alcoholics resume drinking and appear to be able to avoid excesses (Pattison, 1966 and Quirk, 1968 and Reinert, 1968). Here again a clear definition of social drinking is difficult to obtain, especially when moderate and social drinking are compared. Some researchers believe that moderate and social drinking are value judgments and that ". . . moderation for one person may be excess for another" (Hayman, 1967).

Finally, there has been no clear-cut demonstration that drinking during therapy will cause treatment to fail (Pattison, 1966 and Vogler, 1970). For example, an alcoholic may resume drinking while he experiences improvement in a major psychological area of his life and be able to avoid excessive consumption. True, occurrences may be few in number, but none the less, they do occur (Anant, 1968; Quirk, 1968; Reinert, 1968). Furthermore, abstinence is often the prerequisite to psychotherapy or counseling as well as the objective at termination of treatment. It's like having the patient well at the start of treatment. The point is, there are many types of alcoholics and even more probable causes for why they drink. This situation requires flexible treatment approaches and goals.

The diversified and complex nature of alcoholism can result in just as many diversified and complex reactions to its victims from the professional staff of helping agencies. Staff attitudes are very important in determining the approach to treatment and just as important in influencing the results. Stereotypes are still common among some professional people, and the result often is the stereotype gets treated instead of the individual and his total problem.

The lack of agreement about the cause, course, treatment of alcoholism also results in a lack of systematized research from which applicable conclusions can be drawn. For example, one survey of opinions from professional staff who had worked with alcoholics for an average of nine years found that over 71 percent considered abstinence as the preferred criteria for successful treatment goals. However, estimates as to the length of abstinence preferred ranged from total sobriety, one day at a time, to two years continuous abstinence (Einstein, 1970).

At the present state of our knowledge we can reasonably expect that one-third of the alcoholics in treatment will do well. The remainder may relapse from time to time, and some of these individuals will get worse. A survey of 103 state hospitals found rates of improvement ranging from 30 to 40 percent to as high as 70 to 80 percent. Regardless of the treatment program, most reported 33 percent improvement after therapy (Jeppe, 1962; Kendall, 1966; Myerson, 1966; Pattison, 1966; Vincent, 1969).

Alcoholism is still not accepted by some people as a legitimate illness that requires treatment. Although alcohol intoxication can result in a life threatening situation for the alcoholic, many hospitals do not provide the necessary services. Out of the 5994 short-term general hospitals in the United States registered by the American Hospital Association, it is estimated that only 53 percent of them admit patients with a primary diagnosis of alcoholism (AHA, 1972). The need for reform continues.

REFERENCES

Alcohol Abuse. A summary for parents and students on alcohol abuse. Pamphlet, Los Angeles County Board of Supervisors, Supervisor Warren Dorn, 1972.

Alcohol and Alcoholism. A Police Handbook. The Correctional Association of New York, 1971.

American Hospital Association. Personal correspondence. Chicago, Illinois.

American Medical Association: *Manual on Alcoholism.* 1968.

Anant, S. S.: Former alcoholics and social drinking: An unexpected finding. *Can J Psychol, 9:*35, 1968.

Coburn, D. R.: *Robinson to Driver to Easter.* The Correctional Association of New York, June, 1967.

Dorris, R. T., and Lindley, D. F.: *Counseling on Alcoholism and Related Disorders.* Beverly Hills, Cal., Glencoe Press, 1968.

Driver, R. J.: The U.S. Supreme Court and the chronic drunkenness offender. *QJSA, 30*(1): Part A, March, 1969.

Einstein, S.; Wolfson, E., and Gecht, D.: What matters in treatment: Relevant variables in alcoholism. *Internat J Addictions, 5*(1): March, 1970.

Erskine, H.: *Alcohol and the Criminal Justice System: Challenge and Response.* U.S. Department of Justice, Law Enforcement Assistance Administration, National Institute of Law Enforcement and Criminal Justice, January, 1972.

Goff, D. H.: *Legal Status of Alcoholics-Social Welfare Implications.* The Correctional Association of New York. Paper presented at the National Conference on Social Welfare, San Francisco, California, May 30, 1968.

Goff, D. H.: *Criminal Responsibility and the Alcoholic.* The Correctional Association of New York. Paper presented at the 14th International Institute on the Prevention and Treatment of Alcoholism, Milan, Italy, June, 1968.

Goff, D. H.: *The Courts and Public Drunkenness Offenders: The Outlook.* The Correctional Association of New York, June, 1970.

Hayman, M.: The myth of social drinking. *Am J Psychiatr, 124,* 1967.

Hutt, P. B., and Merrill, R. A.: Is the Alcoholic Immune from Criminal Prosecution? (mimeo) Reprinted from *The Municipal Court Review,* July, 1966.

Jellinek, E. M.: *The Disease Concept of Alcoholism.* New Brunswick, N.J., Hillhouse, 1960.

Jeppe, C. B.: The prognosis and treatment of alcoholism. *S Afr Med J, 36,* 1962.

Keller, M., et al. (Eds.): *First Special Report to the U.S. Congress on Alcohol and Health from the Secretary of Health, Education, and Welfare.* Department of Health, Education, and Welfare, Publication No. (HSM) 72–9099, December, 1971.

Kendall, R. E., and Staton, M. C.: The fate of untreated alcoholics. *QJSA, 27,* 1966.

Lunde, S. E.: Generalization of results in studies of aversion conditioning with alcoholism. *Behavioral Research and Therapy, 8,* 1970.

Myerson, D. J., and Mayer, J.: Origins, treatment and destiny of skid-row alcoholic men. *New Eng J Med, 275,* 1966.

National Council on Alcoholism, Inc.: *Facts on Alcoholism.* 1971.

Nimmer, R.: The public drunk: Formalizing the police role as a social help agency. *The American Bar Foundation,* No. 6, 1970.

Nimmer, R.: *Two Million Unnecessary Arrests.* American Bar Foundation, Chicago, 1971.

Pattison, E. M.: A critique of alcoholism treatment concepts. *QJSA,* 27(1), March, 1966.

Picken, B.: *Olive View Medical Center Drug Program.* Los Angeles County Department of Hospitals, August, 1970.

Pencock, T. A.: The frequency of alcoholism among self-referred persons and those referred by the courts for psychiatric examination. *Can Med Assoc J,* 87, 1962.

Pittman, D. J., and Gordon, C. W.: *Revolving Door: A Study of the Chronic Police Case Inebriate.* Yale Center of Alcohol Studies. Glencoe, Ill., Free Press, 1958.

Quirk, D. A.: Former alcoholics and social drinking: An additional observation. *Can J Psychol,* 9, 1968.

Reinert, R. E., and Bowen, W. T.: Social drinking following treatment for alcoholism. *Bull Menn Clin,* 32, 1968.

Room, R.: *Assumptions and Implications of Disease Concepts of Alcoholism.* Paper delivered at the 29th International Congress on Alcoholism and Drug Dependence, Sydney, Australia, February, 1970.

Room, R.: *The Effects of Drinking Laws on Behavior.* Paper presented to Society for the Study of Social Problems, Denver, Colorado, August, 1971.

Rubington, E.: The alcoholic and the jail. *Federal Probation,* 29(2), 1965.

St. Louis Detoxification and Diagnostic Evaluations Center Project Summary. St. Louis Metropolitan Police Department, St. Louis, Missouri. LEAA Grant #284 (S.093), 1970.

Saslow, G.: New views of the alcoholic. *Rehabilitation Record,* 10(1), 1969.

Stern, G.: Handling public drunkenness: Reforms despite Powell. *Internat J Addictions,* 5(1), March, 1970.

Taber, C. W.: *Taber's Cyclopedic Medical Dictionary,* 10th ed. Philadelphia, F. A. Davis Co., 1965.

Task Force Report: Drunkenness. President's Commission on Law Enforcement and Administration of Justice, Washington, D.C., U.S. Government Printing Office, 1967.

Utah School of Alcohol Studies. University of Utah, Salt Lake City, 1968 Manual Supplement.

Vincent, M. O., and Blum, D. M.: A five year follow-up study of alcoholic patients. *Rep Alc,* 27(4), 1969.

Vogler, R. E., et al.: *Electrical Aversion Conditioning with Chronic Alcoholics: Follow-up and Suggestions for Research.* Research supported by Grant No. 11–14 from the California Department of Mental Hygiene, April, 1970.

Vogler, R. E., et al.: Electrical aversion conditioning with chronic alcoholics. *J Consult Clin Psychol,* 34(3), June, 1970.

Yates, A. J.: *Behavior Therapy.* New York, John Wiley and Sons, Inc., 1970.

Chapter 7

LAW ENFORCEMENT AND PHYSICAL DISABILITIES

RICHARD E. HARDY, JOHN G. CULL, WILLIAM A. CRUNK, JR.

- ■ BLINDNESS
- ■ EPILEPSY: CHARACTERISTICS WHICH MAY CAUSE SUSPICIONS
- ■ MULTIPLE SCLEROSIS
- ■ CEREBRAL PALSY
- ■ REFERENCES
- ■ SUGGESTED READINGS

BLINDNESS

BLIND PERSONS often are victims of misunderstanding by professional persons, police, correctional officers, and the lay public. Many people are concerned about approaches they should use in helping blind persons in times of need. Almost all persons without some background and knowledge concerning blindness feel insecure and uncomfortable when they are in the company of individuals who are blind.

The law enforcement and correctional officer should remember that blind persons are much more similar to him than unlike him. They are different in one major respect. They have suffered the psychological impact of a major disability and have adjusted or are in the process of adjusting to this impact.

Many persons hold negative attitudes toward the disabled and these attitudes, of course, influence their reaction to all disabled persons. A good example which illustrates this well is the changing terminology used to describe disabled persons. When a term or description becomes so emotion-laden that its use is prejudicial to a group, the term is changed. During the past fifty years, the number of changes indicate to some degree the depth and diversity of prejudice. Crippled has been changed to handicapped; idiot, imbecile, and moron, once good clinical terms, are no longer acceptable prefessional terms; leprosy has become Hansen's disease; the blind are becoming visually impaired; the poor are now the disadvantaged; the epileptic now has a convulsive disorder; and a few years ago the severely disabled became the catastrophically involved by an act of Congress.

Police officers can do a great deal to change public attitudes toward visually handicapped persons. This can be done by relating with blind persons in an intelligent manner. One factor which the police officer should remember is that many persons who are legally blind are not totally blind. Legal blindness is defined as 20/200 vision in the stronger eye with best correction and/or a visual field limited to 20° or less. In other words a person is able to see at 20 feet what he should be able to see at 200 feet and/or his visual field is constricted in the better eye to 20 percent or less (Hardy and Cull, 1972). It is not difficult to see how vision of this type could cause an individual to stumble and appear awkward especially when he has recently sustained an injury which might cause this amount of visual loss or when for some other reason he has not adjusted well to his visual level.

In addition, many blind persons have moving eyes (Nystagmus) or irritated eyes. In some cases the police officer has felt that these individuals were intoxicated and has not realized that they are people who are functioning with a disability.

Some blind persons who have not accepted their disability become quite upset and naturally so when help or aid is offered to them in an awkward manner or when they feel they are able to function well without assistance. The police officer should realize that this is a natural and normal human reaction to functioning under difficult circumstances. In some cases their reaction represents denial (a rejection, often unconscious, of an obvious fact which is too disruptive to the personality or too emotionally painful to accept). The blind person, in other words, softens reality by denying the obvious fact that he does need assistance at times.

The police officer and corrections worker should realize that blind persons are people first and blind second. There are no magical tricks to use in dealing with them, but some practical approaches and steps can be of considerable value.

When the police officer offers assistance to a blind person, he should do so directly. He should just ask "May I be of help?" He should speak in a normal tone, not raising his voice and address the blind individual directly. When addressed directly the blind individual is better able to locate the police officer than when the officer is walking by asking a question.

In guiding the blind person, the officer should permit the blind person to take his arm. A nice way to offer an arm is to say, "Here is my left arm" (or my right, whatever the case may be). He knows then how to locate your arm, and he will respond to your motion much as a dancer follows a partner. Never "grab" the blind person's arm; he cannot anticipate your movements if you do so.

In walking with a blind person, the police officer should proceed at a normal pace; hesitating slightly before stepping up or down; and being certain not to drag the individual over a curb. After crossing a street, the officer should see that the blind person is started straight in the direction he wants to take. The officer should caution him of any unusual obstacles ahead such as low awnings or construction.

In giving directions, the officer should not point. He might say for instance, "Three blocks ahead, cross third intersection, turn left two and one-half blocks and the building is on your right." The officer should not identify intersections by street names because the blind person cannot read the signs. And, he should not use the tall white building as a landmark; since the blind person cannot see it.

Many of these suggestions sound elementary, but all persons have difficulties in instructing blind persons and helping them when these concepts are not thought out in advance.

In showing a blind person to a chair, place his hand on the back of it. Do not try to push him into it. His touch will tell him the type, width, and height of the chair.

When food is being served to a blind person who is eating without a sighted companion, the menu should be read to him. This should include the price of each item. The police officer may find that he can instruct waitresses and waiters concerning proper procedures. As the waitress places each item on the table, the blind person's attention should be called to it; "Here is your water." If the blind person wishes his meat to be cut or his food served from a casserole dish or a platter he will request help; however, it is never bad to offer help. The officer will have questions about blind persons from time to time from various people.

When conversing with a blind person, use normal terms as well as normal tones. He may greet you by saying, "It is good to see you again." Speak directly to him and remember if your gaze wanders, your voice follows your gaze.

Blind persons may ask a police or corrections officer about the amount of money they have if there is confusion. If the police officer has been requested to count a blind individual's money, he should hand him the bills separately and identify each denomination as it is handed back. This is not necessary with coins because blind persons know them by touch.

A police officer should always identify himself as such when he approaches a blind man. This is done since the blind person may ask for help that he would not ask from others.

Above all, do not pity the blind person. Thousands are successful workers and many more are working toward independence through state-federal programs of vocational rehabilitation.

EPILEPSY: CHARACTERISTICS WHICH MAY
CAUSE SUSPICIONS

The word epilepsy originates from a Greek word meaning "a taking hold of; a something seizing the subject as though it were outside himself." Through the years various myths (epilepsy causes insanity; epilepsy is catching) have arisen about epilepsy. It is one of the oldest known diseases and the least understood.

Laws have been very firm about epileptic people, but most have been updated in recent years. The following restrictions are still found in reference to epileptics:

1. RESTRICTIVE OR DISCRIMINATORY LEGISLATION—one state prohibits marriage by persons with epilepsy. Some states authorize sterilization of epileptics. Ten states will not give driver's licenses to most epileptics.
2. MILITARY—persons are rejected for military service with epilepsy.
3. EDUCATION—some schools will not accept epileptic children.
4. EMPLOYMENT—25 percent who have normal intelligence are unemployed due to epilepsy.
5. INSURANCE—automobile and health insurance are almost impossible to obtain. Life insurance often is much higher than standard rate.

Epilepsy is just a general name given to the symptoms of a number of disorders of the nervous system. A general definition is one that describes epilepsy as a disorder of the central nervous system, marked by sudden and periodic lapses of consciousness and distinctive usually measurable disturbances in the electrical discharges within the brain. Seizures take on various forms, depending on the nature of stimulation to the brain, region of the brain where disturbances start, severity, and spread of the discharge. Although every type of seizure is not classified as epilepsy, repeated seizures generally are labeled such.

Epilepsy is not limited to sex, age, or race. It is found in all age groups, all races, and both sexes. An estimated 500,000 to 1,800,000 people experience some type of epilepsy.

Most doctors do not believe epilepsy is inherited. Research has shown that some families do have inherited tendencies that make it easier to develop seizures. Nonetheless, even the carrier of this tendency may go through life seizure-free if no precipitant factor is added. It is estimated that 10 to 12 percent of the population fall into this group labeled "latent epileptic."

The only sure way to diagnose epilepsy is by an electroencephalographic (E.E.G.) report and a history of events preceding a seizure or unusual behavior followed by a complete physical examination including x-rays and often a spinal tap of the lumbar spine.

NORMAL BRAIN WAVE OR E.E.G. PATTERN

EPILEPTIC BRAIN WAVE OR E.E.G. PATTERN

In addition to diagnosis, an E.E.G. also helps in determining the proper medication for control of these seizures.

The four different forms of seizures are characterized as follows:

1. *Grand Mal*—general convulsions, with loss of consciousness, stiffening, muscle movements and jerks of limbs and/or trunks, neck, eyes, face. Irregular noisy respiration, drooling, and dusky blue or pale color apparent.

   Many patients, experience an AURA, feelings of impending doom, unpleasant odors, odd sounds, tingling of skin, and spots before eyes before the convulsion.

   In the postictal state (after a seizure) patient may experience drowsiness, fatigue, or sleep.

2. *Petit Mal*—generally appears to be merely a blank stare or rapid blinking of eyes, sometimes accompanied by small, twitching movements. Seizures last 5 to 25 seconds, can occur as often as 100 times daily, usually in persons aged 6 to 14, though sometimes in adults.

   In the postictal state, individual's activity resumes as if nothing happened.

3. *Focal—or Jacksonian*—attacks which start in one part of the body and may remain entirely limited to that part. Often they occur without loss of consciousness. However, there may be a spread of the "disorderly discharge" through the entire brain terminating in a generalized convulsion just as *grand mal*. Can appear as pure motor attacks (jerking arm) or sensory seizures with numbness to some part of the body. Rarely painful, dimming of vision or blindness or even episodes associated with formed images experienced.

4. *Psychomotor*—occurs at any age and has the most complex pattern of behavior. These seizures may be characterized by: chewing and lip smacking, staring and confusion, abdominal pains and headaches, color changes, spots before the eyes, buzzing, ringing in the ears, dizziness, fear, rage, anger, and postictal sleep. This may last from a minute to several hours. After the attack, patient is unable to remember what happened. In some patients, night or day walking, picking at or taking off clothes, rubbing the hands, may occur. These purposeless motions occur often and may be controlled by medication.

Males seem more prone to psychomotor epilepsy whereas *petit mal* is more frequent in females.

A further classification is found in epilepsy. A convulsive disorder resulting from a demonstrable lesion noted by a neurological examination or x-ray is known as symptomatic. The convulsive disorder with no definite apparent cause is called idiopathic.

If one were to make several general statements of fact about epilepsy, these would be:

1. Seizures alone are rarely the cause of death.
2. Mental deterioration is not caused by seizures alone. This usually only occurs when infection or trauma to the brain is also found.
3. The epileptic may seem dull or mentally slow when actually his controlling drug is causing this effect.
4. The only major seizure occurrence that should be considered a possible source of death is called *status epilepticus*, which is a state in which there are so many reoccurring convulsions that the patient does not regain consciousness and could die from exhaustion.
5. The "epileptic personality" is a result of society's pressures and ignorance rather than from seizures or convulsions.
6. Epileptics make good workers in society's industries.

Treatment for epilepsy takes on a threefold approach: environmental adjustment, surgery, and/or drugs. A normal life style should be sought wherever possible. Surgery is only possible in a few symptomatic cases. Drugs are used in hopes that they will completely control seizures with minimum possible side effects. The most common drugs used are:

1. Dilantin®
2. Phenobarbital
3. Mysoline®
4. Mebaral®

A basic goal and rule to follow to reduce anxiety toward seizures is "nothing to excess, everything in moderation." Avoidance of over-fatigue and tension is necessary in that these provoke seizure occurrence.

It is very important that the person with epilepsy be taught that his problem is not "different," "strange," or "horrible," but is in the same class as diabetes or a fractured leg or arm. It is therefore advisable to "take it easy" but enjoy life also.

In coordination with the problem of epilepsy, the Epilepsy Foundation of America has prepared a *Working Program Guide for the Planning, Development, and Promotion of Information and Training for Police, Firemen, Airline Cabin Crews, and Other Groups in Contact with the Epileptics.* The basic program consists of a meeting between law enforcement personnel, the presentation of what epilepsy is from a medical point of view, the kinds of symptoms that law enforcement personnel may see, first aid trips, a film which shows seizures, and an opportunity for a question and answer period. Foundation literature is provided as additional resource material for the officers.

The epileptic person, just as the cerebral palsy (C.P.) and multiple sclerosis (M.S.) patient, exhibits many characteristics that are "out-of-the-ordinary." Because seizures are the form in which epilepsy occurs, people in the area near the epileptic may become frightened and alarmed and as a result notify the police. Out of sheer ignorance about this condition the bystander may run away for fear of "catching" the seizure when in actuality his assistance was needed by the epileptic. It is true there is little you can do for the person himself, but you can clear the area of objects which if fallen on would cause injury.

When the police arrive they may look on the occurrence as a drunken sickness. Hopefully, they would be well acquainted with epilepsy and know they should not restrain the epileptic. If they do not know and attempt to restrain the person, they will meet with resistance and force which in turn could cause the police to assume the epileptic is resisting them. Anger could result and harm could come to the epileptic person.

A person having a *petit mal* seizure will tend to just stare or blink his eyes. If spoken to, he would appear to ignore the speaker or seem almost unconscious. Drugs, alcoholism, and defiance may be an assumption made by the police.

A *grand mal* person usually falls to the ground also exhibiting signs of drunkenness.

Periods of amnesia are suffered by the psychomotor epileptics. Their whereabouts, name, or address may be completely forgotten and they may be confused with someone under the influence of outside forces. These epileptics also do other "abnormal" things. They may chew continually with nothing in their mouths, mumble, or move their heads back and forth, exhibiting signs of mental retardation.

The epileptic also has little control of his excretory system during a seizure and therefore may have embarrassing situations resulting from this problem.

Vision problems are also experienced by epileptics. This may cause stumbling and problems in getting about in one's environment. Suspicions may be aroused upon seeing these actions.

Others experience breathing problems and heavy, irregular respiration. People could mistake this breathing problem with heart trouble or a heart attack and therefore try to restrain or force the epileptic to lie down or go with them. The epileptic in turn could respond with force or even rage. This could cause police problems.

The epileptic, after the seizure usually sleeps (especially *grand mal* patients). If he is spotted by police while sleeping, which could be anywhere, police misconceptions could arise as to loitering, drunkenness, and drugs.

Drug therapy side effects must also be considered. After administration of the drugs, drowsiness can occur. Senses can be numbed and reflexes slowed. The epileptic could appear "dull," "indifferent," and even "defiant" to police questioning.

We have a long way to go before understanding epilepsy but the opinions and facts about it are much improved over the past. With the help of the various agencies, it is hoped one day it will be a disease that will be understood and accepted easily.

MULTIPLE SCLEROSIS

Multiple sclerosis, more commonly known as "MS," is a crippling disease of the neurological functioning of the human body. The major area this attacking crippler seems to affect is the brain and spinal cord. The destructive process that occurs in multiple sclerosis is the disintegration of the myelin tissue which coats the nerves. Myelin tissue is then replaced by scar tissue. When these scar tissues or sclerotic plaques are found in the body in place of nerve tissue, an obstruction of function of the simple (to "normal" people) life activities occurs. Activities such as walking or speaking become truly frustrating and at times impossible.

Multiple sclerosis can attack at any age, but the majority of people afflicted with MS are between twenty to forty years of age. Strangely enough, the disease seems to strike more women than men and more Northerners than Southerners. For a reason unknown to experts in this field, MS seems to strike in cold climates more than in warm climate regions.

This disease is progressive but not contagious. People afflicted with multiple sclerosis seem to go through various alternating conditions throughout their lives. They can go from being totally incapacitated to leading a normal routine life within just a short time. They seem to experience periods of exacerbations or worsening, then periods of stability and possibly even remissions or improvement. The exacerbation period often occurs for approximately six weeks interspersed with remissions of months or even years. Unfortunately, with each exacerbation period further permanent damage usually occurs.

One of the problems the afflicted have had has been in determining the course their disease may take. There seems to be no definite path which multiple sclerosis follows: With each patient the disease differs markedly.

There is no known cure for multiple sclerosis as yet. Throughout the years, doctors and scientists alike have tried a little of everything in hopes of finding the answer to the problem. No drug has been found to cure MS, but studies are now being done on ACTH, a hormone. Even if this drug is proved helpful it will only eliminate some of the symptoms and not cure the disease. Actually, all that can be done now is to establish good care and work on building general resistance, being careful not to become fatigued, and avoid contact with infection and disease. Research will continue and there is hope a cure will be found.

People suffering from multiple sclerosis might easily arouse suspicions in those around them because of various characteristics or symptoms they exhibit. Due to poor coordination from interference with the brain and spinal cord the MS sufferer may show the same signs as someone under the influence of alcohol or drugs. Many tend to stagger and/or tremor severely. Simple tasks such as walking now become forced and strained and usually quite strange in nature. Others may show jerking movements of the body, especially the head, causing it to sway back and forth, back and forth. Spasticity is another characteristic of multiple sclerosis often seen along with the dragging of the feet. People with this characteristic also may exhibit gestures that are odd to most people. Because MS sufferers experience periods of dizziness and loss of balance they may stumble and fall. This too tends to call attention to their behavior.

When talking to an MS sufferer, we can easily observe other factors which cause further suspicion. Many have speech difficulties which causes their speech to be slurred and unclear. They tend to be forgetful and their attention span is short. So, naturally, when conversing with other people, the MS sufferer may not seem to have complete control of all his senses. Along with these characteristics, many MS sufferers have vision changes and nystagmus. They may have double or blurred vision or even temporary blindness. Difficulty in seeing, in itself, even without the nystagmus would tend to call attention to the sufferer.

Multiple sclerosis patients experience a continuum of emotions from periods of euphoria to depression. Many sufferers cannot cope with their problem and have deep depression and sorrow. This in turn causes moodiness and irascible behavior. As a result of these emotions, the MS sufferer may become involved in situations of anger and trouble. On the other end of the continuum, the euphoric sufferer will exhibit signs of giddiness and will attempt to blot out his problem. In attempts to do this, they will seem to over react and become overexcited and responsive in situations involving interpersonal relationships.

Another characteristic common to multiple sclerosis is poor bladder and bowel control. Besides the embarrassment and anxiety this causes, others may be led to believe this person does not have complete control of himself, possibly due to an outside influence, such as alcohol. This certainly is a problem which is difficult to disguise in public.

Lastly, a characteristic common to all MS sufferers is fatigue. It takes very little to cause fatigue for the person with multiple sclerosis. They may exhibit signs of weakness, listlessness, indifference, and even signs of obliviousness when actually the only problem is exhaustion.

The people afflicted with multiple sclerosis do unfortunately display characteristics which are not "normal" for most individuals. Those coming in contact with multiple sclerosis, due to lack of knowledge may become suspicious and inquisitive about the person they see and may even confuse this person's actions with that of a person under the influence of outside forces.

CEREBRAL PALSY

Cerebral Palsy refers to a condition not a progressive disease characterized by a group of concurrent symptoms. It is a motor disability caused by a brain dysfunction and damage to the central nervous system. Those with cerebral palsy do not have voluntary control of muscular movements. Two national cerebral palsy organizations have defined cerebral palsy in the following manner:

> The American Academy of Cerebral Palsy defined Cerebral Palsy as, "any abnormal alteration of movement or motor function arising from defect, injury, or disease of the nervous tissues contained in the cranial cavity (1953).

> The United Cerebral Palsy Associations were more inclusive, "Cerebral Palsy embraces the clinical picture created by injury to the brain, in which one of the components is motor disturbance. Thus, cerebral palsy may be described as a group of conditions, usually originating in childhood, characterized by paralysis, weakness, incoordination or any other aberration of motor function caused by pathology of the motor control center of the brain. In addition to such motor dysfunction, cerebral palsy may include learning difficulties, psychological problems, sensory defects, convulsive and behavioral disorders of organic origin (1958).

As one can see from the definitions above cerebral palsy is not limited to neurological disabilities and almost always includes many secondary and associate handicaps. Handicaps such as speech difficulties, perceptual difficulties, learning disabilities, and/or emotional disabilities are a few examples of possible secondary conditions.

To say there is one known cause for cerebral palsy would be

untrue. Experts do not actually know what the cause is, but they do realize there are crucial periods in the life of a child when the brain damage can be pinpointed. Doctors estimate that 30 percent of cerebral palsy is caused by factors operative prenatally.

Genetic and inherited conditions fall under prenatal causes. Also any shock or injury received by the fetus during pregnancy can result in injury to the central nervous system and thus cause cerebral palsy. Conditions such as anoxia, anemia, shock, heart condition, metabolic status of mother and the Rh factor all can be contributing prenatal factors.

Perinatal conditions seem to account for 60 percent of all CP cases. Injury seems to play the most important role in this period. Breech birth, brain hemorrhage, and a loss of oxygen seem to be the most prevalent injuries.

Postnatal conditions contribute the least amount of CP cases. Only 10 percent of all cerebral palsy occurs after birth. Childhood diseases, high fevers, poisoning, and/or strangulation account for specific reasons of postnatal cerebral palsy.

Illingworth, (1958) after studying cerebral palsy, discovered that many factors of this condition correlate. He found:

1. There is a higher than average incidence of CP in males (75%).
2. There is a higher than average incidence of multiple pregnancies —about 6 percent compared to average of 1.2 percent.
3. There is a higher incidence of previous miscarriages and still-births.
4. Anoxia is probably the most important single factor in CP.

Cardwell, (1956) after a study on cerebral palsy also found some relationship between IQ and cerebral palsy. She concluded that of those who come to clinics or are assigned to special classes:

1. About 5 to 6 percent have superior intelligence,
2. About 25 to 30 percent have average intelligence,
3. About 20 to 25 percent have borderline or dull normal intelligence,
4. About 40 to 50 percent have IQ's below 70.

It was brought out earlier that along with the neurological problems cerebral palsied victims almost always suffer secondary handicaps. The above figures show the prevalence of a major associated handicap—mental retardation. A person who is mentally retarded would have difficulty in comprehending many situations he might come in contact with daily. He might react in ways strange to "normal, routine procedures" and therefore cause questions to arise.

About 30 percent of all CP's suffer from a hearing problem. This, of course, contributes to learning difficulties and the problems surrounding the cerebral palsied victim.

Almost all CP victims have speech problems. Several predominate ones are:

1. *Dysarthria*—articulation defect caused by poor motor control,
2. *Delayed speech*—due to mental retardation and cerebral dysfunction,
3. *Stuttering*.

All of those particular problems definitely would cause suspicion. Anyone conversing with a CP might think the person was not in control of all his senses. They might think the behavior shows indifference, when actually the problem may be mental retardation.

Perceptual handicaps are present. Cerebral Palsy sufferers have difficulty in responding to visual and visual motor perceptual tasks. This can cause others to feel the CP is using alcohol or other drugs to blur his mind.

Along with all of these, of course, lie emotional problems. As a result of all the other problems, the CP's have difficulty in coping with their handicaps. They can become frustrated with failure to such a degree that they act out with anger and hatred. They can become involved in fights and cause public disturbances as a result of this frustration.

There is not just one condition called cerebral palsy. Cerebral palsy is the all encompassing title for many types of conditions. CP can be broken down into five subgroups; each with its own distinct characteristics and each exemplified in a different way. Every subgroup has characteristics that might look unusual or suspicious. As each subgroup is described, the symptoms become evident.

The first type, which encompasses the largest number of cerebral palsy victims, is spastic paralysis. An estimated 60 percent of all CP cases are spastic. It is a state of constant tension. It is caused by a lesion in the pyramidal tract—the brain surface.

As a result of this injury, spastics move with jerking, uncontrollable movements. It can affect only one limb, a monoplegic, or even all four limbs, a quadraplegic. The problem arises because the muscles all want to work against each other. A person who is spastic can manipulate the muscle voluntarily because the muscle is normal, but the outcome is slow, explosive, and performed poorly because of the neurological impairment. All of the above conditions, in any routine task, become emphasized, frustrating, and bring a lot of attention to the CP victim. A quadraplegic person would be less likely to be confused with an unlawful person in that his disability is so pronounced. A monoplegic might be confused in a situation because only partial affliction has occurred and his disability may take on the look of a person under the influences of outside factors.

Athetosis is caused by a lesion in the extra pyramidal system located in the fore or midbrain. It seems to account for 30 percent of all CP cases. The athetoid moves with lurching, writhing, and stumbling movements. There seems to be an uncontrolled postural attitude. The athetoid is more fluid than the spastic, but his movements are quite purposeless and unnecessary. In order to complete a task such as eating, many uncontrolled involuntary movements must take place. As the emotions of the athetoid intensify, the number of uncontrolled movements increase. Therefore in a confrontation situation between the athetoid and a policeman, for example, more rapid movements would most likely occur. This in turn might cause the policeman to think the athetoid was being cocky and the end result might be flaring tempers and anger.

Athetosis is divided into six small groups. Each group exhibits a behavior that might cause question or suspicion. These are:

1. *Rotary*—palms of hands move in and out continually.
2. *Shudderlike*—show signs of having chills-facial look is sour.
3. *Tremorlike*—irregular movements of head and body.
4. *Dystonic*—limbs remain twisted for long periods of time.
5. *Nontension*—flabbiness and weakness of muscles.
6. *Hemiathetoid*—only one side affected by condition (Phelps, 1958).

Ataxia, a subgroup of CP is found to be evidenced in only 5 percent of all cases. The basic problem lies in the cerebellum, and therefore the person's balance is affected. As a result of this disturbed equilibrium, characteristics of staggering, stumbling, and falling are found. Because of these factors, the ataxic person has been given the nickname of the "little drunk." If an ataxic person was thought to be drunk and was made to walk a straight line to prove he wasn't, it would be impossible. His equilibrium is just too unbalanced.

Another identifying movement of the ataxic person is his walk. He walks as if he were marching in a parade with a very high step. Strangely enough, his speech is spoken in the same rhythm as his walk. He talks in an explosive manner and this speech would certainly be considered odd. Upon confrontation with the ataxic person, one would notice an uncoordinated movement of the eyes and also a nystagmus. This would cause vision problems resulting in difficulty to function normally. According to Denhoff and Robinault (1960), "various authors agree that over 50% of the Cerebral Palsied victims have occulomotor defects and 25% or more have subnormal vision." The last two types are grouped together because they occur only rarely. Only 5 percent of all CP cases are found in the category of both rigidity and tremor. In rigidity and tremor, the injury lies in the extrapyramidal system. Rigidity is a result of the resistance of agonist and antagonist muscles causing the person to become very stiff.

Tremor results from an interference with normal balance between the antagonist muscle groups. The body exhibits involuntary, vibrating movements of the body. People with either of these might be confused with a person possibly suffering from "cold turkey."

All of these types are distinct and cause the cerebral palsied person many motor problems.

REFERENCES

Cardwell, Viola E.: *Cerebral Palsy: Advances in Understanding and Care.* New York, Association for the Aid of Crippled Children, 1956.

Denhoff, Eric, and Robinault, Isabel: *Cerebral Palsy and Related Disorders: A Developmental Approach to Dysfunction.* New York, McGraw-Hill, 1960.

Fay, Temple: Desperately needed research in cerebral palsy. *Cerebral Palsy Rev, 14* (March–April), 1953.

Hardy, Richard E., and Cull, John G.: *Social and Rehabilitation Services for the Blind.* Sprinfield, Ill., Charles C Thomas, 1972.

Hess, George: *Living at Best with Multiple Sclerosis.* Springfield, Ill., Charles C Thomas, 1962.

Illingsworth, B. S. (Ed.): *Recent Advances in Cerebral Palsy.* London, J & A, Churchill, Ltd., 1958.

Kirk, Samul: *Educating Exceptional Children.* Boston, Houghton Mifflin, 1962.

National Multiple Sclerosis Society: *Multiple Sclerosis.* New York, NMSS, 1969.

National Multiple Sclerosis Society: *Multiple Sclerosis—Facts.* New York, NMSS, 1969.

National Multiple Sclerosis Society: *Multiple Sclerosis—Patient Services.* New York, NMSS, 1968.

National Multiple Sclerosis Society: *Multiple Sclerosis—Research.* New York, NMSS, 1971.

National Multiple Sclerosis Society: *Multiple Sclerosis—The Crippler of Young Adults.* New York, NMSS, 1969.

Phelps, Winthrop: *The Cerebral Palsied Child.* New York, Simon & Schuster, 1958.

Ten Rules of Courtesy to the Blind. Virginia Commission for the Visually Handicapped, 3003 Parkwood Avenue, Richmond, Virginia.

SUGGESTED READINGS

Committee for Public Understanding of Epilepsy: *Epilepsy—the last of the hush-hush diseases.* New York, Committee for Public Understanding of Epilepsy, 1952.

The following were written and published by Epilepsy Foundation of America, Washington, D.C.:

Series A: Children with Epilepsy: a child's view, 1965.

Series A: Children with Epilepsy: a family's role, 1965.

Series A: Children with Epilepsy: a teacher's role, 1965.

Current Information, 1968.

Epilepsy—Questions and Answers, 1967.

Facts about Epilepsy—data pak, 1970.

National Spokesman, June, 1972.

Teacher Tips, 1968.

You, Your Child and Epilepsy, 1966.

National Epilepsy League: *Neurological Disorders and Industry.* Chicago, 1956.

Pennsylvania Department of Health: *Epilepsy—Hope Through Research,* 1970.

SPECIFIC PROBLEMS IN POLICE WORK AND CORRECTIONS

PART III

- Understanding Social and Human Dynamics for Crisis Intervention
- Community Intervention: Applied Behavioral Science and the Law
- The Importance of Language, Racial, and Cultural Differences in Police Work and Corrections
- Groups, Gangs, and Mobs
- Dealing with the Victims of Crime

Chapter 8

UNDERSTANDING SOCIAL & HUMAN DYNAMICS FOR CRISIS INTERVENTION

Edward S. Rosenbluh

A VETERAN POLICE OFFICER recently noted, "I never realized that police were asked to handle quickly and efficiently the variety of delicate . . . crisis situations for which they have little understanding or sympathy." In line with this, the same officer added, "It's grossly unfair to expect these men with a smattering of training . . . to work out these situations. . . ."

When one considers that about 80 percent of a policeman's time is spent in dealing with non-crime related problems, considerably more training is needed in those areas where the officer finds his greatest needs. It has been noted that a large number of injuries to policemen occur in domestic disputes, the one area where most departments offer no training. While there may be some advantages to training specialists in Crisis Intervention, it must be noted that all officers occasionally will be called upon to handle family and friend-type fights, particularly when one notes that about 90 percent of all homicides occur among people who know each other well. It must be noted further that the tone of police-community relations, upon which community cooperation and support are based, is shaped by the crucial role the police play in the resolving of such domestic crises.

This chapter will provide the police officer with some alternatives to the usual response of "take a warrant," which does not solve the problem and often leads to several more runs, possible violence, and arrests. Experience has shown that officers trained in these techniques sustain significantly fewer injuries, make many fewer return runs, and build greater appreciation and support for the police.

The knowledge to be gained will aid the officer to find his own way out of the predicament that the complexities of society force upon him. In reviewing his new tools, the policeman may reflect on the quote regarding Denis De Beauliew from Robert Louis Stevenson's *The Sire De Maletroit's Door,*

> Then, for the first time, he became aware of a light . . . to see anything was a relief . . . ; it was like a piece of solid ground to a man labouring in a morass; his mind siezed upon it with avidity; and he stood staring at it and trying to piece together some logical conception of his surroundings.

SOCIAL CHANGE

Presently we are in one of the few clearly visible social revolutions. Most major aspects of our world are in the throes of change: government, church, society, family, and education, among others. We see draft protestors, church reform agitators, hippies, and black power advocates. With the mass communication facilities at our disposal, everything in the world is at our fingertips. We can have immediate recall of contradictions of our political leaders. We can see the injustices of parts of our society toward other segments. We can view priests on picket lines against the dictates of their superiors.

If the youth have done nothing else they have dramatically pointed out one of the most potent changes that we are presently experiencing. They have illustrated the desire to "Say it like it is"! We hear about the moral decay, the "Death of God," the loss of respect for law. But it has taken the outlandish displays of the "Flower Children" to point out that the only change is in the attempt to make our professed morals fit our behavior.

Social science research has demonstrated that the present-day morals of our youth are no different than those of their parents and even earlier. What has changed, however, is the desire to make the moral attitudes fit the behavior. No wonder the music of today tells us how hypocritical we are and, therefore, not to be trusted.

The days of Realpolitik are numbered. How many of today's future leaders accept governmental pronouncements? Not even their elders choose to accept much of what they hear.

Whatever minor or solitary events occur are immediately magnified, often as curiosities, by the news media. From this glorification, others who, in bygone eras, might not even have known of the event, attempt to emulate its perpetrators and this is, in turn, rebroadcast. Soon, each group feeds upon its publicity and that of its counterparts, and together they motivate and influence new aspirants. One might well speculate that much of today's social change is "created to sell newspapers or 'Mrs. Frump's Frozen Asparagus Steaks.'" This would be more true for the short-lived spectacular events than for the more mundane, long-lasting ones. "Police-Community Relations Conference" does not attract as many consumers as does "Police Riot in Chicago."

However, it should not be construed that without the influence of the mass media there would be no revolution. While some of the startling occurrences might not be widespread, one cannot foment a riot where the people are not primed to explode. There is little likelihood that even Rap Brown could stir up the D.A.R. to rebel, but when centuries of frustration and broken promises are boiling up in the hearts of a people, little encouragement is needed. And when the mass media show how it has worked in one city (In like fashion, have you ever heard of a prison revolt that did not bring promises of reform?), it is often considered worth at least a try in others.

Where, however, does this unrest originate?

SOCIAL HERITAGE

Man's social heritage is the product of his society. It is the result of many achievements over the ages of man's existence. To understand this, we must examine man's relationship with his environment. On one hand, there is the natural environment, such as air, heat, land, water, soil, moisture, flora, minerals, and fauna. On the other, we have the man-made aspects: technology, buildings, institutions, language, art, philosophy, science, religion, and social norms and customs. Each of these environmental aspects interacts with the others continuously and our understanding of man's social evolution requires a careful study of their influences. Culture is, basically, the accumulated products of human society. It includes the utilization of the material objects and social customs and institutions. When these products change, we have cultural evolution. When man's actions and norms change, usually in response to cultural changes, we have *social change*. These changes may be seen in the evolution of social organizations and ways of behavior, such as in religion, art, law, business, education, and social norms.

MATERIAL CULTURE

Material culture accumulates. Different peoples are born into different accumulations of culture. Bone tools may be added to stone tools. Bronze is added to copper, iron to bronze, etc. While man's evolution has changed little since the last ice age, his ability to accomplish many things relies entirely on his accumulated culture. A feral child (one raised by animals) cannot far exceed the culture of its adoptive parents. Twins of genius potential will each realize only that level of accomplishment which his environment will allow. If one is nurtured by scientists while the other is raised in abject mental and economic poverty, the former will probably excel while the latter may never even learn to read. In the same light, a randomly chosen high school student today probably can do more with mathematics than could Pythagoras. In all of the above instances, the development of the individual is based on the accumulation of knowledge available as a base from which to begin learning. Man's accumulation of knowledge tends to be exponential since an innovation is only a combination of existing elements which are cumulative. In the last fifty years, for example, we have more than doubled our scientific knowledge over all that had been known throughout the history of mankind. Some estimates place the current figure at a redoubling every ten years. As interesting as this may sound, it is also frightening. As we increase the innovations, we also increase the likelihood of innovation. Each new idea provides the building block for more new ideas which, in turn, make newer ideas possible, *ad infinitum.*

There is a greater likelihood of cultural change in the United States than among the Burmese and South Sea Islanders simply because our cultural base is so much larger. We already have accumulated such vast stores of knowledge that we cannot do anything but develop even more and more knowledge. Each new answer raises a hundred new questions which must be answered.

SOCIOCULTURAL INERTIA

As an object at rest tends to remain at rest, and one in motion tends to remain in motion, so a society which has been doing things in certain ways tends to continue doing them in that way, even when new and better ways evolve. That such a condition is a problem can be seen in our societal delineation of conservatives, moderates, and liberals. For the conservative, we often move too fast, for the liberal, we usually move too slowly. The moderate, on the other hand, seems to see merit in both approaches. Social security is now well accepted by even the conservatives, but it was not always so. Medicare took over twenty years to gain acceptance. Industry lived through a number of severe panics before the Federal Reserve Banking system was developed.

Even customs may prevail beyond their logical (for the times) inceptions. Mistletoe was once thought to contain magical powers because of its ability to remain green in a lifeless winter tree. It was used, because of its religious connotations, in Druid and early Christian ceremonies. We no longer accept any mystical effects of mistletoe, but it retains an integral part in our Christmas festivities. This type of belief is illustrated by the broad spectrum of superstitious behavior found throughout all cultures. Examples are knocking on wood, lighting no more than two cigarettes on a match, eating chicken soup to cure illness, and the food taboos as practiced by different religions. Many of these practices had, at one time or another, some practical utility, but are now simply done, "because we always do them." Such cultural forms of behavior as customs, beliefs, and religious ritual survive because they meet the psychological need of security. All men strive for safety. When doubt is raised, due to fact or superstition, man seeks to reestablish equilibrium through tried and true methods. These practices will tend to survive as long as they do not lead to worse circumstances than those which tend to precipitate them. They may not help, but "Let's play safe."

Sociocultural inertia provides security in other manners also. One of the most prevalent is the perpetuation of vested interests. Socioeconomic status is quite unequally distributed. The group that has the major portion of the "success goals" of society is loathe to permit changes in the societal structure which might alter this distribution. Of course, those at the lower end of the hierarchy are more likely to institute and support such change. Our society is based on the competitive theme that "If you gain, I must lose." Therefore, those with vested interests in schools, the labor force, churches, and politics tend to resist changes that "threaten" their security. "If representatives of another group enter the labor market, I may lose my job." Fear of uncertainty is a strong hindrance to change and leads to the response "Let well enough alone."

CULTURAL LAG

Since change comes as a natural occurrence in a growing society, there is always the problem of adjustment. Unfortunately, the various parts of modern culture do not change at the same rate. Since all aspects of a system must be interdependent, changes in one aspect cause readjustment in other aspects. When one part of a culture changes first, through some innovation, there is often a delay in dependent changes in other parts of the culture. Such can be seen in our legislative deliberations. A large number of our state legislatures meet only every two years for short periods of time. It, therefore, takes a considerable time for needed statutory reform to catch up with the realities of an ever-evolving society. What worked two years ago may be fearfully outmoded.

Much of the problem arises because of the variegated society in which we live. With so many ethnic and religious subcultures we have many forces pulling in different directions and at different paces. What is a necessity to one group is sacrilege to another. Customs become mores because of the strong approval of them by members of the group. When a group decides that certain norms are to be enforced, group pressure is brought to bear upon members who would transgress. Certain emotional values become attached to these norms and change is resisted, partly through habit, social pressure, fear of the past, and inertia—they have worked before. In effect, these norms have become institutionalized and institutions such as family, church, political party, nation, resist change.

VEHICLES OF CHANGE

Many cultural changes are generated by changes in the material culture. The mass technological revolution of the last half century has so altered our physical culture that the life style lived even during the first quarter of the century is no longer possible. Many who, today, think nothing of telephoning across continents can remember when private phones were almost impossible to obtain. Those of us who marvelled at the adventures of Buck Rogers or even Captain Video find it hard to understand the "so what" attitude of today's child toward moon landings. Reality does not allow for wonderment. A child born into this age of space flight sees nothing strange in such innovation. With each new day, discoveries in medicine, engineering, communications, nuclear physics, biochemistry, etc., proliferate; and each new discovery leads to many more. The culture within which we grew up no longer exists. The old "tried and true" methods no longer work. While it is natural to seek security in the "known truths," these truths, themselves, often do not hold up. The fact that a given culture has done something in a certain way does not mean it is the only way. Different groups have different values. Who is to say which is correct, or if any is relevant to today's needs. When society resists all changes to the extent that cultural lags accumulate, we have wholesale change called revolution. One might say that the rapidity of technological progress has developed so many cultural lags that today's youth is in a revolution. The old answers of family, church, and government no longer fit the questions. If they did, there would be no lag. The fact that problems exist points only to the need for totally new approaches.

RESULTS OF CULTURAL LAG

A great many social problems such as war, crime, vice, and disease arise from the inability of man to adapt to evolving cultural conditions. Much of our unhappiness, nervousness, and mental illness is equally founded in such difficulties of adaptability. All of these problems are merely man's improper responses in attempting to cope with a dissonant world. If nothing changed, man could cope by applying old methods. When these methods no longer solve our problems, we may either seek new courses of action which will meet the modern conditions, misapply old coping behaviors, or curse the changes and those who represent them. Needless to say, only the first will work in the long run. Those who choose the latter two are only putting off the inevitable and will eventually find themselves alienated from society. This is not to say that all social change is good, but neither is it bad simply because it is different than "what we have always done."

SOCIAL PROBLEMS

Aside from improper coping responses such as individual emotional illness, society is plagued with large scale problems directly traceable to inability to adjust. Crime is such a problem. As noted earlier, socioeconomic conditions preclude many citizens from enjoying those success goals deemed important by society. The fact that these material goods are unachievable by legitimate means does not make them less desirable, but achievable only by illegitimate means. Another basis for increased crime rates is the proliferation of what is considered a crime. As soon as society determines that a certain thing should not be done or should be done in a certain way, anyone who does not conform is a deviant and, therefore, a criminal. Many of our most respected citizens today were "criminals" during prohibition. But, since the law has changed, we can overlook this today.

Sex problems are equally controlled and caused by societal norms. Where divorce is illegal, the remarried is adultrous. What is accepted courting or extramarital practice in some cultures is immoral in others, and each group is convinced "good" is on its side.

MASS COMMUNICATION AND ADVERTISING

Our society is ruled by the Gross National Product (GNP). Industry is predicated on producing ever more and different articles while developing a need for them in a public that is not always aware of what it has been missing. We were not aware of the need for deodorants until a major soap manufacturer let us in on the problem of B.O. (body odor). We now have sprays for underarms, feet, hair, mouths, and "private areas." We continually hear that we cannot sleep, relax, digest, reduce, communicate, work, or eliminate without pills. We are now, more than ever, a product-oriented society. Whatever we are upset about can be fixed by some manufacturer's brainchild. If we are troubled by the "drug culture," let us first seek the cultural changes which led to this product-oriented escape. If we are to solve this "problem," we must first recognize the cultural gaps that the practitioners of escape fear.

THE CHALLENGE OF SOCIAL INSTITUTIONS

A society acts through its institutions—government, school, church, family. As society is confronted with new problems brought about by the changing societal environment, these institutions must change their approaches. As individuals must adapt to survive, institutions which hold society together must adapt if society is to survive the pressures of cultural change. In effect, a stable society is one whose institutions are capable of making necessary changes in their coping behaviors. As noted above, there are tremendous pressures for social change building up today, and the issue is whether or not the institutions charged with maintaining our societal equilibrium can or will respond to these pressures. The underlying assumption on which our society is founded is that social change, no matter how rapid or sweeping, will occur whenever such change is necessary for societal survival. Our major institutions have not yet dealt effectively with some of the major problems of society which have come into focus during the last decade. Examples of these areas of concern to many of our citizens are: racial and ethnic inequality, particularly with regard to economics and education; powerlessness of the rural and urban poor; our national interference in external affairs as they seem to affect our GNP or national goals. When each of these factors is weighed carefully, only the hypocrisy of our institutional stands appears as an overriding consideration. We speak of equality, but protect vested interests; we abhor dictatorships that do not grant us special privilege, but support those that do; we tell the young to work within the system for change, but keep them out of the system or degrade them when they differ in opinion. A society whose institutions are not functioning to manage and promote change is unstable. If we are to handle effectively the inevitable social change, we must first understand it, not just decry it.

HUMAN DYNAMICS

The human being, while possessing individual traits, is always a member of recognizable groups. While we can easily differentiate between specific persons within a group, we can also determine which persons belong to different groups by observing how they react toward the same stimulus situation. What appears funny to an American may be meaningless to an Englishman or Frenchman. A hearty burp after a meal is a sign of good manners in some cultures, but is totally unacceptable in ours. Foods that are delicacies to some ethnic groups are taboo to others. Moslems and Jews may not touch pork. Mormons may not use coffee or tea (stimulants).

Such "do's and don'ts" which signify the differences among groups are representative of their group structures. Groups can be large or small, formal or informal. They run from small family groups, through religious groups, to entire countries. The League of Nations and the United Nations have been attempts to extend "groupness" to combinations of countries. People form groups to solve problems. Problems take many forms: raising children, social interdependence, recreation, spiritual inclinations, welfare needs, human rights, fraternal desires, among others. When there is no need, there is no group. However, people do not just form groups by saying they will. They must first recognize the problem and be convinced that working with others will alleviate it. When they reach this conclusion, the group members begin to develop ways of doing things. They determine what may or may not be done by group members and how things will be done by them, particularly in situations that are important to the group. Along with this, the group begins to set up its influence hierarchy. Those that seem to provide more answers to the problem move up in leadership responsibility. Those who offer the least, move down. When a leader loses the ability to solve problems, because better problem solvers appear or new and different problems develop, new leaders will be chosen. This, then, is the basis of group structure.

FRAMES OF REFERENCE

The individual member of any group (family, church, fraternal, work, national) seeks some clue as to how he ought to respond in situations where his group holds specific views. These rules for acting are called norms. Of course, when these norms are written down and enforced by society, we call them *laws* (statutes, ordinances, regulations). Norms, however, are not the only frames of reference, although they do influence the development of the other types.

Another aspect of these points of reference are attitudes and opinions. Opinions, for the most part, do not influence major decisions. They are more or less fleeting and are easily changed. No commitment to principle is made in an opinion, and if one is proven false, no self image is lost. However, attitudes are more central to the ego structure of the individual. They are built up slowly, over years, usually beginning in childhood. Often, one is never even aware of having learned them. However, everything we know, including attitudes, is learned through being rewarded. When parents believe something, they tend to reward the child for expressing the same view and to not reward him (or even punish him) for expressing other views. This is the basis for deep-seated ethnic prejudices and strong political beliefs. Therefore, when one attacks a person's attitudes, he is attacking that person's ego structure. When one's ego structure is attacked, his self-image suffers. For this reason, logical discussion of areas of strong belief, such as religion and politics, are extremely difficult. The same can be said for beliefs and values which are closely intertwined with, and in many instances the same as attitudes.

These aspects of one's ego structure are not based only on parental beliefs, but on internalized social norms, from whence many of the parental values also come.

The following diagram of the frame of reference will demonstrate the basis for observed behavior.

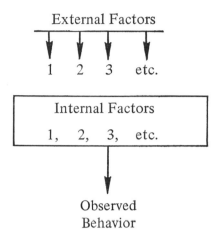

The behavior manifested by any individual is a direct result of the interaction of *Internal Factors* such as attitudes, beliefs, values, and feelings and *External Factors* such as social norms, peer group influences, physical situations, and incoming communications. As a social stimulus situation makes itself known to an individual through his senses, he seeks to interpret it so that he may respond in a manner consistent with his own belief structure. Human beings seek to always understand and control their environments. An important method of such control is to interpret the world in line with the internal psychological structure. It is only when such an equilibrium between beliefs and reality can be maintained that the individual ego is contented. When this balance is destroyed through faulty attitudes, new norms, or disagreements with others, the individual will seek to rebalance the structure by seeking new information, by accepting new norms, or by blaming others for "forsaking old proven ways." The self-image is, thereby, protected.

The self image is, of course, the way the individual sees himself and desires to be seen by others. This image that a person seeks to project guides his thinking and behavior. However, the self image is often in conflict with the real self. Oftentimes the man who seeks to project the rough masculine countenance is merely attempting to prove to himself that he is not a coward. In the same light, the woman who seeks acclaim as a beauty may be trying to prove to herself that she is a worthy human being. Of course, seeking success is not necessarily wrong. For if all humans were contented there could be no progress.

Considering the earlier diagram, we might modify it thusly.

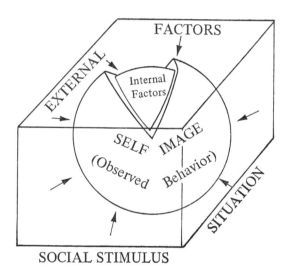

Under this new interpretation, the *observed behavior* is a manifestation of the self image which seeks to retain an equilibrium between the external stimulus situation and the internal attitudes, feelings, and values with which the individual enters the situation.

COMMUNICATIONS

Man is the only animal that we are certain of that can retain, organize, and manipulate the environment by reference to ideas formed from within himself. However, the symbols we use to express inner thoughts are usually arbitrary. That is, words display little natural relationship to the physical objects they represent. For example, does the word "whale" look like the giant sea mammal? On the other hand, we have many words which do not even relate to any physical objects, e.g. What does "eternity" look like?

All groups of humans possess the physical organic equipment needed to make the sounds of all known languages. But, this does not mean that all sounds mean the same to all people. We find, for instance, that the same meaning may be expressed by different words (symbols) in different languages. What we do not always realize, however, is that the same word may have different connotations for different people who use the same language. What, in parts of our country, would be a small paper bag—a poke—could well be the start of a fight in other areas. To "crack the window" may mean open it slightly for some Americans, but an unexpected glass repair bill for others of their countrymen. Such obvious differences in local usages are easily seen, but what of the more subtle alternative connotations that may crop up within the same city, workgroup, or family. This type of misunderstanding might best be expressed by the following statement: "I know that you believe you understand what you think I said, but I am not sure you realize that what you heard is not what I meant." In effect, it must be asked, "Are we communicating"? To communicate is to exchange information, ideas, or attitudes. If we are not in agreement on the meanings of our symbols, then we are not truly communicating.

Communication and Its Significance

Without the ability to communicate, man would be in the same predicament as the lower animals. The most intelligent horse knows little more than did his ancestors. The best-schooled dog can still do only tricks learned through association of trial and error, behavior and reward. Neither of these animals will be able to convey any of his knowledge to his grandchildren or great grandchildren. If we cannot communicate, there can be no history. Each new discovery must be rediscovered by every generation. There is no base of knowledge on which to build.

Only through communication can we begin to understand each other. And only through understanding can we have co-operation.

To communicate is to interact—to send a message and to evoke a response. Often we invoke ritualistic forms of communications called "manners." No real meaning is usually inferred by "How are you"? nor is any thought given to the response "Fine"! Both statements merely produce the effect of group cohesion.

Communications should not be thought of as only verbal. Many messages are carried in the bodily movements we make to accompany our conversations. If we lean toward the individual with whom we are conversing, we infer interest. If we lean away and look around, we express boredom. The disapproving look of the teacher immediately informs the misbehaving student that he ought to mend his ways. The hand signal of the traffic police-man says much to the driver approaching the intersection.

Elements of Communication

The act of communicating can be broken into three basic elements.

1. The Communicator (individual, group, institution) sends a message which seeks to impart some meaning.
2. The Receiver (individual, group, institution) interprets that which has been sensed.
3. The Receiver responds, based on his evaluation of the original communication.

To be particularly noted is that people do not react based on the reality of a situation, but on their interpretation of the situation. An important aspect of this interpretation is the form of the communication. If the message is to get through, it must be concise and accurate. In spoken and written messages, words must be chosen that are known to have the same connotation for both sender and receiver. To account for such mutual under-standing, it is necessary for the communicator to be aware of any feedback (response from receiver that gives clues as to how message received) which might allow him to resubmit parts of his message for better understanding.

Proper Use of Feedback

Feedback is basically reverse communication. It is reported that Chinese merchants used to watch the pupils of potential customers' eyes. Since the form of trade involved bargaining, it was important for the tradesman to know when the client was interested in a specific item. Armed with such knowledge, the seller could then keep the price on that item high. The method used by these merchants was to observe whether or not the eye pupils expanded. We now know that such occurs when we see things that interest us and this message was not wasted on the alert salesman. The initial communication would be the presentation of items with the implied query, "Are you interested in this"? The enlarging pupil would, then, be the feedback.

We often think of communication as merely delivering messages from Sender to Receiver.

Such a diagram illustrates simple messages as "Come here," "Have a smoke," or "Let's eat." However, as soon as any interpretation is required, as in "Don't touch the stove," where voice tone could imply further meaning, we must expand our diagram.

Depending, in part, on the sender's implied signals and on what the receiver is prepared to hear, the received message may be distorted beyond recognition or be more understandable. Good communications must be considered a two way street. Sender and receiver represent a system, all parts of which must be atuned to each other, or the system breaks down. Such a breakdown can be seen when personalities take precedence over meanings. If A says, "I don't think this will work," and B sees this as a personal attack, he might totally ignore the inferred advice that "We ought to rethink this," and defend his ego with, "Who are you to tell me how to do this, I've been doing this job for 15 years." Obviously, A and B will not soon solve their problems, particularly if A now feels he must defend his own ego. Such difficulties are regular happenings in interactions between labor and management, police and citizen, white and black, worker and supervisor, and parent and child. The distortion can be on either side or both when communications break down.

Success in Communication

To make the received message closely approximate that which was sent, the possibility of distortion must be removed before the message is sent. Communications must begin in an atmosphere of mutual trust. To build a relationship of trust we must be aware of the needs and values that each of us brings to the situation. It is just these attributes that determine how our words and motions will be interpreted. These needs and values form the frame of reference against which our communications will be judged. Mutual trust involves being aware of the different frames of reference that govern our behavior and allowing different interpretations that could be put on significant words.

When a message is sent, the trusting receiver must seek to interpret it from the context of the sender's frame of reference and not his own. In turn, the sender must be similarly aware of differing points of view so as not to respond negatively to undesirable feedback. Mutual trust requires the commitment that "I accept and trust you, although I cannot accept what you are saying."

When this trust is developed, our earlier statement might be rephrased to:

"I believe I understand what I think you said, but I am not sure that what I heard is what you meant."

CRISIS INTERVENTION TECHNIQUES

There are a number of interrelated reasons that place various disputes in the hands of the police. There was a time when our society was not so complicated and the family, relatives, or neighborhood could handle such problems. However, with the social mobility present in today's world, these meaningful relationships no longer exist. To decry their absence will not help, so we must find new approaches. Some type of public intervention is now necessary. While mental health and social service systems have, in some areas, begun to develop the round-the-clock responsiveness necessary, the police must still bear the brunt of the problem for very valid reasons:

1. They are constantly on patrol and can respond anywhere in the city on short notice.
2. Many such disputes involve violence or possess the potential for violence, and only the police are prepared and legally able to handle this.
3. There is such a proliferation of governmental service agencies that, in a crisis, where one is motivated by fear, the police are the most likely to be contacted—they are open seven days a week, twenty-four hours a day.
4. When properly trained, the police officer knows to whom else the disputants may be referred after the immediate crisis is alleviated.
5. Possibly of greatest importance is the fact that the major mission of law enforcement is crime prevention and peace keeping.

The techniques most useful in such crises are those developed by mental health practitioners as effective in dealing with interpersonal conflict. They are, for the most part, common sense. The following eighteen principles will provide a large part of the proper frame of reference to allow the police officer to turn a potentially volatile situation into a possibly helpful encounter.

1. Prevent violence by separating the disputants (in different rooms if possible).
2. Allow only one person to talk at a time.
3. Switch officers so that the stories can be checked out.
4. In listening to the stories, try to find out what each individual contributed to the conflict.
5. If one of the disputants holds himself to blame, find out in what ways the other shares the blame.
6. Ask questions so as to get the details as clear as possible.
7. Find out if there has been a previous history of this kind of behavior.
8. See if the history goes back to other relationships or to similar ones in the present.

9. Give each person the opportunity to speak in detail.
10. Bring the disputants together to tell their stories to each other. Again, make sure only one person speaks at a time.
11. Point out similarities and discrepancies in the stories.
12. Point out the part that each is playing.
13. Get a reaction from both sides about what the officers say they see is going on.
14. Ask what they plan to do in response to what has transpired and to the officers' reactions. If they seem to understand and say they want to try to work it out, accept it.
15. If you disagree with their response, suggest that they seek other help. If necessary, make a referral.
16. Tell them that if there is another dispute and they see that they are coming close to violence or to repeating the same pattern, they should go again for counseling or contact you.
17. While noting that there will be further difficulties, assure them that if they sit down and talk, they can, at least, come out in the open and try to resolve it.
18. Make sure they know your name and leave your card if you deem it advisable.

REFERENCES

Bard, M. and Berkowitz, B.: Training police as specialists in family crisis intervention. *U.S. Justice Department Report*, PR 70–1.

Driscoll, J. M.; Meyer, R. G., and Schanie, C. F.: Police training in family crisis intervention. Unpublished Report, University of Louisville, 1971.

Margolis, Clorinda, and Fox, H. G.: Rap and rapport: Police and mental health pros. *The Police Chief*, Dec., 1971, pp. 46–48.

Phelps, L. G., Schwartz, J. A., & Liebman, D. A. Training an entire patrol division in domestic crisis intervention techniques. *The Police Chief*, July, 1971, pp. 18–19.

Rosenbluh, E. S., and Reichart, W. A.: Community intervention: Applied behavioral science and the law. Unpublished manuscript, Bellarmine College and Louisville Division of Police, Louisville, Ky., 1971.

Rosenbluh, E. S.; Reichart, W. A., and Hyde, C. J.: Is the policeman obsolete? *The Police Chief*, May, 1972.

Chapter 9

COMMUNITY INTERVENTION: APPLIED BEHAVIORAL SCIENCE AND THE LAW

EDWARD S. ROSENBLUH AND WILLIAM A. REICHART

- ■ METHOD
- ■ EVALUATION
- ■ DISCUSSION AND CONCLUSIONS
- ■ REFERENCES

It must be remembered that there is nothing more dangerous to manage than the creation of a new system. For the initiator has the enmity of all who would profit by the preservation of the old institutions and merely lukewarm defenders in those who would gain by the new ones. The hesitation of the latter arises in part from the fear of their adversaries, who have the laws on their side and in part from the general skepticism of mankind which does not really believe in an innovation until experience proves its value. So it happens that whenever his enemies have occasion to attack the innovator they do so with the passion of partisans while the others defend him sluggishly so that the innovator and his party are alike vulnerable (Machiavelli in *The Prince*).

BEHAVIORAL AND SOCIAL SCIENTISTS have, for years, bemoaned their lack of influence in the governmental processes that seek to resolve the problems of society. It is only recently that these specialists have actually realized that their loneliness was

159

due to their own failings: they talked only with each other and did not make any concerted effort to intervene personally in their communities.

One such area of dire need is that of law enforcement, particularly in the realm of police work. For the majority of our country, the police are still in a Neanderthalic stage. To evolve from this level and become a professional, the police officer must be reinforced for updating his knowledge. Also, new and better methods, not just hardware, must be continually made available to him. For most police officers in our country, education is unavailable, even though the Federal Government is pouring millions into this area. In many departments, the most highly educated are those in planning offices, communications sections, or the property room, since they are the only ones with set schedules that match available college courses. However, the beat man, who is in contact with the public, cannot get the classes he needs. In many instances, even when he so desires, he cannot get the time off, and if he does, he may be forced to miss a large proportion of classes because of court appearances or emergencies. Even when departmental policies allow for proper scheduling, the archaic chain-of-command often precludes the motivated officer from realizing his desires. Commanding officers often look upon gaining of new skills as detracting from business as usual—"You need bodies on the street." There is little realization that proper education can make a small number of men more valuable than a large number of uneducated troops.

A police sergeant was once heard to state that the policeman is required to make decisions in a split second that nine wise men on the Supreme Court may take months to ponder, and yet we make it difficult for anyone with more than a high school diploma to be on the force. In many departments, the college graduate is considered a "smart ass" who is just trying to prove something, or who will stay only long enough to "write a book."

When innovative programs are begun, the Neanderthal will tell you, "This is a bunch of crap. What you need is to make the people afraid of you." When Crisis Intervention Programs, such as those of Morton Bard in New York (1970) and Jim Driscoll in Louisville (1971) or Behavioral Interaction Training such as we have been running for three years in Louisville (Rosenbluh & Reichart, 1971), the Neanderthal states, "You can't coddle those bastards, you gotta be tough. You can't let 'em think you're soft. That's what's wrong with policing today, you gotta be a social worker." Of course, in the more enlightened departments, when such an attitude is recognized, the offender is removed from public contact and put where he is less likely to do damage. However, this is not always possible, particularly when such a mentality is found in a commanding officer who can influence all with whom he comes in contact. The cubbyhole often used in departments around the country for such ne'er-do-wells is, unfortunately, the Community Relations Bureau. This, of course, demonstrates the administrative lack of commitment to new methods of policing, but shows merely a desire for Federal funds which are then channeled into a beefing-up of old unworkable procedures.

Instead of testing future commanding officers for their understanding of behavioral management techniques, our civil service boards ask, "What is the length of a nightstick." Instead of following the European tradition of sending new commanding officers to management training programs, we often put them right to work with no attempt to see that they have developed any behavioral skills. What is needed are controlled validation studies for promotional tests, similar to those for recruit selection that Melany Baehr, John Furcon, and Ernest Fromel (1968) have been doing in Chicago, and we are doing in Louisville (Rosenbluh & Reichart, 1971).

As noted above, departmental composition is often at fault for the archaic tradition of U.S. policing. Considering themselves paramilitary organizations, police departments have adopted the military chain-of-command, but without its working philosophy. Even in the military, chain-of-command is cumbersome and wasteful, but in the hands of city hall, it is often counterproductive. While the patrolman is admonished to "go through the proper channels to register a complaint," he often finds that he is disciplined by all commanding officers, in person, without going through the chain-of-command in reverse. We then wonder why morale is low. The Neanderthal will tell you, "If they just paid us more, our morale would go up." The enlightened officer—the professional—will note that we would then have more highly-paid malcontents. Yes, more money is needed, but without a drastic overhaul of the structure, there can be no progress. We cannot say that what is needed is a totally non-military structure, with one director, some administrative heads, and several strata of patrolmen of different skill levels, but such is an inviting possibility. However, it is strongly recommended that if our police departments are to mimic the military structure, they had better employ the same safeguards employed by the military when its chain-of-command breaks down. If we are to have the many layers of command, as are to be found in most departments, then we must supply an inspector general who can handle complaints without retaliatory discipline of the plaintif. We should also have trained counselors to aid with personal problems and educational specialists to keep abreast of new opportunities.

It has become clear that there must be an amalgamation of the behavioral scientist and the police specialist if the future is to become bright. City planners must work with the police; the police and other officials must work with psychologists and sociologists. We can no longer just talk to ourselves. It is not the police against the community; it is the police of the community.

The policeman often feels himself alienated, he feels that he must prove his masculinity. Past approaches to police-community relations have been to set up a separate branch of officers to provide the police-community relations services. This, as Black and Labes (1967) state, is like extending the olive branch in one hand and the night stick in the other. If the system is going to work, one should either remove the policeman's alienation, or, preferably, the alienated policeman, if he cannot be saved. At least, we can seek to help the majority of the policemen now on duty so that they do not look upon every arrest as a test of their masculinity. They must learn to withstand taunts without striking out. They must be taught that the greatest cooperation obtains when neither side is forced to lose all face. One of the earliest police rules came more than one hundred years ago for the London Metropolitan Police, the first professional police force in the Western world. It stated that an officer is never " 'justified in depriving anyone of his liberty for words only, and language, however violent . . . is not to be noticed. A policeman who allows himself to be irritated by any language whatsoever shows that he has not a command of his temper, which is absolutely necessary in an officer with such extensive powers by law' " (*Time*, 1968).

There is but one certainty involved in group activity and community sentiment—change. As a result, policemen must be continually undergoing formal or informal training. Officers must keep abreast of law, social movements, technology, community changes, police ethics, and improved police procedure.

Each peace officer should be a community relations agent for the police—on *and* off duty. In his every contact with citizens he modifies the public image of the police and thereby sets the tone for later police-community contacts.

For twenty-five years researchers have sought means to help policemen be better public servants while helping the community accept and appreciate their function. Recently, interest in this area has intensified as police-community relations have degenerated. Because the problem has been a chronic one, and because a great number of factors have contributed to it, no simple, sure-fire remedy is possible. One key to the cure is to find new and better ways to make both the community and the police realize that the police are an integral part of the communities they serve.

While self-defense, search and seizure, arrests, handling firearms, etc., are vital parts of policing, policemen must now be more than technicians; they must be artists skilled in the art of meeting the community as persons able and willing to communicate, understand, and help others. Policemen cannot be professionals, no matter how impressive their arrest records or their investigative techniques, without recognizing the sociological and psychological impact they can have on the community, and without continually seeking to upgrade their professional education. As society has enlarged and become more specialized and complex, its demands on the police have changed both in type and number. Consequently, the police role must be expanded to include a variety of new abilities. It has been estimated that as much as 90 percent of the average Louisville police officer's time is spent in activities other than actual crime prevention. Louisville police commendably provide the best ambulance and emergency service to be had. They also have shown great ability in many areas of diversified crisis intervention (e.g. domestic, minority group protests, riot activities, etc.). Because such a great portion of policework is social in nature and service-oriented, officers must be aware of the various ways in which they can help or hurt their public image, not to mention the channels of communication with the community which may be jeopardized by an unwary officer untrained in elementary human dynamics. All policemen must now be equipped with at least a basic understanding of human behavior, attitudes, and motivation. Because of the nature of the job they do, the constant public contact, police have always had to wear the hat of the psychologist and the sociologist, to an extent. Police need not be social workers or psychoanalysts, but the need for law enforcement officials to understand and be personally involved in people is crucial (Hendrix, 1971).

Unfortunately, the national public image of the police is at its ebb for a number of reasons. First, the punitive and authoritative nature of police work has contributed to the negative image. Other factors (incompetent policemen, abuse of police power, ignorance of officers about the community) have also hurt. Of course, not all the blame can be assigned to the police, but the police, it seems, must take the first steps to reconcile the present situation before a positive public image can evolve (Earle, 1970).

Policemen must realize that they are constantly in the eye of the public and that the public image of law enforcement can be made more favorable only through adequate police-community communication. Each side must come to understand the thinking and actions of the others. By design, police and community must work *with*, not *against*, one another.

In order to actually "know" a community, officers working an area must be aware of the formal and informal groups in that area. They are vital because they can be so very influential in shaping the thinking of an individual or even an entire sector. In one sense, community groups are attitude determiners, and a prime target for police-community relations work (Hendrix, 1971).

There has been little need for teaching our police that the average middle-class or working-class White is a human being with feelings, problems, and hangups who needed to be treated humanely, because it was from these ranks that most policemen have come. However, with the increasing voice that our inner cities have achieved, the policeman has been attacked by many for his inability to understand the problems and frames of reference of the inner city inhabitants. The difficulty has arisen because of the frustration faced by the individual officer as he attempts to deal with a person from a culture he cannot completely understand. In concert with and as a response to this, the young are beginning to present unexpected problems for the community.

The growing consciousness of this problem has led social scientists to insist that policemen receive more specialized training to aid in the required interaction with these ethnic and racial groups. However, short of requiring a college education with extended study in social science, most police officers have had little opportunity to gain an increased awareness and understanding of the problems facing them. Since the education mentioned above is not now feasible, another method must be found. If no solution is forthcoming, large and small cities face much grief as the two sides (police and antagonists) continue to clash in many small skirmishes which can only lead to greater frustration for the sides.

METHOD

The objectives of the several projects begun by us in Louisville were to offer police departments acceptable and feasible ways to extend to their members an insight into the complexities and problems of the people with whom they must deal. Face to face confrontations and lectures have not been notably effective.

Beginning with the landmark research of Kurt Lewin (1964)

in the 1940's, it has been demonstrated (also Bloom, 1953) that "Lecturing may lead to a high degree of interest. It may affect the motivation of the listener. But it seldom brings about a definite decision on the part of the listener to take a certain action at a specific time." The mass approach places ". . . the individual in a quasi-private, psychologically-isolated situation with himself and his own ideas. Although he may, physically, be part of a group listening to a lecture, he finds himself, psychologically speaking, in an 'individual situation'" (Lewin, 1964, p. 203). Lewin adds "Lecturing is a procedure in which the audience is chiefly passive. The discussion, if conducted correctly, is likely to lead to a much higher degree of involvement" (1964, p. 203). If we are seeking to develop attitudes, we cannot afford to stress only information (McKeachie, 1962). As Lewin and others (Dressler, 1959; Meyer, 1936; Rosenbluh and Reichart, 1971; Terry, 1933) have amply demonstrated in their research, if commitment is to obtain, group discussion must be utilized.

In the first of the present series of studies, small groups of twelve to fifteen police officers met in seminar fashion with two program directors who sat opposite each other at all times. While one spoke, the other would monitor the group for signs of interest loss or misunderstanding. The directors of the program were both social scientists in social psychology and political science. One or the other was periodically spelled by other behavioral scientists with some law enforcement experience or by a police officer with social science training. The program has been running since July 1, 1969 and some four hundred patrolmen, commanding officers, and recruits have been contacted.

The syllabus is as follows: Each course lasts five weeks, with two classes of two hours each per week.

1. *HUMAN DYNAMICS*—What is man, how does he develop?
2. *USE AND ABUSE OF WORDS*—How and why do communications break down?
3. *CRIME AND DELINQUENCY*—Dynamics of Delinquency.
4. *LEADERSHIP*—Understanding the frame of reference of the followers.
5. *URBAN PROBLEMS*—The physical city and its social atmosphere.

The seminar discussions are tied together so that one flows into the next. Stress is placed on the continuity of human interaction as opposed to the discontinuity too often stressed, even in our colleges. Officers are encouraged to offer personal beat-problems for group consideration. In addition to these impromptu cases, actual case histories of the Louisville Police Department are used in each seminar discussion to provide a test situation in which the officers might apply the new knowledge they have gained.

The first session of each five-session seminar is begun with a group interaction exercise such as an adaptation of the prisoner's dilemma game or the moon trip necessity checklist exercise, in order to both break the ice and develop an understanding of the need for cooperation in human interaction.

Program directors, who have been deputized, continually accompany requesting officers during duty hours, both day and night, to better understand their problems and procedures.

Since it has been noted that the term "Police-Community Relations" has become anathema to the average policeman throughout the country, because of the, often, one-sided militant diatribes leveled against them in such programs, the program has been titled "Police Leadership Seminar." Participants are informed that true leadership entails the understanding of the people with whom one deals. It quickly becomes clear that the seminar is geared toward community relations, but, by this time, a trust of the directors and an interest in the material has been developed. Stressed throughout is the fact that the directors are not there to "tell them how to be good policemen," but to provide them with information upon which they may draw for frames of reference in deciding how to handle their day-to-day problems.

A major adjunct to police training was the adaptation of small group techniques to what we have called Behavioral Interaction Training which seeks to provide a fertile learning environment for about thirty to forty police officers at one time. Developed for Louisville's Experimental Police District, this approach utilizes specialists in the above listed seminar areas plus those of Crisis Intervention, Black Culture, Groups and Roles, Community meetings, Authority, and Juvenile Delinquency, who present some resource material and then partake in question and answer periods and small group discussions with the officers. Included in the forty-eight hours of concentrated training are several films utilizing professional actors and two crisis-trained Louisville police officers who seek to work out typical confrontation situations related to each of the resource presentations. Using a "trained" and "untrained'" sequence for each situation, new discussion is then generated around each of these stimulus films.

A major portion of this community intervention program is the Police Behavioral Scientist-Counselor project. Along with classroom-type training, another approach has also become necessary. What often passes for a brutal or unsympathetic police officer is usually a sincere individual who simply does not possess the alternatives for behavior which might turn an unpleasant encounter into a helpful meeting. Experience has demonstrated that a trained behavioral scientist, riding with officers and noting methods of reaction, can often supply just such alternatives. From such observations, many useful suggestions for procedural and management changes have been forthcoming. With this innovation, the project directors have been able to offer a municipal police department, for possibly the first time, a continuing counseling and observational service to help police officers to understand and adjust their techniques of law enforcement when dealing with members of new and evolving life styles.

There has been some minor research into police selection, but the only comprehensive studies have been that conducted by Baehr, Furcon, and Froemel (1968) at the University of Chicago and our present study (Rosenbluh and Reichart, 1971). A few masters theses have been written in this area, but little of substance is available. If any concerted effort has been made to determine what a police officer is and how to select him other than the two noted, it has not been disseminated to the scientific or law enforcement communities.

Not only must standards be set for the Louisville area, but eventually, norms must be developed in cities of different sizes and in varying areas. To assume that results of the Chicago study, or the present one, are sufficient to select policeman throughout the country would be to disregard one of the basic tenets of the scientific method—to beware of making dangerous overgeneralizations. Cities of different sizes and different make-ups may require different types of policemen. Only comprehensive research programs can adequately assure this vital need.

It had been decided to exclude tests specifically aimed at assessment of a global intelligence quotient since this is accomplished by the Louisville Civil Service Commission. Furthermore, tests favoring the white middle-class citizens have been excluded in cases where black citizens will be taking the tests. The selected tests covering the areas of personal background, work interests, mental abilities, aptitude, temperament, and personality, as described by Baehr, Furcon, and Froemel (1968), have been given to the veteran patrolmen and are now being administered to each of the new recruits joining the force in the first year of a two-year evaluation period. The following are those tests used in this program: (Two added by Bellarmine).

Personal History Index. This index is based on past performance and experience in relation to future job success. It lasts from five to fifteen minutes.

Closure Speed. Basically assesses the subject's ability to unify complex situations when these situations appear disorganized or unrelated.

Perceptual Speed. Essentially a visual thinking test. Uses diagrams, drawings, etc., and the subject is asked to identify likenesses and differences.

Closure Flexibility. This measures subject's ability to keep a figure in mind in the face of distraction.

Tol Scale. This test measures degrees of tolerance for unusual and threatening circumstances.

Rokeach Dogmatism Scale. This test assesses dogmatic thought and prejudices.

Test of Social Insight. Tests reaction of individual in an interpersonal and social situation.

Press Test. A test of individual's performance under stress situation.

Temperament Comparator Test. Tests permanent temperament tracts of subject.

EMO Questionnaire. Screening procedure for emotional health.

Arrow Dot Test (IRS Modification). Prediction measure of relative strength of Id, Ego, and Superego, i.e. impulsive behavior, ability to function realistically, and value system.

The significance of such a study is that veteran policemen, while being trained in community relations, can also provide a large sample on which potential selection procedures will be worked out. Only if we weed out the potentially dangerous officers can we truly develop a police force well versed in the essentials of good community relations as it pursues the just and equitable enforcement of the norms of society.

EVALUATION

To date, only the initial Leadership Seminar has been subjected to a reputable, although not complete, evaluation. In order to evaluate the approach, an anonymous questionnaire was administered during the last session of each seminar. Behavioral objectives, in the form of case discussions, were used throughout the Program.

The results from this questionnaire are quite favorable and show a great degree of acceptance on the part of the officers for the small group interaction approach as well as for the material presented and discussed.

Each officer, with the exception of one, enthusiastically stated that, although he began with much trepidation, many new insights had been gained. A particularly significant result was the feeling evinced by most participants that someone was concerned about their needs and feelings and would perhaps be in a position to communicate, to the top command, their frustrations and suggestions, anonymously, thus providing somewhat the same services as an ombudsman.

This preliminary evaluative technique lends credence to the tentative conclusion that the officers are gaining a better understanding of urban problems and the ticklish position in which they are placed as enforcers of the law in our 20th Century urban society. Hopefully, their increased knowledge and understanding of urban problems and community relations will have an influence on their actions and behavior as they perform their law enforcement duties.

Evaluative support has also been forthcoming from the Director of Safety, Col. George C. Burton, and the Chief of Police, Col. C. J. Hyde, who stated:

"Officers from the rank of Patrolman to Assistant Chief of Police have been among the different classes completed. The value of this training program, in my opinion, is best evaluated by the noticeable change in attitudes in officers of all ranks that have completed this two weeks' training, toward the management problems experienced not only at the Chief's office level but at district and bureau levels. Suggestions by the graduates of these classes for the betterment of the Department have been more numerous and when criticism is experienced they are usually accompanied by a suggestion for improvement. The attitudes toward the public served also mirrors the positive aspects to this training program."

The Experimental District Program and the Police Selection Project are still being evaluated.

DISCUSSION AND CONCLUSIONS

Throughout this program, reference is made to the psychosocial factors associated with the manner in which members of a particular community act. It is important that officers realize that certain types of crime can be associated with areas of low income, broken homes, unemployment, and a variety of other neighborhood characteristics. Though police are not in a position to remove all causes of crime, it is possible to make oneself familiar with certain correlates of criminal behavior. To do this, police must contact the community and learn about it from within. Police isolation, the association of peace officers only with fellow officers, is a primary reason why police either are not aware of the sociological characteristics of an area or do not make full use of this information. Sociologists study the group composition of society and the manner in which groups function. They become aware of the physical cultural characteristics of an area, as well as the effects of group activity on the general attitudes of the community. Policemen, too, must be attentive to the functioning and characteristics for groups and areas, for these largely determine the values and attitudes toward law enforcement and the police to be found in an area. Officers must note social classes and formal and informal leaders within a community. It is the policeman's responsibility to know his community and how to communicate with it. From such knowledge and subsequent actions will police relations become community relations.

As the police officer seeks a frame of reference which will help him out of his predicament, he may reflect on Denis De Beauliew's quote from Robert Louis Stevenson's *The Sire De Maletroit's Door,*

> Then, for the first time, he became aware of a light . . . To see anything was a relief for Denis; it was like a piece of solid ground to a man labouring in a morass; his mind seized upon it with avidity; and he stood staring at it and trying to piece together some logical conception of his surroundings.

REFERENCES

Baehr, Melany E.; Furcon, J. E., and Froemel, E. C.: Psychological Assessment of Patrolman Qualifications in Relation to Field Performance, LEAA Project 046, U.S. Department of Justice, 1968.

Bard, M.: Training Police as Specialists in Family Crisis Intervention, U.S. Department of Justice, PR 70–1, 1970.

Black, H., and Labes, M. J.: Guerrilla warfare: An analogy to police-criminal interaction. *Am J Orthopsychiatr,* 37:666–670, July, 1967.

Bloom, B. S.: Thought process in lectures and discussions. *J Gen Educ,* 7:160–69, 1953.

Dressel, P., and Mormier, Margaret F.: *Attitudes of Liberal Arts as Viewed by Faculty Members in Professional Schools.* New York, Columbia University, 1959.

Driscoll, J. M., and Schanie, C. F.: Impact of Family Crisis Intervention Training of Police. Presented at Kentucky Psychological Association Convention, Louisville, Kentucky, March, 1971.

Earle, H. H.: *Student-Instructor Guide on Police-Community Relations.* Springfield, Ill., Charles C Thomas, 1970.

Hendrix, E. M.: Behavioral Science Aspects of Policing. Experimental District Training Manual, Louisville Division of Police, 1971.

Lewin, K.: Group decision and social change. In MacCoby, Eleanor E.; Newcome, T. M., and Hartless, E. L.: *Readings in Social Psychology.* New York, Holt, Rinehart and Winston, Inc., 1964, pp. 197–212.

McKeachie, W. J.: Procedures and techniques of teaching: A survey of experimental studies. In Nevitt, Sanford (Ed.): *The American College.* New York, John Wiley, 1962.

Meyer, G.: An experimental study of the old and new types of examinations: 11, Method of study. *J Educ Psychol,* 23:30–34, 1936.

Rosenbluh, E. S., and Reichart, W. A.: Small Group Interaction Approach to Police-Community Relations Training. Southern Society for Philosophy and Psychology, Athens, Ga., April 8, 1971.

Rosenbluh, E. S., and Reichart, W. A.: Police Selection and Community-Relations. Presented at 1st. Annual Mid-States Institute on Police and Community Relations, May 17, 1971.

Terry, P. W.: How students review for objective and essay tests. *Elem School J*, 33:592–603, 1933.

Chapter 10

THE IMPORTANCE OF LANGUAGE, RACIAL, AND CULTURAL DIFFERENCES IN POLICE WORK AND CORRECTIONS

WAYNE S. GILL

It is a terrible, an inexorable, law that one cannot deny the humanity of another without diminishing one's own. James Baldwin, *Nobody Knows My Name*

POLICE OFFICERS SOMETIMES, before they know better, refer to bilingual persons as having a language barrier. By analogy, this is like a man whose yard is separated by a property line, insisting that the line is the *neighbor's* property line. In fact, if one individual is monolingual while another is bilingual, it is more logical to speak of the monolingual individual as having a language barrier than the bilingual one. If one is able to look at the language-racial-cultural differences in this light, the way is open for mutual understanding.

People differ from each other in so many ways and it is always difficult to generalize. Whenever we make statements like: "All women are . . ." or "Most children will . . ." or "Older people often . . . ," we are making generalizations and we must always take in consideration the fact that there are so many exceptions as to make the generalization itself close to meaningless. The fact is that prejudices are born from just such generalizations and our seeming inability to recognize an individual once he has been assigned to his general group.

We are all, in fact, members of many groups simultaneously. One may be a member of the Jones family, the Clarkstown College student body, the Republican party, the Lions Club, etc., all at the same time. Indeed, we may generalize about any and all of these groups, but to make a statement about the group, it does not at all follow that the same could be said about all members of the group. We may say that the Jones family is close-knit, that people at Clarkstown College tend to be intellectual and scholarly, that the Republican party is conservative, or that the Lions Club is service-oriented. The fact that an individual holds membership in all of these groups may not necessarily give us any significant information about him as an individual.

There has been considerable misunderstanding over the years brought about by this simple inability to make the distinction between an individual and the group. A rather humorous example of this occurred many years ago when intelligence testing first became popular. One newspaper editorial complained that scientists were spreading the word that half the people in the United States were below average in intelligence.

Because of the fact that language, racial, and cultural differences are so much more obvious and permanent than club membership, party membership, or even family membership, we tend to generalize more freely about them. This tendency, however, is not without its dangers. It is so easy to over-generalize and lose the individual by assigning him to a racial or cultural group. This activity gives a false sense of security because it makes the person assume erroneously that he has knowledge of the person, obviously knowing his racial or cultural group.

Then again, for many individuals, differences in people are apparently frightening or threatening. They tend to close their minds and attempt to isolate themselves from individuals who are different from themselves. For a country like ours, with a reputation of being the great "melting pot of civilization," such an attitude robs us all of valuable experiences. Not only that, the evils of segregation and group isolation have robbed many of their birthrights as citizens.

Racism takes several forms. As an example, have you ever considered that to label adhesive bandages "flesh colored" is a subtle way of announcing that the U.S. is a "white only" society? While we have claimed that America is a land of many ethnic and racial groups, the language and the ads in America still too often reflect a one-group perspective. Too many of the symbols in American society have been created for a racially homogeneous population. It should not be surprising that it was more than 300 years before the African comb was made commercially in America. Generations of black children grew up thinking something was wrong with their hair because a conventional comb would not go easily through it. Straight hair was better than kinky hair because the small teeth of the comb were made for it. As another drugstore example, sunglasses are exclusively designed for the bridges of European noses, certainly not for the oriental.

Symbol imperialism reflects a racist perspective and in so doing supports the myth of white superiority. Across the Cobo Hall in Detroit there is a large statue with European features called "The Spirit of Detroit." It is ludicrous in its absurdity as Detroit has nearly 700,000 Blacks and they find no identification with that symbol. In a multiracial situation all persons should be able to participate in the symbol or share in the event. Thus, the playing of "Dixie" in integrated schools can no more be allowed than playing "The East Is Red" at an American football game.

Such racism, however subtle in its execution, is a source of considerable dissonance in America. The fixation with symbols reflecting the white group perspective would not be so bad in a society of all Whites, but it is an imposition in a multiracial society and it must be changed (Smith, 1972).

Griffin (1961) in his book, *Black Like Me,* tells how the doors of social, cultural, and economic advancement are kept closed.

> Ignorance keeps them poor and when the town-dwelling Negro is poor he lives in the ghetto. His wife has to work usually and this places the children without parental companionship. In such places where all of man's time is spent just surviving, he rarely knows what it means to read a great book. He has grown up and now sees his children grow up in squalor. His wife usually earns more than he. He is thwarted in his need to be father to the household. When he looks at his children and his home, he feels the guilt of not having given them something better.
>
> His only salvation is not to give a damn finally or else he falls into despair. In despair a man's sense of virtue is dulled. He no longer cares. He will do anything to escape it—steal or commit acts of violence—or perhaps try to lose himself in sensuality. Most often the sex king is just a poor devil trying to prove the manhood that his whole existence denies. This is what the whites call the 'sorry nigger.' Soon he will either desert his home or become so unbearable that he is kicked out. This leaves the mother to support the children alone. To keep food in their bellies, she has to spend most of her time away from them, working. This leaves the children to the streets, prey to any sight, any conversation, any sexual experiment that comes along to make their lives more interesting or pleasurable. To a young girl who has nothing, has never known anything, the baubles she can get—both in a kind of crude affection and in gifts of money—by granting sex to a man or boy appeal to her as toys to a child. She gets pregnant sometimes and then the vicious circle is given impetus. In some instances the mother cannot make enough money to support her children, so she sells her sex for what she can get. This gets easier and easier until she comes up with still another child to abort or support. But none of this is 'Negro-ness.'

As if these troubles were not enough, the poor and uneducated are easy prey for unscrupulous businessmen. Recently housing schemes have been uncovered in Philadelphia, Boston, Wilmington, St. Louis, Chicago, Miami, and Detroit. In these schemes, the "fast-buck artists" connive with the most unsuspecting applicant to defraud the Federal Housing Administration by listing income that they do not have in order to qualify for housing. Later, when the purchaser is unable to make the payments, the dealer buys it back at an appropriately deflated price, kicks out the welfare tenants by raising their rents, and then starts the whole cycle over with another victim. So far, the U.S. Attorney's office said, at least 2500 and perhaps as many as 5000 poor families have been sold worthless houses and turned out into the streets (*Newsweek,* 1972).

These kinds of exclusions, however, are not confined to any one minority group; they are for the most part general for all disadvantaged groups. Statistics released by the Department of Health, Education, and Welfare (1969) show that there are more than 35 million disadvantaged persons in our land today; 8 million of them are in central cities, 12 million in surrounding suburbs, and 15 million in rural areas. ("Disadvantaged" is defined as individuals with an annual income of $590 or less and families earning $3,000 or below.) More than most American citizens, the disadvantaged suffer from inferior and inappropriate courses in school, low educational attainment, lack of vocational skills, unsatisfactory work histories, inadequate income and financial resources, poor medical care and physical health, substandard houses, and limited opportunity to select the neighborhood in which they live.

THE DISADVANTAGED

Contrary to popular belief, the disadvantaged have values and objectives which are similar to those of the middle class—security, advancement, money, achievement, and happiness. Their psychological, social, and physical needs create a strong desire for immediate security which in turn interferes with long-term planning. Their preference for short-term goals offering tangible pleasures is often seen by the outsider as lack of motivation and poor judgment.

Because they are outside the mainstream of society they may speak a nonstandard English which hinders communication and learning in a middle-class environment. Their attitude is often self-defeating and passive, and their social behavior is maladaptive with crime, behavioral disorders, and emotional disturbance more prevalent than in the general population.

Heller (1966), Madsen (1964), and Kluckhohn and Strodtbeck (1961) are among many writers who have stressed that differences in cultural orientation lead to different views toward ambition, competitiveness, interest in education, and other attitudes and values that bear directly upon aspiration and ambition. Bruckman (1961) found that the vocational expectations and aspirations of Mexican-American eighth-grade children in South Texas were lower than those of other ethnic groups such as Negro and Anglo. These findings were maintained when the data were analyzed within the father's occupational level. Bruckman reasoned that unless there is an increment in vocational placement from one generation to the next, the children of people now at the bottom of the occupational ladder will tend to remain there. Change in vocational status of the Mexican-American is possible and is occurring; however, the relative position with other ethnic groups is still low. Perhaps one aspect of raising the present status of vocational and educational achievements lies in the area of directly attempting to increase the children's levels of aspiration.

Racial and cultural minorities have always been over-represented in the disadvantaged in this country. This, of course, is not due to any inherent inferiority, but rather to the additional problems of cultural and language assimilation which must be achieved. In addition and perhaps more important, prejudices held and fostered by the dominant group lead to serious discrimination in jobs, education, and social activities.

THE SELF-IMAGE

An even more subtle influence is often found in the very self-image and self-expectation related to minority group membership. Self-images are, for the most part, derived from parents, teachers, and "important others" during the developmental years. The expectations which others have of us influence to a great extent our achievement. Research by a school district in California, for example, showed that when the expectation level of teachers was manipulated by telling them that the children in their classes whom they had believed to be retarded, were shown to have higher I.Q. scores, teacher's expectations immediately rose as did the self-images of the students. Surprisingly, the achievement levels also increased markedly. Thus, it may be argued that when an individual believes that he is inferior and through our subtle cues finds this inferiority is re-enforced, he comes to accept it as true and behaves accordingly. It was found, for example, when Chinese-Americans anglicized their first names, they have significantly more American acquaintances than the nonchangers, read fewer Chinese publications, and were more familiar with American magazines and far better adapted to American cultural tastes. They were a bit more competitive than the nonchangers (*Human Behavior,* 1972). It may be that a person's name is a symbolic representation of his social identity. It often establishes sex and ethnic identity, may indicate family status or religion, and imply patterns of social interaction between the bearer and others.

Another interesting example is the American image in this country. Recently the Wooden Indian Bar in the Americana Hotel in New York has been closed because four Indians said the establishment was an insult to their race. They objected to the cigar-store figure as a kind of "connotation of the dumb wooden Indian." Similar objections can be heard for the use of Indians as mascots by various schools and sports activities.

POVERTY

The poverty related to the disadvantaged often has been hidden. People have a natural tendency to play down or forget that which is unpleasant. The procedures for reporting unemployment as well as errors in census figures have combined to give a minimal feature of poverty in America. Consensus of findings from research shows that employment outcomes for the disadvantaged are as good as, or better than, those for the physically and mentally disabled clients conditionally served by vocational rehabilitation. From 50 percent to 90 percent of the graduates of the programs for the disadvantaged secure jobs. The disadvantaged in work orientation programs have a high dropout rate but it is not higher than that of many other programs. The probability of a client's success appears to vary directly with the length of time he spends in the program (Department of Health, Education, and Welfare, 1969).

IMPLICATIONS FOR LAW ENFORCEMENT AND CORRECTIONS

Basic Assumptions

The professional in law enforcement or corrections must believe that it is worthwhile to work with disadvantaged people and realize that they have suffered injustices which can be remedied. The professional must expect some hostility and motivation problems and should respond to them in helpful, nonpunitive ways. There must be an attitude of equality. No law enforcement officer nor correctional officer is ever superior to his client. All men are created equal. While the law enforcement officer and correctional officer may have certain skills which the individual does not have, the same is true of the individual or he has certain skills not possessed by the law enforcement officer or correctional officer. Each has different skills but neither the professional nor the nonprofessional is inherently *superior*. The professional realizes that in one way he is dependent upon the nonprofessional for his job and, but for certain accidents of time, circumstances and opportunities, the roles each plays could easily be reversed.

Communicate

All possible channels of communication should be open. The law breaker is often suspicious of the professional in the correctional system, believing that he represents the establishment. The law enforcement officer or correctional officer, by subtle means, may in fact re-enforce the suspicion. Advocacy on behalf of the offender is especially important for success with the disadvantaged. The professional should learn the language of the ghetto, the barrio, or the disadvantaged group. He need not necessarily speak it, as this might be seen as false, but he should certainly understand it. The use of indigenous workers is important in developing a sense of trust. The professionals who themselves have been among the disadvantaged are, other things being equal, especially suited to serve this group.

It is also recommended that the professional develop as close personal friends some members of the disadvantaged group. This should not be the public offender with whom the professional is working, or is apt to work with because the dual relationship will be confusing to both. However, it is a good idea to know members of the offender's own group on a personal basis. It is hard to be prejudiced against acquaintances or friends, and it is broadening to the personal experiences of the professional in law enforcement and corrections.

Police Standards

In recent years more rigorous standards of professional conduct and behavior have been developed and taught in order to effectively carry out the complex police mission. Dr. Robert B. Mills of the University of Cincinnati (APA Monitor, 1972) warned that unless standards for police conduct are raised quickly, policemen will be the continuing object of hostility for some groups. He recommended a "new breed" of impartial and professional police and called for testing new recruits to weed out the emotionally unfit. As head of the University of Cincinnati's Criminal Justice Department he has developed a series of behavioral "survival traits" including seven personal attributes which identify positive characteristics such as sensitivity toward minority groups and social deviates and flexibility. Other attributes are identified through a process of peer review and playing out roles under ambiguous circumstances. Through proper selection and training it is hoped that the often current stereotype of the policeman as a sadist can be completely displaced.

Meeting Human Needs

Problems of the disadvantaged are often complex and interrelated and may include such needs as housing, health, transportation, and food. Enforcement and correctional officers can be most helpful in directing individuals in need to appropriate community agencies, thereby perhaps preventing crime by reducing the needs in socially acceptable ways.

Problem Solving and the Underprivileged

One of the functions often overlooked in police training in the past has been the very important educational function of police work. The poor and underprivileged whose needs have been frustrated are often tempted to "play the long shots." A man who is within two weeks of finishing an expensive training program may suddenly quit and go to a distant city when he hears of a vague possibility of a job opening—even in an unrelated field. A woman with very limited financial resources may spend a week's income to take her sick baby to a folk healer. Another person may borrow money from a loan shark at an exorbitant rate even though a credit union was available at the place of employment. Such poor decision making often lands them in trouble; much of crime is an attempt, albeit maladaptive, to get out of trouble. It follows then that at least some crimes can be prevented by helping people find alternate and more effective solutions for their problems.

The Importance of Self-Respect

There is an almost universal need for feelings of self-respect. This should be recognized, built on, and developed. Without self-respect, progress is possible only if built on threats and coercion. But that kind of progress is short-lived and unworthy of our kind of society.

If a person is to feel better toward himself, he has to feel some sense of autonomy and some sense of control over his future. In practical terms this means that he has to become as far as possible, the decision-maker, deciding if he wants help in changing and deciding what steps might be taken. No matter how wise the professional and no matter how well-intentioned, the consequences of his acting as the decision-maker for the client can serve only to reduce the interest of the client and to increase his anger.

Moreover, by being permitted and encouraged to become the decision-maker, the client acquires an emotional investment in proving his capacity as a decision-maker and proving the correctness of his decision (Olshansky, 1972).

For the most part, the disadvantaged person knows that something is terribly wrong but with things the way they are, he cannot know that something better actually exists on the other side of law and justice. "We are born blank. It's the same for blacks or whites or any other shade of man. Your blanks have been filled in far differently from those of a child grown up in the filth and poverty of the ghetto" (Griffin, 1961).

SUMMARY

Prejudices are often subtle and deeply engrained in the habit patterns of our very society. Each professional should be aware of their existence and strive to eliminate them, both from the culture and from his own behavior and attitudinal set. Only through self-awareness and self-discipline can mutual understanding among people be ensured. Specific suggestions are offered for working with disadvantaged people.

REFERENCES

Bruckman, Idel R.: Vocational expectations and aspirations in Mexican-American school children. *Internat J Psychol,* 5:1–2, 1971.

Department of Health, Education, and Welfare, R & D Brief, Vol. III, No. 2, Washington, D.C., October 1, 1969.

Griffin, J. H.: *Black Like Me.* Boston, Houghton Mifflin Co., 1961.

Heller, C. S.: *Mexican-American Youth: Forgotten Youth at the Crossroads.* New York, Random House, 1966.

Kluckhohn, F. R., and Strodtbeck, F. L.: *Variations in Value Orientations.* Evanston, Ill., Row and Peterson, 1961.

Madsen, W.: *The Mexican-Americans of South Texas.* New York, Holt, Rinehart, and Winston, 1964.

Minorities. *Hum Behav,* March/April, 1972, p. 39.

Olshansky, S.: The rehabilitation process and public welfare. *J Rehab,* March/April, 1972, pp. 38–39.

Pratt, Bill: New standards for police conduct developing. *APA Monitor, 3,* No. 12: 5, December, 1972.

Smith, A. L.: "White Only" takes many subtle forms in U.S., *San Antonio News,* June 16, 1972, p. 8-B.

The housing scandal. *Newsweek,* April, 10, 1972, p. 61.

Chapter 11

GROUPS, GANGS, AND MOBS

J. Gary May

- INTRODUCTION
- INDIVIDUALS IN GROUPS LOSE THEIR INDI-
  VIDUAL IDENTITY
- HOW DO GROUPS EXERT SUCH POWER?
- "SENTIMENT OF INVINCIBLE POWER"
- CONTAGION
- SUGGESTIBILITY
- PEER GROUP AND JUVENILE GANGS
- GROUPS AND IDENTITY
- THE ADOLESCENT GANG
- MOBS AND RIOTS
- USES OF THE GROUP
- CONCLUSION
- REFERENCES

INTRODUCTION

SPECIAL THINGS HAPPEN to individuals in groups, things which every law enforcement officer, teacher, entertainer, clergyman, or psychiatrist must understand in order to be able to work with more than one person at a time. To make things more complicated, that particularly difficult category of problem people—juveniles—are usually found in groups and gangs. And if youth are hard to understand as individuals, with a group you have your hands full.

There is hope, however; that hope is in understanding some basic facts about groups. If you have a car, the way to keep it trouble-free is to know something about how it works, what maintenance it needs to prevent trouble, how it should be handled to keep it from being damaged, and where to take it for expert help if it needs fixing. A similar philosophy applies to understanding groups. For example, to work with a juvenile gang you must know about the basic mechanisms of group function (what mental health people call "dynamics"). One needs to know what to look for in case of trouble, and as important, how to prevent trouble in the first place. You must know what to do in case of emergencies and how to get help if you need it.

Make no mistake about the power of groups psychologically. They can be incredibly effective in altering behavior, both for good and evil. For the law enforcement officer to underestimate the power of the group can endanger his life and markedly limit his effectiveness.

This chapter will first discuss the basic principles of group dynamics and then will consider several special types of groups which interest the law enforcement officer. These include juvenile groups and gangs, adult groups, crowds, and mobs. Finally, we will discuss the use of groups for treatment and rehabilitation.

INDIVIDUALS IN GROUPS LOSE THEIR INDIVIDUAL IDENTITY

Most of us are raised to think of people just as individuals. It is not part of our usual experience or schooling to consider groups as a separate entity or to consider the group as more than a collection of individuals. This is especially true for the lawman who must by the nature of our judicial system think about the fact that individuals—as separate people—are responsible for what they do. Most people know that groups can affect behavior, at least to some degree. "Don't keep bad company" reflects that idea, but most people do not understand the enormous power of groups on the individual. But the law does not and should not prosecute groups. Because one belongs to a group ("gang") that robs a store, it does not alter his culpability unless he can prove that he was forced physically against his will to participate. In this sense, the law is "black and white." But the understanding of what makes people tick, how they feel and behave is not a black and white matter. Behavior is usually a shade of gray, the result of many factors.

A group can be studied like some study the individual. The group has a psychology, development, natural history, and behavior which one can understand and which operates with certain basic principles and laws.

The incredible power of the group is illustrated in the many places groups are used to get people to respond to the group's demands. Many religious services rely upon the group's bringing the individual along emotionally. Political rallies and demonstrations classically have used the power of the group to change men's minds and wills.

These techniques reached a zenith in Hitler's Germany. The night rallies by torchlight with the music, singing, and chanting along with the emotional speeches had the effect of persuading the crowd to actions that many individuals in the crowd would not agree with nor do alone. More recently the violent demonstrations by groups of young people, who as individuals think of themselves as nonviolent and nonaggressive people, testifies to the power of the group. The group is essential to the military training methods which can take a group of civilian men, each different, many unwilling to be in the service, and in a few weeks mold them and their behavior into effectively trained soldiers. The ultimate of group pressure techniques can be seen in the process of "brainwashing" in which one can obtain incredible changes in people. Given a trained and dedicated cadre who can have complete control over a group, they can bring 80 to 90 percent of a group to behave in any way desired.

HOW DO GROUPS EXERT SUCH POWER?

The question of how a group exerts such power on the minds of men has been studied and questioned by many of the most able and famous mental health professionals. Sigmund Freud wrote a brilliant analysis of the dynamics of groups which is worth considering.

Do not be too quick to think of Freud as the man who invented sex. He wrote about many areas with unparalleled skill. His collected works consist of twenty-four volumes and should not be summarized in a few sentences of cliche'.

Freud quoted extensively from a French psychologist, Le Bon. Le Bon felt that a person's individual identity, differences, and attitudes are obliterated by the group. The group then takes on a "collective mind" which substitutes for the individual's personality.

"SENTIMENT OF INVINCIBLE POWER"

Le Bon felt there were three characteristics of the group which account for the changes one sees. These are a "sentiment of invincible power," contagion, and suggestibility. It is the propensity of the group and its individuals to feel as if they are invincible, that nothing can stop them and that their cause is all powerful. Often the individuals who make up the mob come from a section of society where, as individuals, they feel powerless and are frustrated by feeling unimportant and ineffective. The gangs of recent times have echoed these feelings. Minorities, the poor, and the young have in common a sense of powerlessness, and some individuals feel that they have little to lose. These groups have been the backbone of all historical revolutionary movements (see Eric Hoffer's *The True Believer*). The group for these individuals is especially seductive. But the group's effect can be felt by all who are caught up in it, regardless of their background. The group's values transcend all of the values of the individual. These feelings are partly a function of the size of the group with the larger group being the more powerful. The group is invincible.

The power of the group allows and encourages the individual to yield to instincts which he would have otherwise resisted and repressed. According to Freud, the individual in the group, as he throws off his repressions, displays all the unconscious manifestations of that which is evil in the human mind. This is a way of saying that the conscience and the sense of responsibility disappear. Of all of the aspects of illegal groups, this is the most distressing. A fairly sensible, law abiding individual can become a savage unfeeling killer—foul-mouthed, disrespectful, and unpredictable. The lynch mob of years ago, the ghetto riot of today, the campus rebellion of late often contain many individuals who, alone and with sober thought, would think that they would never do the things they do in a group. The group takes over their conscience, supersedes it, and strips away that thin layer of social restraint which makes it possible for men to live in societies. The same will occur with smaller groups—the "gangs" become their own conscience. We will discuss the gang in more detail later, but the same basic group principles apply.

CONTAGION

Contagion is one of the basic mechanisms of group behavior. It can be observed early in the formation of a group. One can see as a new group forms each individual watching the others closely and the attitudes of the leaders are quickly passed through the group. If one does not conform to the group attitude he is belittled, made to feel quite alone and out of line, and inside he feels anxious and uncomfortable. Regardless of what the individual thinks, the group speaks for him. A theme or idea can begin and is soon accepted by the group. If the group sees one of its members commit an act which may have been unacceptable before, the group condones it and other members of the group follow. If a mob sees one of its members loot a store, other members may commit similar acts. If a peaceful group sees one of its members commit a violent act, others may do the same. Behavior, as well as attitude, is contagious and awareness of the contagiousness is essential to the understanding of the management of the group.

SUGGESTIBILITY

The third dimension of the group is equally important. It is suggestibility. It means that the group alters the individual's conscious personality. Le Bon made the comparison between the individuals in the group and the individual under hypnosis. The individual's feelings, thoughts, and behavior are bent by the group and, according to Le Bon, the individual is not conscious of his actions. He is no longer himself. Freud said, "The group is extraordinarily credulous and open to influence, it has no critical facility, and the improbable does not exist for it."

PEER GROUPS AND JUVENILE GANGS

The first part of this chapter may carry something of a misconception. We have talked about the problems of groups; that is, what's bad about groups. We must also discuss what's good about groups, for groups have far more potential for good than evil; groups are an important part of normal growth for all humans. Much of that which we feel we are, our self-image, is related to the groups with whom we identify.

GROUPS AND IDENTITY

If we find out about who a person *is* we often find that he is more than Mr. John Jones, individual. He is John Jones, policeman or doctor, Texan or New Yorker, Methodist or Morman, young or old, bowler, football fan, or country club golfer. He can be a Democrat or Republican, belong to the PTA, NAACP, FOE, or Weight Watchers. As one can see, a part of our identity—the substance of who we are—is defined by those with whom we associate. An outstanding example of this is our national identity and how strongly most Americans feel about being an American. Even if being an American means association with the two hundred million others who are quite different than the individual, the feeling of belonging is still very strong.

However, if groups are important to adults they are even more important to adolescents who, at times, appear to lose all of their individuality to the groups with whom they associate.

Where does all of this begin? It begins with birth (unless you were a twin, triplet, etc.) which is a rather individual experience between you and your mother. Even at birth, however, you belong to certain groups (usually those of your parents) without knowing it. You are of a specific nationality, race, and sex; you will probably be raised in the religious beliefs of your parents and hold many of the values of their groups (at least for a while). Of course, baby doesn't know all of this yet.

Even a preschooler will watch other children and sometimes imitate what they do (what is called "parallel play") but not see himself as of the group. In fact, it is only as children become of school age that they consistently become involved with other children. In school some of the group identifications become very important. "I am Jimmy Jones, ten years old, I'm in the fourth grade, I am a boy (and don't care much for girls), I belong to the Red Devils baseball team, and I have my friends." Jimmy thinks very highly of his friends ("They are the greatest"—although his mother may not share his opinion), overvalues the Red Devils ("We're the best team in the league and if we had better pitching and the umpires had been fair, we would have won a lot more than two games this season"). The point is that even by ten years old a child has developed firm identification with his groups, to the point that he overvalues the group, refuses to hear criticism of the group, and will defend them regardless of the facts. In other words, he is already showing the effect of the group on his value system, sense of reality, and individual identity. His school and peer groups have a profound effect that may alter the child's earlier exclusive identifications with his home and his parents. The group does this by using the mechanisms we discussed earlier of feeling of invincible power ("nobody can beat the Red Devils"), contagion ("Okay, boys, talk it up in the outfield"), and suggestibility ("Come on, Charley Brown, you know you can strike him out"). Groups are good. They are absolutely essential to normal growing up and adult life. For a person to be without group associations will often be a sign of real problems with emotional adjustment. Nonetheless, as much as we value our groups and want our children to identify with them, well balanced development also should include the solid roots of individual identity that serve to resist the power of less desirable, dangerous, or destructive groups.

A fascinating demonstration of the power of peer groups was conducted by Scherif. He set up a summer camp for boys eleven and twelve years old. These were normal children, from normal homes, who did not know one another when they came to the camp. The boys did not know that they were part of an experiment. When the boys arrived at camp they were all housed in one large bunkhouse. Then in a few days, after the staff had found out from each boy who his best friends were, the boys were divided into two groups, separating the "best friends." Each group then went on a hike. Like all groups of strangers in some common activity, the group spontaneously developed organization and leaders. Some boys would be on the top of the heap and others would be at the bottom. For the boys who didn't do things "right" there would be the "silent treatment," ridicule, or threats. Each group developed its own special jokes, secrets, and ways. The groups markedly overestimated the skill and ability of the boy who was their leader and seemed to "put down" the lowest members of the group.

Scherif tried two experiments with the groups. The first had as its hypothesis that "when two groups have conflicting aims, i.e. when one group can achieve its ends only at the expense of the other, their members will become hostile to each other even though the groups are composed of normal, well-adjusted individuals." To prove this they had a "tournament of games." These were the usual things—baseball, football, tug-of-war, etc. Although the boys were good sports at the start, it soon changed to name-calling and intense rivalry. It then turned the camp into a real battleground—night raids, name-calling, and scuffling. Each group became more solid, cooperative, and increased in morale, all in response to their new "enemy."

The next problem was how to put the groups back together in a harmonious way. The staff tried "pleasant social contacts." Movies together, eating together, etc. The results were predictable; the movies and the dining room became the battlefield.

The next hypothesis became "Just as competition generates friction, working in a common endeavor should promote harmony." In order to test this they arranged for the water supply to break down. The groups had to search together to find the water main break; they worked together harmoniously. Also, in order to have an extra movie the groups had to chip in together and had to vote on which one to get.

The staff arranged for the food truck to break down. The boys tied their tug-of-war rope to the truck and all pulled together to get it started. Gradually the hostility between the groups began to decrease. New friendships between the groups developed. The groups wanted joint campfires, treated each other to goodies and renewed their earlier friendships.

The experiment demonstrated several important concepts. The commonly used approach to bring rival groups together through social activities will often fail. There was much more success when the groups worked together on a common endeavor.

There are many social lessons in the research by Scherif. Our great cultural emphasis on competition can often be destructive. The weak, less effective are the scapegoats and will have a great need to find a group in which they can be accepted and by banning together become more powerful. This is the beginning of the formation of the gang.

THE ADOLESCENT GANG

What you call a "gang" is up to you. Many people loosely refer to a group of three or more boys as a "gang." Although the major emphasis of this part of the chapter is on the violent gang, the importance of "gangs" and groups in adolescence should be clear to the law enforcement officer. The psychological elements which bring about the violent gang can also be the most effective approach to treating and rehabilitating the youthful offender.

Adolescence is a time when the principle psychological task is to begin to find one's identity. Identity is an individual thing and for the adolescent it involves the psychological differentiation of one's self from his parents. The younger child will often speak of himself in terms of his parents: "I'm Johnny Jones, Jr., I live on Maple Street (in my parents' house). I go to Lincoln Elementary School. When I grow up I want to be a policeman like my father, and I live with my mother, father, brother and sister." You would also find that he, for the most part, shares his parents' beliefs (religious, political, etc.), values, and prejudices.

When he becomes an adolescent in order to find *his* identity it, by definition, implies that it cannot be the identity of his parents. He can be like his parents, but he cannot be himself and his parents, too. This emotional separation from the parents can be a time, at best, of some stress and, at worst, a time when the adolescent rebels with such force and anger as to end up in serious trouble with the law.

Adolescence is a complicated time. There are many issues which are of importance to the law enforcement officer as this is an age when many kids become his "clients." The teenager is a complex person. He does not become a "man" overnight, although in some cultures the transition is that abrupt. In some primitive tribes the child will be raised by the women until he is of age (thirteen or fourteen) and he is initiated into the world of the men where he lives after that time. That is not done in America. Becoming a "man" is a process which seems to take between five and ten years. At seventeen a boy may be six-three, weigh 220 pounds, be tough as nails and still not have the right to be on his own. Conflict often occurs. *Playboy* defined adolescence as "a hair-raising experience." Yet this is also an age of growth. The adolescent can be one of the most interesting and stimulating of people to work with. If you have any understanding of what the adolescent is going through they can often be easy to reach and gratifying to help.

Let me give you an example. If the policeman understands that one common, perhaps universal, feeling in adolescents is depression, he will have found a way to reach many teenagers. The depression comes, in part, from the fact that growing up means giving up some things. He has to give up the pleasant dependency of childhood where he didn't have to worry about where he was going to live, if he was going to have something to eat, what clothes to wear or who was going to look out for him. Perhaps more important is that he didn't have to worry so much about himself, particularly in terms of his self-control. His parents made it clear what he could do and just as important, what he could not do. They set his limits, told him which friends he could see, kept him out of trouble.

Adolescence changes that—one is more and more on his own. One loses that feeling of protection and limit as he takes those functions on himself. It's scary and it's sad, too. Any time one loses something, depression will result. Most adolescents are depressed part of the time. Out of their depression they will often, unknowingly, try to get their parents to treat them as children again. For example, suppose it's five o'clock on a Saturday morning and on your beat you pick up three fifteen-year-old boys wandering around a shopping center. None of them have a record, all come from "good" homes, but you have been aware that the boys have been on the edge of trouble. You want to prevent, if you can, further danger of delinquency. What can you do?

In counseling the boys, it's best if you can deal with them individually. If you try to relate to the three of them as a group, they may try to maintain "face"—show their buddies how tough they are and how they can defy authority. If you can take two of them home and talk individually to the third you might try to get at some of his feelings of sadness (not just anger) at being picked up by the police ("How do you feel, son, about my picking you up?"). He will be mad and perhaps scared, but he will also be sad about it.

Too many police officers react to the teenager's anger with anger in return. There is very little positive or productive one can get from the anger. If you recognize the depression you may have something which will demonstrate to the adolescent that you have some understanding of his feelings. When you take him home it is important to encourage the parents to recognize that they are asking for increasing trouble until they see this kind of behavior as being a demand from the teenager that the parents limit him. The adolescent feels that since his parents let him get into trouble it indicates that they don't care about him. It leaves him vulnerable to his own drives and impulses which he is having trouble controlling. It also justifies the defiant behavior by allowing the rationalization, "They don't care what I do anyway." By appealing to the teenager's sense of depression you can help reinforce the parental sense of limits. "You must be feeling pretty bad about having to go home and face your parents." "I'll bet you really don't want to be in trouble with the police." "I'm always sad to see kids start into trouble."

Out of some of these same emotional issues the adolescent becomes particularly inclined to seek the approval and acceptance of his peers. If he has to give up his tie to his parents, he still requires a sense of approval and acceptance from some quarter. He turns to his friends. The peers begin to give what the parents used to offer—a value system, a model for identification, a sense of acceptance (or rejection), and a validation of the individual's sense of identity. Obviously not all or even most groups are "bad." They are an essential part of the adolescent's growing up. But they can also be sources of real trouble.

The violent group is of real concern to the police officer and to the society he is to protect. Much has been written about the violent gang, some of which should be read by every police officer. Here we will attempt only to summarize some of the literature about gangs.

It is difficult to get an overall picture of the current prevalence of violent juvenile gangs. In the author's personal experience the violent gang was a very pervasive and dangerous force in the city of Denver, Colorado in the late forties. Much of the gang activity seemed similar to that of the "Dukes" as portrayed in the movie "The Blackboard Jungle." The gangs were very active in weekend warfare which led to considerable injury and occasional death. The gangs were only loosely drawn on racial lines, generally more representative of neighborhood or school groups. The gangs were often vicious, would engage in violence against other adolescents even when there was no provocation. (A friend of mine was shot as he walked up to his porch after a football game. He belonged to no gang. Some kids shot him as they drove past in a car for "no apparent reason.") Of course, in a psychiatric sense there is no such thing as an action without reason—it is the challenge to explore and discover the reason. Nonetheless, the gangs were and are still dangerous. The most dangerous, in the author's experience, have been the girl gangs. They are less common and seem to be made up of very disturbed girls. A gang behavior is culturally much more deviant for a girl than a boy.

For some reason, the prevalence of juvenile gangs in smaller cities appeared to decrease between the forties and mid-sixties. Then racial strife reignited the "need" for gangs in minority groups.

The gang now seems to be returning in strength in some cities. *New York Magazine* recently reported on the "return of the New York Street Gang." This was accompanied by the headline, "Are you ready for the new ultraviolence?" It is interesting that some of these gangs have taken a very violent attitude against the heroin pusher. Weingarten believes that it was heroin use by the gang members which destroyed the gangs a decade ago, and the gangs of today see heroin use by a member as an offense which they punish.

Gangs are not a new thing. They have been around for decades, perhaps centuries. Herbert Asbury in 1927 published the book, *Gangs of New York*, which was primarily about adult gangs, including that most famous of adult "gangs," the Mafia, which is more (in a psychological sense) a criminal organization than a gang. Although in 1898 Sheldon described gangs in a sociological and psychological sense, the most important early study was by Thrasher who studied gangs in the 1920's. The importance of the social, neighborhood, and parental substrate for gang formation was stressed in this early writing. Included also was the importance of the psychological aspects of the adolescent improving his self-conception and public identity (his "reputation").

The more modern authors have greatly refined both sociological and psychological analysis of gangs. For the police officer who works with gangs the study of the writings of the recent authors is vital to the understanding of what makes gangs tick. Much of the literature is well summarized in Yablonsky's *The Violent Gang* which should be read by anyone who works with gangs. Yablonsky refines some of the concepts of Cloward and Ohlin and divides gangs into several categories. Knowledge of the type of gang should alter considerably the psychological approach to the gang. It is essential that the law officer recognize the type of gang with which he is dealing. Yablonsky defines three types of gangs: delinquent gangs, violent gangs, and social gangs.

The delinquent gang is dedicated toward illegal acts which bring about some gain, primarily theft of various descriptions. Violence is only a by-product. Yablonsky states that most of the members of this type of gangs are emotionally stable, future career criminals who may reflect a social "sub-class" which condones the illegal activity.

The social gang is different. It seldom involves itself in delinquency or violence. It will generally center about a place—a drugstore, a clubhouse, etc. These members come together because they like each other and have mutual interests. The members are the most stable of gang members, less inclined to be emotionally disturbed, and the gang serves the needs of society more effectively. For the police to confuse this type of gang with the other two types would be a great tragedy, for these are the gangs that, with proper handling, can help prevent rather than foster illegal and antisocial activity. Here the police can help prevent disorder by working with these groups.

The violent gang is cut from another cloth. These gangs exist to offer immediate gratification to the impulsive needs of the members. The leadership is characterized by megalomania and feelings of invincibility. These are often members who are so disturbed as to be inacceptable in society, whose self-conception, at the root, is so severely impaired that they establish identity only in the company of others like themselves and by "demonstrating" their physical superiority over others, Yablonsky states:

> "In summary, violent gangs appear to originate in order to adjust individual emotional problems, for reasons of "self-protection" and defense, for channeling aggression, in response to prejudice, because of the peculiar motivations of disturbed leaders or because of a combination of these factors mixed with special external conditions produced by "enemy gangs.""

Yablonsky has a great deal more to say regarding the communities role in gangs, the movement of gangs into the suburbs, the nature of the psychological makeup of the gang members, and the role of prejudice. Prejudice deserves a bit of special mention because it is so often a "cover-up" for the violent feelings within the individual and is a reflection of his emotional problems. Since at its psychological base the aggression cannot be directed toward its real objects, usually people too close to home, prejudice offers a substitute. It has the added characteristic that it also serves as the rationalization for the expression of the violence. "You can't trust those niggers" (or waps, or spicks, or chinks, etc., depending on where one lives) and "you have to do it to them before they do it to you." So, one's violence is excused, justified, and perhaps applauded by the group. Prejudice has served as the excuse for much of the bloodshed through man's history and yet implies the underlying emotional instability of the prejudiced individual.

Of most concern is how to approach the problem of gangs. Yablonsky discusses this, too, and is worth reading. He says, ". . . One must keep in mind that his ultimate goal is not the 'redirection of the violent gang into constructive activities' but its eventual dismemberment." He emphasizes the importance of the "detached worker" sometimes supplied by the police department in working with the gang. He feels the beginning approach is to not work with the core members and leaders but to try to strip away the more marginal members by getting them into other activities and interests. The approach to the core member, usually a sociopathic and difficult to reach individual, is far less satisfactory. The conventional approaches of psychotherapy and criminal institutions (even of the new "reformed" variety) have little success with this individual. Many, including Yablonsky, have emphasized that since the gang plays such importance in the makeup of the sociopath, a group approach is most likely to reach him. Yablonsky has considerable hope, for group approaches such as Synanon, and it does seem to contain the basic elements which may bring about the change if change is possible.

The fact of the matter is that there are some people who cannot be reached. We do not have the knowledge or techniques to change them. Psychotherapy is primarily for people who have an intense personal desire to change and then it is still a great deal of work and effort. To bring about change against one's will is extraordinarily difficult. If there is an answer, it will probably be in the prevention of the antisocial character in the first instance, but even that requires techniques we have yet to develop.

MOBS AND RIOTS

As groups get larger and more emotional there is greater danger. The possibility of a large group of people becoming a mob is one of the most frightening aspects of group psychology.

All that we have said so far about the group taking over the conscience and restraint of the individual, about its enormous power of suggestion and the group dictating the behavior of individuals, coalesce in the specter of the riot.

We have witnessed the upsurge of riots and violence in the decade of the sixties. For many, this was the first experience they had had with riots. All of America was overwhelmed by what they saw happening on television. The fact that it had come to this was a disturbing experience for most viewers. The racial upheaval of the civil rights movement, followed by the peace demonstrations on the campuses and in Washington were witnessed by millions via the television.

Marshall McLuhan in *The Medium is the Message* talks of our now being one large "global village" in which we share, through television, all of the events, particularly the disastrous ones, of other humans everywhere on the globe. The communication satellites makes it possible to see exactly what is happening in China or Vietnam at the same instant it takes place.

Into this caldron of enormous psychological pressure the police have been immersed and, unfortunately, have come out smeared in the public eye, with the upsurge of many vehement and dangerous generalizations regarding all law officers everywhere. It is clear that in many instances the police officers did not realize what they had gotten into. They had little understanding of the psychology of the mob and they made some public mistakes. There may be no way to totally avoid mistakes, bad publicity, or even injustice in the midst of the overwhelming emotional conditions of a riot. However, some reflections may be helpful. None of these will take the place of the intensive training necessary for the police officer in the handling of riots.

It is too often thought that riots are new to America. We had long been aware of the student demonstrations in other countries but had the idea that it couldn't happen here. How wrong we were. Our national heritage contains the skeletons of our past. In 1831 there was the bloody racial insurgent of slave Nat Turner with the death of fifty-five in two days. In 1863 there was perhaps the worst of American riots in New York. It was stimulated by the draft with conscription of the poorer men (you could pay three hundred dollars to the draft board and not have to go) to fight in the Civil War. The riots began where the draft lottery was being held. It lasted four days and involved some seventy thousand participants. The police force was slightly over two thousand. The crime and violence were indescribable. Murder, lynching, looting, and burning were all a part of the riot. It began to direct itself toward the black population and many were robbed, beaten, and lynched. It was only when sufficient troops were brought in that the riot subsided.

The history of riots must include the many bloody and violent confrontations between labor and management. In 1892 there was the lockout by the Carnegie Steel Company followed by management's attempt to bring in a private police force (The Pinkertons). The riots which followed led to considerable bloodshed and injury.

One of the great tragedies is that, with the movement of history and time, the law enforcement officer, by representing the status quo, may be maintaining a lost cause. The causes of repeal of slavery, labor's right to organize and to strike, civil rights, and even peace, have become causes to correct moral flaws in our society. This certainly compounds the problem of the law enforcement agencies. They cannot let lawlessness occur without a response, but if they respond with force or brutality they become the issue themselves and receive the brunt of the mob's anger. Every effort must be made to avoid that kind of confrontation.

The psychological nature of the riot is such that the law enforcement officer can, by following his instincts, play into the riot—help to fuel its disorder—if he is not careful. For example, not all the participants of a riot are the same, just as all riots are not planned. Monte and Leinwand say:

> "However, not all those who participate in the riots have knowledge of the plan. They may be victims of mob psychology practiced on them by a small but forceful minority. To the extent that not all participants are instigators of the riot, the outcome of such conflicts cannot be predicted or controlled."

The psychological principles discussed at the beginning of this chapter must be considered. The mob develops from a group who may feel that they are assembled to represent or discuss a situation about which they, as individuals, have strong feelings. It may be civil rights, a war, labor practices, or other issues. Most do not assemble with the idea of violence. They may be feeling a sense of moral outrage or simply be "fed up" which contributes later to their susceptibility to the group. As the emotions spread contagiously through the group of already suggestible people a dangerous mood may develop. As noted before, the group takes over some aspects of the conscience of the participants. Nonetheless, violence may not occur until there is some act to provoke the moral outrage of the group, to allow them to express their anger to gain retribution. Their mood will be moral outrage which then rationalizes the most immoral of acts.

If the law enforcement agent acts in such a way as to justify the sense of moral outrage then the riot is likely to begin. Let one serious provocation, one act of "brutality," take place and the restraint is broken.

The development of the riot as described by Monte and Leinwand:

> ". . . (begins as) gradually a larger crowd gathers. An incident occurs that triggers an emotional outburst . . . The thread of reason is lost as blind fury engulfs the group . . . Plans for violence are made . . . An object of simmering hatred is selected. The mob, both terrified and causing terror, lawlessly tramples upon such opposition to its conduct that may develop . . . As they move and shout, they become like a stone rolling down the mountainside. Gathering pebbles and rocks along the way, they avalanche through the streets, destroying property—often their own . . . and the police or military must be brought into play. Here is force against force, and the result can only breed deeper dislike and distrust . . ."

There is evidence that many lessons have been learned by the law enforcement agencies in the past few years. Witness the difference in handling of the demonstrations between 1968 and 1972 at the Democratic National Conventions. The 1972 Convention was characterized by the police's attempt to clearly avoid provocation of the youth. Space and facilities were provided for the dissident groups. By allowing the leaders of the groups an almost unlimited opportunity to express themselves the group soon became bored, not angry. Their energy was dissipated in nonviolent ways. The authorities seemed prepared in terms of numbers and discipline to prevent a violent response from the police and handle any violence in the crowd.

Contrast this to the events of 1968 as reported by the Walker Report:

> ". . . the police had been put on edge . . . tho nature of the response was unrestrained and indescriminate. Police violence was made all the more shocking by the fact that it was often inflicted upon persons who had broken no law, disobeyed no order, made no threat. These include peaceful demonstrators, onlookers, and large numbers of residents who were simply passing through, or happened to live in the area where confrontations were occurring. Newsmen and photographers were singled out for assault, and their equipment deliberately damaged. Fundamental police training was ignored and officers, when on the scene, were often unable to control their men." . . .

Here there was police provocation of the mob. Undoubtedly, the police were reacting to exactly the same group psychology as the mob itself. Within the police group it appears that the breakdown of the individuals' training and their reaction of violence rather than arrest represents the fact that the group took over these men's conscience and they acted, in many cases, with less restraint and thought than they would have as individuals. This, in turn, inflamed the mob (and much of the nation, too) and served to justify the mob's lawlessness in striking back. The police of Chicago suffered serious public disdain and lack of public confidence.

As much as we are concerned with the psychology of the rioter, it is equally important to be concerned with the psychology of the law enforcement officer assigned to riot duty. After interviews with some men who have served on riot duty some suggestions may be made regarding the approach. As a society, we have been concerned exclusively with the mind of the rioter. We should also consider the feelings and emotional needs of the law enforcement officers who approach the riot problem. One National Guardsman whom I interviewed pointed out a number of factors worth considering:

When the riot duty began the unit was assigned to a ghetto area where there had been some racial trouble and looting. When the unit arrived, it was something of an adventure, perhaps even a lark. It was as if it "wasn't real." The Guardsmen were in good humor and while on the street were in good spirits. They had no trouble taking some of the passing insults of the neighborhood residents. They were on duty long hours, sixteen hours or more, which at first was not so bad. However, when they were finally relieved, they found that they were bivouacked at a local school on uncomfortable cots and with very limited bathroom facilities; so limited that one could not take a shower. The food was limited and poor. Their sleep was fitful and unsatisfying.

By the time the Guardsmen were out on the street again they were tired, much of the humor was gone, and they were both on edge and dissatisfied. The fear began to mount. They began to wonder what they would do if things really did get bad. They found that they had some doubts if their leaders knew what they were doing. They were distressed by some of the contacts with the police who, in some instances, were calloused, prejudiced, and seemed eager for a chance to "bust some heads." The Guardsmen found that they did not have the power of arrest and there was little they could rely upon except their weapons.

By the third day, particularly after they were late in being relieved, the anxiety began to mount, they were very irritable, and prone to flare up at any provocation. They felt dirty, tired, and frightened. There was more talk from the Guardsmen of wanting some "action".

For the rest of the duty the Guardsmen were irritable, tired, dirty, and in a real sense, dangerous. It only requires one "incident" on the part of one law enforcement officer or Guardsman to inflame the mob into a riot. Therefore, it is essential that the emotional and physical needs of the officers be considered and cared for in order to help prevent the riot.

It is a common phenomenon that when some men feel fear or anxiety they react with anger which serves as a defense against feeling afraid. This means that the feelings are directed outwardly and, if it occurs in a law enforcement officer, can lead to unnecessary and unauthorized aggression.

Wherever possible the availability of lethal weapons should

be limited. Gases, batons, rubber bullets, etc., can do more to prevent riots than the use of the deadly weapons. Some weapons, although not deadly, can inflame the mob (and the public) such as dogs, cattle prods, and even fire hoses. It is important that the police and their allies be protected. If they feel safe in doing their job, they are less likely to respond with "excessive" force. Shields, helmets, and other protective clothing help. There may be something to be said for tanks or armoured personnel carriers for the protection of the police.

It has been a rule when dealing with a violent mental patient that the patient is far less impressed with the size of an attendant than with the number of people present. To control a violent patient one gets together as many people as possible to move in on the patient. He will almost always back down in the face of clearly numerically superior force. The same might be said for the riot. It is important to have plenty of people on hand. The situation will get out of control if the law officer feels alone, shows fear, and if the crowd senses it.

Effective communications are important with the officer being in a position to know that he can always ask for help. Effective radio with reserves to back one up can help the officer's feeling of security. This must be backed by command's effective demonstration that they are in firm control of the situation, know what they are doing, and can be relied upon to do what they say they are going to do. If a man has been told that he will be relieved at twelve o'clock, he should be relieved at that time. Officers must have control of their men. If an officer has a man in his command who is not reliable, very prejudiced, volatile, or inclined not to follow orders, it is better to keep him at a "desk" job during a mob disturbance. One man can create the one incident which can turn a gathering into a riot.

In a very important paper, G. T. Marx of Harvard discusses police behavior during riots in the past. Marx describes some shocking incidents of the "police as rioters" in which there have been clear examples of murder of innocent and nonthreatening citizens (usually Negroes) by police. More common have been the situations where the police have been passive in the face of mob violence or lynch mobs (particularly at the turn of the century). He then discusses the problem of "police partiality," again seen, particularly in the white against black riots of the past.

Marx goes on to point out that there have been some real changes in police behavior in the 1960's. He states:

> "Considering the absolute number, size, intensity, and duration of recent disorders, there has probably been much less police rioting, less brutality, and relatively less injury inflicted upon Negroes by the police. . . . Where police rioting has been present—as in Watts, Newark, and Detroit—this tends to be primarily in the latter stages of the disturbance as police are unable to control the disorder and as they become subject to the same collective behavior phenomena as blacks (such as the breakdown of social organization, rumor, panic, etc.)."

Marx makes a number of additional points of importance to the law enforcement officer, which I can only briefly summarize here. It would be of value for any law enforcement officer to read the paper by Marx. He discusses some of the mistakes that have been made in past riots. These include inappropriate control, strategies, lack of coordination among and within various control units, and the breakdown of police organization. Associated with inappropriate control strategies include the mistakes of crowd dispersal (dispersing a peaceful group has led to rioting), failure to negotiate, seeing all Blacks as rioters, official anticipation (anticipation and preparation covered by the public media for a riot when none was about to happen), inappropriate response to sniping, and undue use of force.

The violent sixties have passed and with the first years of the seventies there seems to be less mob action. Perhaps the mood of the country has cooled or perhaps the police have learned some of the lessons regarding how to prevent the group from becoming the mob. The handling of the national political conventions in 1972 seems to point to the fact that many lessons have been learned. In Miami, at the Republican National Convention, there was to be the "last" of the anti-war demonstrations. The police prepared for the demonstrations in some remarkable ways, including not dispersing the demonstrators but accommodating them by having a place for them, complete with sound system, to demonstrate across from the convention hall. There everyone could speak his mind until all grew weary of the sound of indignation. In addition, the police supplied the leaders of the antiwar groups with police two-way radios so as to allow them to be continually aware of what the police were doing, be able to check out rumors, and communicate with police when there were problems or questions. The police were clearly in evidence in adequate numbers, seemed rested, in good humor, well fed (the television had pictures of the police eating), not tense, nor apparently looking for trouble. In spite of the desire of some of the student leaders to start the riot, it simply didn't happen. Those who broke the law were arrested, the police used limited violence, and as a result got a positive press reaction, and were impressive in their decorum. It demonstrated that it can be done, even though the Miami police got some criticism for being "too soft" with the youth. It demonstrates that the police "can't please them all," but must maintain a spirit of intelligence with an understanding of the psychology of the mob.

USES OF THE GROUP

As we end our discussion of groups it is again important to emphasize that the group is neither good nor bad in itself. The use of groups for the treatment of many kinds of people with many kinds of problems has been well established. In mental health, group therapy is one of the leading treatment approaches for all types of disorders with all age groups under many different conditions.

The use of groups with the criminal offender is often the treatment of choice. The group can often reach a person who otherwise is unresponsive to individual treatment approaches. Most prison systems have developed group treatment facilities.

Group therapy is an increasingly popular and widespread approach to treatment and rehabilitation in correctional institutions. Arnold and Stiles, reporting in 1972 on surveys of correctional institutions, found that 79 percent of prisons were using group methods (compared to 35 percent in 1950). In one-fourth of institutions virtually all of the inmates are in group programs.

The leadership of the groups, in most cases, is being shared by mental health professionals with other correctional workers. Groups were noted to be especially effective with emotionally disturbed and neurotic offenders, sex offenders, alcoholics, and first offenders. They found poorer results with habitual thieves and professional criminals. Nonetheless, the prevalence of group treatment methods is increasing in correctional facilities with more prisoners being involved in groups.

In the treatment of the delinquent, the group is the treatment of choice. Because much of the delinquent's behavior is in response to a group, it is the group that can change his behavior to more acceptable lines. The techniques are interesting but do not fit the limits of this chapter. For those who are interested in the group approach, it is interesting to get involved in a group itself; and, if the opportunity is available, to become an observer (or co-leader) in an ongoing group.

CONCLUSION

Groups are of special interest to the law enforcement officer. They affect the behavior of most of the clients with whom he deals. He must know and understand the power of the group over man's behavior. Since the law enforcement officer has to deal with the most extreme alterations of human behavior and with the most seriously disturbed of the population, he can benefit from becoming something of a behavioral scientist. There is a great deal known about behavior and why it occurs. Although many questions remain to be answered, present knowledge can be of real help to the policeman. To take a college course in group psychology or abnormal psychology can also be very helpful.

Nonetheless, no matter how much training the policeman may have, there is advantage in his having available professional mental health consultation. This can usually be arranged through the auspices of a local community mental health clinic, a university medical school department of psychiatry, or through a local private practicing mental health professional. Such consultants can serve by holding workshops and education programs. They can consult with you on the handling of difficult situations and help with police public relations. Also, the local and state mental health associations offer an interesting series of booklets, films, and programs to help the police officer deal with the abnormal offender.

The law enforcement officer and the mental health professional, in some real ways, are in the same business and often deal with an overlapping population. We have much to learn from each other. So, in that sense, we belong to the same group.

REFERENCES

1. Arnold, W. R., and Stiles, B.: A summary of increasing use of "Group Methods" in correctional institutions. *Internat J Group Psycho-Ther, 22:*77–92, 1972.
2. Asbury, H.: *Gangs of New York.* Garden City, N.Y., 1927.
3. Cloward, R. A., and Ohlin, L. E.: *Delinquency and Opportunity: A Theory of Delinquent Gangs.* Glencoe, Ill., The Free Press, 1960.
4. Freud, S.: *Group Psychology and Analysis of the Ego,* translated by Strachey, James. New York, Bantam Books, 1960.
5. Hoffer, Eric: *The True Believer.* New York, Harper and Row, 1951.
6. Le Bon, G.: "Psychologie des foules," quoted by Freud, Sigmund. *Group Psychology and Analysis of the Ego.* New York, Bantam Books, 1895.
7. Marx, G. T.: Civil disorder and the agents of social control. *J Soc Iss, 26:*19–57, 1970.
8. May, J. G.: Army basic training as a group phenomenon. *Am J Orthopsychiatr, 39:*224, 1969.
9. May, J. G., and Main, W.: We just want to help you. *Ment Hyg, 53:* 638, 1969.
10. Olmsted, M. S.: *The Small Group.* New York, Random House, 1959.
11. *Report of the National Advisory Commission on Civil Disorders.* New York, The New York Times Company, Bantam Books, 1968.
12. Sargant, W.: *Battle for the Mind: A Psychology of Conversion and Brain Washing.* Baltimore, Penguin Books, 1957.
13. Sheldon, H. D.: The institutional activity of American children. *Am J Psychol,* 425–428, 1898.
14. Sherif, M.: Experiments in group conflict. *Sci Am, 195:*54–58, 1956.
15. Thrasher, F. M.: *The Gang.* Chicago, University of Chicago Press, 1926.
16. Weingarten, G.: *East Bronx Story—Return of the Street Gangs.* New York 5:*31–37, March 27, 1972.
17. Yablonsky, L.: *The Violent Gang.* Baltimore, Penguin Books, 1970.

Chapter 12

DEALING WITH VICTIMS OF CRIME

John M. Macdonald

- The Role of the Victim
- Interviewing the Victim
- Reactions of Victims
- Comforting the Victim
- Conclusion
- References

President Johnson's Commission on Law Enforcement and Administration of Justice noted that one of the most neglected subjects in the study of crime is its victims: the persons, households, and businesses that bear the brunt of crime in the United States. Certainly the victims of crime too often receive inadequate help from law enforcement agencies and from society. The focus is upon the criminal and more attention is paid to his rehabilitation than to the rehabilitation of his victim who may have received grievous physical or emotional injury.

There is general public sympathy for the unfortunate victim, but until recently there has been little concerted effort to meet his needs for help. Some countries have enacted legislation to provide financial aid for physically or mentally disabled victims of crime. Much can be done by police officers not only to aid victims but also to protect them from further victimization. The focus of this chapter is on the role of the victim and on the provision of comfort to victims of robbery, rape and physical assault.

Police officers seek the cooperation of victims in order to solve crimes and to convict the offenders. Officers give emergency aid to injured or emotionally distressed victims. They provide guidance for those victims who are fearful that the criminal will repeat the offense or seek vengeance for the victim's contribution to his arrest. Often offenders are quickly released on bail, and while at liberty they may indeed attempt to coerce the victim into silence. Officers also give advice to likely victims of crime. These tasks are complicated by the fact that victims sometimes contribute to crimes against them.

Often too sharp a distinction is made between the criminal and his victim. The offender is invariably seen as a scoundrel indeed, and the victim is viewed as a knight in shining armor. Experienced police officers know better. The bank customer who is shot down by a robber as he walks into the bank is an innocent victim of circumstances beyond his control. But some victims provoke the crime or give an untruthful account of the circumstances of the crime because they themselves have committed an illegal act or for other reasons. A minority of "victims" have either set up the crime or have otherwise participated in it. Some "victims" make false reports of crime.

Compassion is essential in the provision of comfort to the victim of crime. But compassion alone is not enough and without understanding may not be helpful at all in some cases. Skill in helping victims is derived in part from knowledge and experience. Awareness of the possible roles of the victim in the crime contributes to an officer's ability to respond appropriately to the victim's distress. These roles will be reviewed.

THE ROLE OF THE VICTIM

The Victim Precipitates the Crime

In 26 percent of 588 criminal homicides in Philadelphia reported by Wolfgang, the victim was the first to show and use a deadly weapon, to strike a blow in an altercation—in short, the first to commence the interplay or resort to physical violence. In cases of victim-precipitated homicide the victim (62 percent) was more likely than the offender to have a previous arrest or police record. Wolfgang gives the following examples.

> A husband accused his wife of giving money to another man, and while she was making breakfast, he attacked her with a milk bottle, then a brick, and finally a piece of concrete block. Having had a butcher knife in hand, she stabbed him during the fight.

> In an argument over a business transaction, the victim first fired several shots at his adversary, who in turn fatally returned the fire.

> During a lover's quarrel, the male (victim) hit his mistress and threw a can of kerosene at her. She retaliated by throwing the liquid on him, and then tossed a lighted match in his direction. He died from the burns.

> A victim became incensed when his eventual slayer asked for money which the victim owed him. The victim grabbed a hatchet and started in the direction of his creditor, who pulled out a knife and stabbed him.

> During an argument in which a male called a female many vile names, she tried to telephone the police. But he grabbed the phone from her hands, knocked her down, kicked her, and hit her with a tire gauge. She ran to the kitchen, grabbed a butcher knife, and stabbed him in the stomach.

An even higher incidence of victim-precipitated homicide was reported in Chicago where 32 percent of the homicides were so classified. These figures may be too low as victims may precipitate homicide not only by resorting to physical violence but also by words and looks in an emotionally charged situation. Harsh criticism, belittling sarcasm, or a contemptuous glance in a moment of crisis may tip the delicate balance between a homicidal threat and homicide.

A man estranged from his wife took a taxi to her home. During an argument with her he produced a pistol and fired at her. The gun misfired and his wife scornfully commented "Big deal." He responded "Let's try again" and shot her several times. Even if she had not provoked him further he might well have shot her, but her comment was surely unwise. Other wives during arguments with impulsive assaultive husbands have provoked them by comments questioning their masculinity or by other slighting remarks.

One wife during a heated argument with her husband over the custody of their children suddenly told him that he was not the father of one of the children and that his brother was the father. He slashed her throat with fatal outcome.

Other wives have responded to production of firearms during an argument with provocative comments such as "What are you going to do, big man, kill me?" and "You haven't got the guts to kill me." A wife who had suffered repeated beatings and homicidal threats kept on display in her living room a gift from a man she had lived with while separated from her husband. Following one threat with a loaded shotgun she told her husband "Go ahead, you might just as well kill me."

Police officers seldom have the opportunity to help the victims of homicide as the majority are beyond help by the time officers arrive at the scene of the crime. However, the victims of attempted homicide, homicidal threats, assault, and rape do survive and can be helped. Furthermore a significant number of these offenses are probably victim precipitated. A survey by the District of Columbia Crime Commission of the victim offender relationship among 131 aggravated assault victims showed a resemblance to the victim offender relationships in criminal homicide. Only 19 percent of the aggravated assault victims were not acquainted with their assailants.

Amir introduced the term "victim-precipitated rape" to refer those rape cases in which the victims actually—or so it was interpreted by the offender—agreed to sexual relations but retracted before the actual act or did not resist strongly enough when the suggestion was made by the offenders. The term applies also to cases in which the victim enters vulnerable situations charged with sexuality, especially when she uses what could be interpreted as indecent language or gestures or makes what could be taken as an invitation to sexual relations. Amir (1971) found that 19 percent of 646 forcible rapes in Philadelphia were victim-precipitated.

The Victim Is Also an Offender

During the armed robbery of a business establishment one of the employees was shot and seriously wounded in the presence of several customers. Police investigation later revealed that the

wounded employee had set up the robbery and one of his ac-
complices shot him accidentally. A parking lot attendant on duty
alone at night was severely beaten by one of two robbers. It was
later discovered that the attendant was an accomplice in the
crime and he had instructed one of the men to hit him in the
face in order to convince the police that it was a genuine robbery.
However, the man overplayed his role.

It is not unusual for employees of gas stations on duty at
night to hand over the money from the cash register to a friend
and then call the police to report an armed robbery. Genuine
victims of armed robbery may themselves be involved in illegal
transactions which culminate in the robbery. Thus a drug pusher
may be held up by his client or a drug purchaser may be robbed
by a man who has offered to sell him narcotics. Similarly, men
in search of homosexual partners or prostitutes may be held up
either in the street or in an apartment by the homosexual, the
prostitute, or an accomplice. Thus they are both offenders and
victims.

The person who commits suicide is both an offender and
victim. Occasionally a person who has made an unsuccessful
attempt at suicide will claim that he was the victim of a physical
assault or armed robbery in order to avoid disclosing his suicidal
act. Thus a woman who shot herself told police that a man broke
into her home, and she shot at him with a revolver. She did not
succeed in shooting him and he attempted to disarm her. During
the struggle she was shot and wounded in the arm.

The Victim Thinks He Is an Offender

The person who buys an apparently expensive diamond ring
or an apparently new television set under the mistaken impression that he is buying stolen property sees himself as an offender.
It is not unusual for shady characters who deliberately contrive
a furtive manner to create the impression without actually saying
so that they are selling stolen merchandise at bargain prices.
When the buyer discovers that the diamond is a fake or that the
television set does not work, he calls the police to make a false
report of armed robbery. He does not disclose the sale but claims

to be the victim of a street stick-up. If the suspects he describes are arrested, the true story comes to light.

The Untruthful Victim

Genuine victims of assault, robbery, rape, or other crimes often give false accounts of the crime to the police. A man who is ashamed because he handed over his wallet to an unarmed assailant will report that he was robbed at gunpoint. Two girls who willingly went for a ride in a car with some youths and were later forcibly raped tell the police that they were kidnapped at knifepoint while walking home and later raped. The story is changed slightly to avoid the wrath of their parents for going out with strangers.

Owners of grocery stores, gas stations, and other businesses sometimes exaggerate the extent of their loss in order to profit at the expense of their insurance companies. Similarly a householder may overestimate the value of items taken in a robbery at their home. A wife who is severely beaten by her husband may claim that she was assaulted by a stranger in order to avoid public scandal.

The Victim Who Is Not a Victim

False reports of crime occur more often than is generally recognized. In 1971 almost 7 percent of all reports of aggravated robbery made to the Denver Police Department were found on investigation to be false reports. Such reports were made for a variety of motives as, for example, to obtain money from an insurance company, to cover theft from an employer, to explain loss of money in a poker game in order to avoid the anger of a wife or parent, and to explain default in payment to a creditor: "I was robbed, if you don't believe me, call the police."

False reports of rape are made to explain pregnancy in an unmarried girl or in a married woman whose husband has been in Vietnam during the previous year; to obtain an abortion in those states where rape is a legal basis for termination of pregnancy, and to obtain revenge on a lover who has transferred his affections to another girl.

A desire for attention from friends and relatives and a desire for newspaper publicity may underlie false reports of kidnapping and other crimes against the person.

The Delusional Complainant

A not infrequent problem facing a busy police department is the person who makes bizarre complaints or continually pesters the department with baseless reports of burglaries or makes false accusations against his neighbors or work mates. It is important to distinguish between the harmless eccentric and the potentially dangerous person who suffers from paranoid delusions. Unfortunately it is not easy to formulate rules for distinguishing between these two groups. The manual, *How to Recognize and Handle Abnormal People,* published by the National Association for Mental Health is perhaps the best available guide for the police officer.

It is not, however, always a simple matter to arrange for psychiatric examination of the person suspected of insanity as he may be unwilling to agree to this and there may not be sufficient information available to justify involuntary commitment to a psychiatric hospital for diagnostic study. Whenever a person has false ideas that people are plotting to kill or harm him the need for psychiatric assistance is imperative. The individual with persecutory delusions all too often feels justified in taking the law into his own hands when he fails to obtain the help he expects from the police.

The writer has examined two patients who committed murder under these circumstances. A middle-aged woman had delusions that her husband was having sexual relations with their teenage daughter. The police department, on receipt of her complaint, arranged for physical examination of the daughter. The woman did not accept the results of the examination which showed that her daughter was a virgin and she later shot and killed her husband. A railway worker complained to a sheriff's office that officials of the railroad union were doping him. The complaint was recognized as being absurd, but no attempt was made to obtain psychiatric examination and the man subsequently murdered one of his imagined persecutors.

INTERVIEWING THE VICTIM

The police officer who obtains the report of a crime from a victim will be alert to any clues which might suggest that the victim provoked the offense, set up or otherwise participated in the crime, or is giving a false report of crime. The fact that the victim is uncooperative, belligerent, or is giving false information does not rule out the possibility that he is a genuine victim, but shows the need for further inquiry. Unlikely or improbable events demand an explanation, yet truth is sometimes stranger than fiction.

Inconsistencies should be noted. Victims who claim that they vigorously resisted an assault may show no sign of physical combat, not a hair is out of place and there is no sign of physical injury. Similarly the appearance of some victims of rape is not in accord with their account of the struggle. Girls who protest that they have fought their way out of muddy ditches through brambly undergrowth do not always look as if they have done so (Simpson, 1962).

An explanation should be sought for a victim's delay in reporting an offense, for his presence in areas notorious for drug sales or illicit sexual activity, for his failure to follow established business procedures to prevent loss of money in a robbery, for poor descriptions of assailants despite prolonged observation of them, or for any contradictory statements. A melodramatic quality in the reporting of an offense arouses question. In his inquiry the police officer should be neither too credulous nor too skeptical.

In all cases of assaults, threats, attempted homicide, or rape, care should be taken to ask the victim the nature and extent of any prior relationships with the offender. Victims often will not disclose such vital information and may indeed convey the impression that the offender is no more than a casual acquaintance when this is not the case. Direct questioning may reveal that the assailant is a former common-law husband or close friend. Inquiry should be made regarding previous reports of crime by the victim involving the same or other assailants.

REACTIONS OF VICTIMS

There is great variation in the patterns of response of victims of crime. A middle-aged woman who has had her purse snatched from her without suffering any physical injury may show more distress than another woman of similar age who has suffered several physical injuries in a mugging. A single anonymous telephone call with homicidal threats leads to a panic state in one girl whereas another is quite unperturbed when someone fires a shot into her room and the bullet hits the chair that she is sitting on. When warned by detectives that her unknown assailant might return she calmly replied "Oh well, I'll take my chances."

Some victims are more upset over the loss of money or some personal possession than over physical injury. A girl who was raped by a man who broke into her apartment in the early hours of the morning did not bother to inform the police. When she discovered the following evening that the rapist had stolen $12 from a dresser drawer she made an immediate report to the police.

In a multiple shooting the surviving victim may show less concern than officers who respond to the scene of carnage. Sometimes there is a delayed reaction to a horrifying or frightening experience. The victim who seems unaffected shortly after the crime may start sobbing the next day when a mug shot identification is made at police headquarters.

One young married woman who surprised a burglar in her home was shot three times and pistol whipped. Despite her injuries she was able to run to her neighbor's home where she explained what had happened and made appropriate arrangements for the care of her children before being taken to the hospital. However, for many weeks after her discharge from the hospital she was handicapped by her fear that the assailant would return. She refused to remain at home alone, her sleep was troubled by bad dreams, and she reacted with alarm to sudden noises.

> I'm convinced he won't come back but I'm not completely convinced. I'm still scared. I can be in a rollicking mood, next day I'm

depressed. I wonder how long this panic depression fright will last. When I go in a dark room I feel apprehensive. I know there's no one in there but I'm terrified. I'm clinging on to my husband. I can't be left alone for 20 minutes. I could not be in this house alone at night. If someone touches me lightly on the shoulder I jump a mile. There is a real depression. What am I going to do with my life? I wonder if I'll ever get over it.

Sutherland and Scherl (1970) in their study of thirteen white young adult victims of rape found a similar sequence of reactions falling in three distinct phases, extending over a period of weeks or months. Their findings may well be applicable to other victims of physical assault.

Phase One: Acute Reaction. In the moments, hours, and days immediately following the rape, the victim may show shock, disbelief and dismay or may be in an agitated incoherent state. In this early phase the initial reaction is often succeeded by great anxiety.

Phase Two: Outward Adjustment. This is a period of pseudo-adjustment in which the person turns a blind eye to the rape and dismisses the importance of the occasion. The victim attributes the crime to blind chance ("It could have happened to anyone") and looks upon the offender as sick. Anger and resentment toward the assailant and distress over the event are subdued in the interest of a return to ordinary daily life. The woman often asserts that she must get back to work as if nothing more traumatic than a sprained ankle had occurred.

Phase Three: Integration and Resolution. This begins when the victim becomes depressed and feels a need to talk about her experience. Her earlier attitude of "understanding the man's problems" gives way to anger toward him for having "used her" and anger toward herself for having permitted and tolerated this "use." Diagnosis of pregnancy, the need to go to a police line-up for identification of the assailant, a marriage proposal, a glimpse of someone who resembles the rapist—these or many other situations may introduce phase three. Frequently it is not possible to identify a specific precipitant. Instead the victim finds herself thinking more and more about the rape and does less well at her work.

COMFORTING THE VICTIM

The immediate objective of a police officer interviewing a victim is to obtain, as quickly as possible, information likely to lead to the prompt arrest of the assailant. The officer who quietly but firmly questions the victim may well be a source of comfort even though he is seeking answers to his questions rather than dealing with the feelings of the victim. A few preliminary and concluding remarks may be directed toward reassuring the victim. Usually the officer is too busy making out an offense report, providing information for the radio dispatcher and checking the crime scene to spend much time with the victim.

If the victim is in great emotional distress, it may be necessary to seek outside help which is usually available in the emergency rooms of large general hospitals. A relative or neighbor may be willing to care for the victim overnight or arrange transport to the home of someone who can care for the victim. Some victims who have been attacked in their own homes are unwilling to remain there the night following the crime, especially when the husband is absent from the home for any reason.

Before leaving the victim, the officer will attempt to answer any questions the victim may have regarding the offender and his offense. The victim may wish to know whether the offender is likely to return, what steps can be taken for self-protection and what help can be expected from the police. Advice on these issues is sometimes forgotten almost as soon as it is given and one must be patient when the same questions are repeated over and over again.

One of the most useful devices a person has is to talk about a source of tension. Talking about the crime over and over again serves to relieve great anxiety and distress. Merely allowing the victim to tell and retell his story may be sufficient for the moment. Some would-be therapists mistakenly feel they have to do something, preferably something more dramatic than listening to a repeat recital of the crime.

The officer should be careful not to expect the victim to think the way he does. He should not expect the victim to present his information in an orderly manner. He should not expect the victim to adopt a detached objective attitude. He should remember that some people hear only that which they wish to hear and he should not be dismayed if his advice is disregarded.

The role of the follow-up investigator is important, especially when there is a delayed reaction to the crime. At this time the victim is usually better able to think coherently about his experience and to take appropriate steps to deal with his problems. He may still feel a need to talk at length about the crime, but there is less pressure of speech and his attention to other matters can be obtained more easily.

Rape Victims

It is difficult for a police officer to comfort a rape victim if he is embarrassed or ill at ease. Experienced sex detail detectives are able to talk to victims in a detached yet not insensitive manner. The inexperienced officer should cultivate this approach and should ask himself whether he is restricting his inquiries and his attempts to comfort the victim because of his awkwardness. Strong feelings whether of sympathy for the victim or prejudice against her may make it more difficult to respond effectively.

What the victim will tell about the assault on herself will depend on whether the officer seems interested and concerned or unfriendly and impatient. The better informed the officer is about the offense the better equipped he will be to offer help. If the victim feels guilt over any of her behavior which may have contributed to the rape, it may be useful for her to talk about this. She is unlikely to voice self-criticism if she senses a strong negative reaction on the part of the officer.

Her distress may be over perverse sexual acts such as fellatio rather than over the rape. She may be so embarrassed that she will not volunteer any information on the offender's deviate sexual behavior. Yet when questioned directly she may reveal the real source of her distress.

A valuable service for rape victims is a home visit by a nurse from the Visiting Nurse Service. In Denver almost all rape victims are taken to Denver General Hospital for medical examination and treatment. The hospital usually requests the Visiting

Nurse Service to call on the victim on the day following the rape as victims seem to appreciate help more readily when it is offered promptly. If the initial visit is not made until several days later when the emotional crisis has subsided and the need for help is less apparent, the woman may refuse to talk about the rape and its consequences.

The majority of victims welcome the nurse and will often interrupt her explanation for the visit with a torrent of words about the rape and their fears that the man will return or will attack a member of her family in fulfillment of earlier threats to discourage a report to the police. The nurse provides advice on questions regarding venereal disease, pregnancy, police protection, and return to work. If psychiatric help is requested she will provide the telephone number and address of the nearest mental health clinic.

Police departments in cities which do not provide help through the Visiting Nurse Service or through hospital clinics for rape victims should request such help from local metropolitan hospitals.

Police officers are sometimes more sensitive than physicians in their approach to rape victims. Too often rape victims who are taken to a hospital by the police have to wait an hour or more in the emergency room before being seen by a physician. They are sometimes examined without privacy, understanding or compassion. Particular care should be taken over child victims of rape.

Sometimes the parents of a young girl will cry rape and demand a physical examination when in fact the only basis for their accusation is their suspicion that their daughter has misbehaved sexually. Police officers should be aware of the psychological trauma which may result from a vaginal examination at a very young age, and should not allow themselves to be intimidated into taking steps which are not justified by a careful review of the parental complaints.

Victims of Indecent Exposure

Some victims of indecent exposure become greatly alarmed because they fear that the exposure is a prelude to rape or other bodily assault. Indeed some rapists do approach their victims either nude or partially exposed, but not usually on a busy street in the daytime. Although exhibitionists are properly regarded as posing slight risk of physical injury, a few of those men who expose themselves also commit forcible rape. Fearful reactions to exposure are more common in children than in adults. Sleep may be disturbed by frightening dreams and the victim may be afraid to walk alone outdoors. The child victim of indecent exposure seldom requires psychiatric treatment although those parents who are unduly alarmed may require psychiatric guidance.

Sex education in schools, increased license in literature and everyday language, exhibitions of erotic art, underground newspapers with sexual advertisements (especially of penile prostheses) peep shows and "art" cinemas, pubic hair and simulated sex in movies as well as increasing acceptance of nudity on the stage may eventually deprive the exhibitionist of his victims. Who will be left to be startled or shocked? Common sense discussion of the problem with adult or child victims should serve to relieve morbid anxiety over an act of indecent exposure.

Victims of Assaults and Threats

Fights between neighbors, between husbands and wives, and between a parent and adolescent son contribute significantly to the work of a patrolman. These disputes are a source of considerable frustration because so often the victim is unwilling to swear out a complaint no matter how serious the bodily injury.

A review of the circumstances leading up to an assault or threat may help the victim to recognize his role in the encounter and show the way to an avoidance of future disputes. Unfortunately domestic disturbances tend to be repetitive and homicide is an occasional tragic outcome. The officer should therefore not confine himself to providing comfort to the victim in time of crisis. He should also make every effort to persuade the victim to seek the help of a family counseling service or psychiatric clinic. He is more likely to involve both offender and victim in therapy if he recognizes that there are two sides to family disputes and the victim is not always free from responsibility for the disputes.

Suicide

A shoe salesman shot himself to death in his car and a young patrolman was told to notify the victim's wife who worked in a nearby supermarket. He walked up to her, identified himself and told her of the circumstances of her husband's death. Unfortunately he did not ask to see her in the privacy of the manager's office and he spoke to her in a monotone as if he was reading to her the contents of a legal document. The majority of police officers are able to perform this difficult duty with tact and understanding. Some officers need advice and guidance.

Threats of suicide as well as actual attempts should never be regarded lightly. Even though the attempt may seem to be more than a dramatic gesture, care should be taken to refer the person to a mental health center or suicide prevention service. Even though the wrist slashing may consist of a superficial cut which requires only a band-aid, even though only a few tablets of aspirin are taken, it does not follow that there is no risk of suicide. The next attempt may be a determined successful act of self-destruction.

Furthermore, persons who make dramatic gestures may succeed in killing themselves even though this may have been neither their desire nor their intention. Hysterical persons make suicidal gestures to gain attention, to arouse sympathy or to frighten others into submission, however fatal accidents are apt to occur: leaning too far out of a window, overdosing with drugs mistakenly believed to be harmless, or miscalculating the arrival of someone to shut off the gas jets may lead to a fatal outcome. Here death is an accident in a dramatic setting.

Suicide by automobile is much more common than is generally recognized. Death by automobile offers special opportunity for concealment of suicide. The person who plans to take his own life may wish to prevent discovery of his suicide to protect his family from disgrace or to ensure payment of his life insurance. All police officers should be alert to this problem. Accidents should not be quickly dismissed as being due to alcohol, sleep, or loss of control at high speed.

When the driver survives the attempt, it may be difficult to obtain an admission of suicidal intent. Police officers, however, should always keep this possibility in mind when investigating accidents. Recently, a police officer found a man sitting in his car which was balanced on the undercarriage over the edge of a 150-foot embankment. The driver said his brakes had failed and a wrecker was called to pull his car back onto the highway. An hour and a half later his body was found in the wreckage of the car at the bottom of the same steep embankment. Relatives reported that he had been despondent over ill health and had previously attempted suicide.

A number of drivers who failed in their suicide or homicide attempts mentioned that police officers volunteered explanations of the auto wrecks. Thus a man who attempted to kill himself and his wife by driving his pickup truck into a tree was told that the wreck was due to a tire blowout. Certainly the tire blew out as the result of the truck hitting an obstruction at high speed. But this was the consequence of the driver's actions rather than the cause of the accident.

A young woman aimed her car at eighty miles per hour at a concrete overpass abutment. Although her car flew through the air for fifty feet before striking the roadside again and was airborne for a further twenty-five feet before coming to rest, she survived serious bodily injuries. The police officer informed her that she had overshot the turnoff from the throughway, had tried to turn too late, and then in her panic she had "frozen" on the wheel and driven into the overpass abutment. She agreed with him as she did not wish to reveal her attempt at suicide. This young woman had worn a safety belt to dispel suspicion of suicide. She was confident she would die in the wreck and her survival was indeed remarkable.

The progression of tire marks considered typical of a driver falling asleep at the wheel—marks on the gravel alongside the edge of the black top followed by a sudden change of direction due to the driver awakening as his car runs onto the gravel and

taking too sharp a compensatory turn of the steering wheel—
may also be caused by the suicidal driver, who swerves the car
slightly before overturning it with a sharp twist of the steering
wheel. Such a sequence may be similar to the tentative superficial cuts found on the person who commits suicide by cutting
his throat; preliminary efforts before the final plunge.

When police officers suspect deliberate suicidal intent, they
are often handicapped in their investigation by their natural
reluctance to press inquiries in the presence of serious injury and
grieving relatives. The great emotional distress of the driver's
wife at the scene of the wreck may not be due to a minor scalp
wound but rather to awareness of her husband's homicidal and
suicidal action. Such awareness may not be shared with solicitous
police officers. Police officers are also handicapped by the natural
reluctance of these drivers to reveal the true circumstances of
the wreck.

Yet these drivers and their relatives will often freely reveal
this information when encouraged to talk about the "accident."
The majority of these persons are impulsive, unstable persons
who more often than not make the attempt very impulsively
following an argument with a lover, marital partner, neighbor,
or boss. Thus a young woman when told by her boyfriend that
he did not intend to marry her drove off at high speed. She aimed
her car at a brick wall but crashed into another car. Another
woman, following an argument with her husband, jumped into
a car and drove into a truck at the nearest intersection.

In contrast, some drivers give considerable time and thought
to selection of a site for suicide. One man drove 160 miles to a
location he had selected two years previously as particularly
suitable for suicide. This was a section of mountain highway
with no guard rail alongside a seventy-five foot drop. He drove
past the spot twice and then spent several hours drinking in a
nearby tavern before driving off the road at the location previously selected. Despite a punctured lung and ruptured kidney,
he survived to face a summons for driving on the wrong side of
the road.

Awareness of the problem of the suicidal driver on the part
of police officers should permit early psychiatric evaluation of

these persons who are a danger to themselves and often other drivers on our highways.

CONCLUSION

There is controversy over the expanding role of the police officer. Some authorities have suggested that officers should perform many of the functions of psychiatric social workers and that police intervention in family and neighborhood disputes should include an active effort to resolve underlying interpersonal conflicts. On the other hand, it has been said that police officers should be police officers, and that the pressure of police work, including immediate response to emergency calls, precludes the time consuming social work role.

A compromise plan involves the use of special teams to provide aid in the resolution of those family and neighborhood disputes which result in requests for police action. In New York City, for example, a group of patrolmen were given instruction in the behavioral sciences at City College's Psychological Center. Part of the curriculum included the staging of mock family disputes, using professional actors. Graduates of the program were assigned to the Family Crisis Intervention Unit. The success of this unit was such that new police recruits now receive ten hours of instruction in crisis intervention.

Every officer should have some instruction in responding to the victims of crime as well as to the offenders. Formal lecture courses are less effective than practical instruction in classrooms, hospital emergency rooms, as well as court clinics and mental health centers. Psychiatrists and psychologists who participate in these programs should be available for emergency consultations and for follow-up review of incidents in which officers have encountered difficulties.

A calm, confident, friendly attitude, an alert observant mind, the patience to listen to a drawn-out talk, combined with the talent for seizing quickly the heart of a problem, the ability to confront a person without causing outrage, tolerance for but not indifference to unusual or disagreeable behavior, the capacity to see beyond the facts presented and to read the minds of men

—all these qualities contribute to an officer's skill in responding appropriately to the victims of crime.

REFERENCES

1. Amir, M.: *Patterns in Forcible Rape.* Chicago, University of Chicago Press, 1971.
2. Bard, M.: *Training Police as Specialists in Family Crisis Intervention.* Washington, U.S. Government Printing Office, 1970.
3. Criminal Justice Commission: Criminal homicides in Baltimore, 1960–1964. Baltimore, 1967 (processed).
4. Macdonald, J. M.: *Rape: Offenders and Their Victims.* Springfield, Ill., Charles C Thomas, 1971.
5. Macdonald, J. M.: Suicide and homicide by automobile. *Am J Psychiatr, 124:*366, 1964.
6. Macdonald, J. M.: *The Murderer and His Victim.* Springfield, Ill., Charles C Thomas, 1961.
7. Matthews, R. A., and Rowland, L. W.: *How to Recognize and Handle Abnormal People.* New York, National Association for Mental Health, 1954.
8. Simpson, K.: *A Doctor's Guide to Court.* London, Butterworths, 1962.
9. Sutherland, S., and Scherl, D. J.: Patterns of response among victims of rape. *Am J Orthopsychiatr, 40:*403, 1970.
10. Wolfgang, M. E.: *Patterns in Criminal Homicide.* Philadelphia, University of Pennsylvania, 1958.

INDEX